THREATS TO MILITARY PROFESSIONALISM
INTERNATIONAL PERSPECTIVES

THREATS TO MILITARY PROFESSIONALISM
INTERNATIONAL PERSPECTIVES

Edited by
Lieutenant-Colonel Jeff Stouffer &
Lieutenant-Colonel Douglas Lindsay, PhD

CANADIAN DEFENCE ACADEMY PRESS

Canadian Defence Academy Press
PO Box 17000 Stn Forces
Kingston, Ontario   K7K 7B4

Produced for the Canadian Defence Academy Press
by 17 Wing Winnipeg Publishing Office.
WPO30836

Library and Archives Canada Cataloguing in Publication

Threats to military professionalism : international perspectives /
edited by Jeff Stouffer and Douglas Lindsay.

Issued by: Canadian Defence Academy.
Available also on the Internet.
Includes bibliographical references and index.
ISBN 978-1-100-21185-5
Cat. no.: D2-310/2012E

1. Military ethics. 2. Military art and science. I. Lindsay, Douglas II.
Stouffer, Jeff III. Canadian Defence Academy IV. Canada. Canadian
Armed Forces. Wing, 17

U21.2 T47 2012   174'.9355   C2012-980176-3

Printed in Canada.

1 3 5 7 9 10 8 6 4 2

ACKNOWLEDGEMENTS

Threats to Military Professionalism: International Perspectives, the latest product of the International Military Leadership Association, represents the continued interest of a small group of researchers to help militaries around the world expand their professional development literature base and their understanding of contemporary military issues. Its members, and especially those that contributed to this volume, must be commended for their continued efforts in moving this project from a simple idea to the actual.

In particular, as with the previous six volumes in this series, it is important to acknowledge the continued support of the Canadian Defence Academy and CDA Press. Our gratitude and appreciation is extended to Melanie Denis of the Canadian Defence Academy Press for her continued work on these volumes and her willingness to accommodate the tight timelines imposed to ensure its timely release. Our sincerest appreciation is also extended to the staff at 17 Wing Publishing Office in Winnipeg, Manitoba who continue to transform these rough manuscripts into a product that we are proud to present.

TABLE OF CONTENTS

TABLE OF CONTENTS

FOREWORD

I am extremely pleased to introduce *Threats to Military Professionalism: International Perspectives*, the seventh and latest volume that the International Military Leadership Association (IMLA) and the Canadian Defence Academy (CDA) Press have collaborated in producing. Established in 2005, the IMLA has collaborated on a variety of multinational research projects, the aim being to develop and share knowledge pertaining to leadership and the profession of arms within the context of the member nations' militaries. These collaborative efforts, of which this series of publications is only one, have greatly increased our collective ability to better explore contemporary and emerging military issues in light of the growing resource constraints faced by individual nations. As such, this volume stands as a testament to what can be accomplished when the efforts of a diverse group of international research agencies are pooled.

Threats to military professionalism abound: some are obvious, others are concealed, a few are emerging and many are already in play. Regardless of their origin or impact, many are intrinsically linked to a nation's culture and history. In terms of origin, threats to professionalism are probably best categorized as being either external (e.g., those that result from fluctuating societal expectations, changes in the geo-political arena, or budget cuts that can both limit the procurement of equipment and decrease opportunities for training, education and deployment) or internal (e.g., scandals, increased bureaucracy, the failure to support a learning environment, or the failure to uphold an established ethos). What is painfully apparent, however, is the vast and insidious impact that such threats can have on military professionalism.

Should a military's professionalism be at all compromised, its capacity to operate effectively in today's complex battlespace will at best be stunted and at worst eliminated altogether. A country's military can undoubtedly do little to influence the external factors that threaten its professionalism. Many of the internal factors, by comparison, are often well within its control. Ensuring that these internal threats are sufficiently addressed will, in turn, help to elicit the support of the public. In so doing, the legitimacy of the military will be established, maintained or even increased amongst the general population, including those individuals, the decision-makers, who are able to control policy and thus exert a moderating influence over some of the external threats. Keeping one's "house in order" and presenting a consistent, healthy and positive image through the execution of military responsibilities

FOREWORD

in a professional and morally responsible manner can, in fact, go a long way in minimizing those factors that threaten to erode professionalism.

Although this volume is many things – theoretical, research-oriented, practical and even at times speculative – I am confident that it will promote lively discussion and debate. One of its main strengths is that it brings to light a multitude of factors that leaders must acknowledge and potentially take pre-emptive action against in order to minimize, if not completely prevent, the damage that such threats can cause. It is only through their identification that we can ever hope to mitigate their detrimental effects. I am also certain that readers will come to better appreciate the complexity surrounding these threats to military professionalism and what they mean for all military forces as they face ever-increasing challenges resulting from the contemporary operating environment. This book represents a significant contribution to that understanding.

Threats to Military Professionalism: International Perspectives is another significant accomplishment of the IMLA and serves to further demonstrate the their sustained contribution to the growing body of international professional development literature. It also continues a unique series of publications from CDA Press that gives the reader an exposure to the inner workings of various international organizations. Indeed, it is a rare and diverse collection of opinions and cultures.

Should you wish to discuss any issues, research or opinions presented in this book, individual members of the International Military Leadership Association, in addition to the contributing authors and their respective organizations, would be pleased to entertain your inquires.

Major-General P.J. Forgues
Commander
Canadian Defence Academy

CHAPTER 1

South African Military Professionalism: Some Critical Observations and Threats

Abel Esterhuyse
Colonel Piet Bester, PhD*

INTRODUCTION

Military professionalism matters. It directly influences, on the one hand, the relationship between the military and its polity and, on the other hand, the effectiveness of military operations. Section 31 of the 1996 Constitution of the Republic of South Africa (RSA) states that, "… the Security Forces as a whole, shall be required to perform their functions and exercise their powers in the national interest and shall be prohibited from furthering or prejudicing party political interest." In order to attend to this matter, *inter alia,* the South African White Paper for Defence states that "… stable civil-military relations depend to a great extent on the *professionalism of the armed forces.*"[1] The question is thus, how is military professionalism understood and operationalized in the South African context and, in particular, what kind of threats does it face in the contemporary South African National Defence Force (SANDF)?

This question can only be answered within the right contextual framework. Consequently, the discussion focuses on how South African military professionalism is shaped, firstly, by questions about the theoretical understanding of military professionalism and the manifestation thereof in Africa. Secondly, it is informed by the historical and policy context of military professionalism in South Africa. The last part of the chapter places specific emphasis on the current nature of military professionalism and the threats and challenges it confronts in South Africa.

THE IDEA OF MILITARY PROFESSIONALISM: MORE THAN HUNTINGTON

The western outlook on military professionalism has always been somewhat Huntingtonian in nature. The Huntingtonian approach is rooted, firstly, in questions about the constituent elements of a typical profession and whether

---

* The views expressed in this chapter are those of the authors and do not necessarily reflect those of the South African National Defence Force.

those elements are recognizable in the military domain. It is, secondly, driven by questions about the best way to de-politicize military forces and at the same time militarize these forces through training and education to ensure their military effectiveness and prevent them from encroaching on the political realm. More recently, however, the debate on military professionalism has moved beyond the point where the professional status of the military is in doubt. More specifically, the debate has shifted toward the military institution with a focus on how to professionalize the military. The focus is, thus, more on the self-concept of military professionals, the nature of the military as a bureaucratic profession and methods to professionalize the military domain through training and education. The publication of *The Future of the Army Profession* by Don M. Snider and Gayle L. Watkins in 2002 was a watershed in this regard.[2]

Underlying this outlook is the view that the military is a typical bureaucratic profession with all the attributes of such a profession. Therefore, the military is, on the one hand, a vocational profession focused on developing expert knowledge on warfighting, the management of defence and the management of peace.[3] It is, on the other hand, a hierarchical bureaucracy focused on applying routine knowledge through operating routines, procedures, and checklists.[4] Thus, a bureaucratic profession requires from military practitioners (and civilians working in the defence realm[5]), the ability to exist and operate almost continuously in two worlds: a bureaucratic military world, the so-called corporate army, and a professional military world, the so-called field army. Each of the worlds is characterized by a unique set of requirements (see Figure 1.1 below).

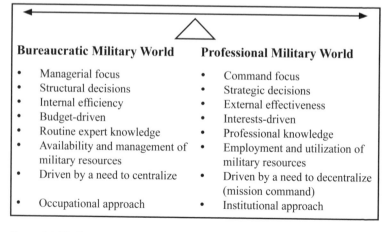

Bureaucratic Military World

- Managerial focus
- Structural decisions
- Internal efficiency
- Budget-driven
- Routine expert knowledge
- Availability and management of military resources
- Driven by a need to centralize

- Occupational approach

Professional Military World

- Command focus
- Strategic decisions
- External effectiveness
- Interests-driven
- Professional knowledge
- Employment and utilization of military resources
- Driven by a need to decentralize (mission command)
- Institutional approach

Figure 1.1: The Two Worlds of Military Professionalism

The corporate army is characterized by all the aspects of bureaupolitics: from emotional meetings, power struggles, negotiations for target dates, and battles over budgets to the famous PowerPoint and signature cultures. It is a "cold" world that displays features of "organized anarchy" where information is often lost or directed at the wrong people or both. In addition, it often happens that the wrong people are trying to solve a problem and that the right people are overlooked or sent elsewhere. The field army, in contrast, typically represents the "front-line" dimensions of military life and often functions in "hot" conditions that are critical, difficult, dangerous, violent, ambiguous and frequently stressful. It is an environment that encourages the cohesion of small groups, trust among its members, the importance of leadership qualities and a "can do" mentality.[6]

It is important to recognize the unavoidable dual nature of the military profession, the absolute need for both worlds in military organizations and, at the same time, the eroding or undermining effect that the bureaucratic military culture may have on military professionalism in a particular military. When the bureaucratic dominates the professional military world, Snider, Emiritus Professor of Political Science at West Point, argues there is cause for immense tension for individual professionals and for the military institution as a whole. Militaries, Snider points out, that do not resolve this tension in favour of their professional side can "die" in the professional sense. In consequence of domination of the bureaucratic military world, military practitioners are increasingly squeezed into bureaucratic moulds. Thus, military practitioners are increasingly treated as bureaucrats or mere employees, and soon become little more than obedient military bureaucrats exhibiting little of the effectiveness of a vocational profession.[7]

In Africa, militaries face a unique set of difficulties that, in most cases, tend to endanger the professionalization of armed forces. African armed forces, more specifically, are known for their widespread interference in the political and economic realms. Militaries find it challenging to interact with parliament, civil society organizations and other civilian entities. At the same time, most African civilian officials lack a deep-rooted understanding of security issues and institutions. Thus, Houngnikpo, Professor and Academic Chair of Civil-Military Relations at the Africa Centre for Strategic Studies, argues productive engagement, cooperation, and mutual respect are elusive and frustration in both the military and political realms is common.[8] Many African countries experience a lack of military professionalism because of a disconnection between the role and responsibilities of those responsible for security and defence policy *formulation* and those tasked with the *implementation* of the security and defence policy.

SOUTH AFRICA

In a discussion of *The Roots and Results of African Military Unprofessionalism*, Herbert M. Howe[9], Assistant Professor of African Studies at Georgetown University, provides a detailed exposition of the reasons underpinning this disconnection between the political and military worlds in many African states and, more specifically, the reasons for the inability of many African militaries to demonstrate both technical capabilities and political responsibility. Firstly, military professionalism in Africa is often negatively affected by ethnic-based recruitment or a process of sub-national favouritism. Of course, many African states are not nation states and are made up of many different ethnic groups. Skewed recruitment often leads to the over- or under-representation of certain ethnic groups in the militaries. Secondly, domestic deployments have an undermining influence on military professionalism, more specifically by severing the relationship with certain parts of the population or the political elite. Very often, domestic deployments discriminate in a subtle way against opposition parties and their supporters, especially when they are from a different ethnic group than the ruling party. Humanitarian aid will, for example, be firstly distributed to those ethnic groups that are part of the ruling party. African militaries are, thirdly, professionally affected by a lack of urgency. Their operational tempo is often not very high. Howe noted, for example, that African states often refrain from interstate conflict and their ability to garner foreign military support has reduced the need to develop capable militaries. This situation often allows governments to structure their militaries for political loyalty.[10] Fourthly, the professionalism of African militaries is regularly undermined by corruption through wasting defence money on irrelevant equipment and focusing the attention of military personnel on private financial endeavours. The procurement of new equipment is frequently accompanied by large-scale corruption. Lastly, many African polities establish special presidential security units to counterbalance the political support of the military. These forces are often a variant of private military companies because they protect the ruler and his regime, rather than defending the nation.[11] In combination, these factors inhibit the development of a culture of military professionalism in many African states. This, unsurprisingly, leads to the question as to the extent to which South Africa has been affected by new thinking about military professionalism and the nature thereof in Africa.

WE HAVE A HISTORY:
MILITARY PROFESSIONALISM BEFORE 1994

The South African military establishment was formalized with the creation of the Union Defence Force (UDF) in 1912. The UDF matured through the years under the tutorship of British officers and non-commissioned officers as a force with a long-standing British heritage of subordination of the military to civil-political authority. During the First and Second World Wars, the South African military was deployed almost as an extension of the British military. The British and western outlook on military professionalism became an institutionalized part of the UDF.

With the rise to power of the apartheid government in 1948, a range of changes were introduced through the reform programs of the Minister of Defence, Mr. F.C. Erasmus. Erasmus served as Minister of Defence in the National Party government between June 1948 and 1959. He introduced a rigorous program of Afrikanerization that included changes in the uniform and rank structure, as well as what some perceived as a purging of the officer corps to rid it of its English ethos, character and personnel. Of course, these changes were part of a much larger Nationalist agenda to place Afrikaners in positions of control and influence in the public service, parastatal bodies, state-owned industries, universities and the media.[12] It has been argued that these changes were aimed at ensuring a nationally-minded officer corps and altering the ethos of the defence force through the replacement of British traditions, customs, conventions and symbols in order to forge a distinctive South African appearance and demeanour.[13]

However, the strategic realities of the Republic of South Africa in the 1960s directed the defence force toward a more realistic approach that was underpinned by the dialectic that was soon visible in the interaction between foreign realities and domestic political dynamics. This specifically concerns the interplay between the beginning of the process of decolonization and independence in Africa in the 1960s, which soon turned out to be a real threat to white rule in Southern Africa, and the black civil unrest and rising expectations of South Africa's black population. In the military, the Afrikaner populism of the 1950s was thus replaced by a more professional orientation and ethos. This was due partly to strategic realities that confronted the Afrikaner establishment from the mid-1960s onwards and partly because of the appointment of a pragmatic military-minded politician by the name of P.W. Botha as Minister of Defence in 1966. Botha's term in office, 1966 to 1980, would eventually cement the military professionalism of the South African Defence Force (SADF) though priority of funding, the introduction of two-year conscription for white South Africans, and a high operational tempo and involvement in wars all over southern Africa.

Botha, more than any other person, was responsible for the political and defence policies and higher order military doctrine that shaped the SADF's institutional outlook. The ideas of total onslaught,[14] rooted in the academic writings of the French General André Beaufre,[15] became the overarching framework shaping the threat perception of the SADF. It provided a relatively simplistic framework for tying the many diverse problems facing the apartheid government, specifically the problem of the *swart gevaar* (black danger), into the western ideological framework of the Cold War – fighting the *rooi gevaar* (red danger) of international communism.[16] This threat perception, together with the increasing isolation of the country through international sanctions, had a defining influence on the professional outlook of the SADF. In particular, it provided the SADF with what Howe describes as a sense of urgency.[17]

Military professionalism in the SADF was rooted in a well-developed professional officer corps. Philip Frankel, senior lecturer in Political Science at the University of Witwatersrand in Johannesburg, noted that the long-standing British heritage of the SADF ensured "… the technical subordination of the military to civil political authority."[18] This tradition was supplemented by various South African statutes that barred its soldiers from any partisan political activity. The 1987 White Paper on Defence, for example, stated explicitly that all members of the SADF "… are by regulation prohibited from taking part in, or encouraging any demonstrations or procession for party-political purposes."[19] Thus, Frankel described the SADF as highly professional in its political relations with the civilian government. The SADF enjoyed functional autonomy in return for its subordination to civilian rule. The absence of political interference from the 1960s onwards led to an absence of factionalism in the military and, thus, less incentive for officers to intrude into government affairs.[20] Over time, though, and primarily because of Magnus Malan's appointment as Minister of Defence, civilian oversight over the SADF declined and specifically in the 1980s, operations were conducted that neither the public nor parliament approved of. In addition, the SADF became an important political entity within the country and though its members and institutional culture were apolitical, the SADF, as an extension of the apartheid government, was not non-political.

The SADF was dramatically influenced professionally by its involvement in a variety of counter-insurgency wars throughout Southern Africa. Counter-insurgency campaigns necessitate a holistic, comprehensive and intellectual approach from militaries. At the same time, the SADF needed to be very pragmatic, particularly in fighting the counter-insurgency campaign in Southwest Africa/Namibia. It had to be very adaptive in approach and in the development of and collaboration with indigenous forces. This was clearly demonstrated in the bureaucratic, structural and organization flexibility in the creation of unconventional military units such as the 32 Buffalo and the 31/201 Bushman Battalions. The indigenization of the SADF's counter-insurgency effort through the creation of white-led ethnic battalions added a very interesting African dimension to the professional blend of British regimentalism and Afrikaner frontierism in the SADF.

As part of the counter-insurgency doctrine, the SADF had to balance an aggressive offensiveness against opposing forces with a caring defensiveness for the local population. Typical of any counter-insurgency campaign, a culture of positive interaction with the local population was encouraged and became a matter of routine for most SADF members. In the context of the United Nations (UN) armament boycott, the SADF had to develop an "outside the box" approach to solutions, specifically with regard to the development of technology. This was clearly demonstrated in the development of countermining technologies and a preference for wheeled vehicles to allow for force projection over long distances. A point that should not be ignored, though, is that the SADF, like all militaries facing a high operational and warfighting tempo, had to place great emphasis on sound tactical training and operational experience. As a result of this and from a professional perspective, the SADF, over time, developed into a very tactically and operationally minded military.[21]

The SADF's involvement in counter-insurgency and the influence thereof on its professional ethos were reinforced through identity politics. On 31 May 1961 the Prime Minister, Dr H.F. Verwoerd, noted that "The Republic of South Africa is the only sure and stable friend the Western nations have in Africa."[22] There is absolutely no doubt that the SADF, as an expression of the white South African society it served, identified itself with the western way of war and, by implication, tried to emulate the kind of military professionalism associated with what Stephen Biddle described as the modern military system.[23] An overview of the characteristics of the modern military system that underpinned the western way of war provides an interesting analysis of the professional approach of the SADF. It is, firstly, an approach to conflict and the use of armed force that places heavy reliance on technology. This does not imply universal technological superiority. Rather, it is an approach in which technology is used as a substitute for numbers and in which technological innovation and the need for the "technological edge" is pursued. Secondly, it is an approach that highlights superior training and discipline as a means to foster cohesion in the technical and tactical realms of war. Training and discipline are tools for the creation of a cohesive fighting force that may consist of culturally and racially diverse groups of people. Thirdly, the modern military system relies on an aggressive military doctrine that has its roots in the Clausewitzian paradigm of total defeat, destruction and annihilation of the enemy. This military doctrine is shaped, though, by acceptance that past examples could and should influence present practice (i.e., the need to learn from experience). Thus, the western way of war is, fourthly, shaped by willingness to accept ideas from all quarters and to adapt to present realities in the warfighting domain. The ability to change and at the same time conserve military practices through an effective system of military training provides for a dynamic military ethos. Lastly, the western way of war is rooted in an ability to finance military changes, technology and war.[24] Biddle highlighted the fact that the modern system poses difficult political and organizational problems that prevent many states from implementing it.[25] It was the SADF's emulation of these basic characteristics of the western military ethos that made it retain "…a functional autonomy highly unusual in Africa during the 1970s and 1980s."[26] There is no doubt that the SADF had an operational warfighting approach to military professionalism.[27]

Through conscription and the reserve force system, the SADF had access to the best manpower available in South Africa. Apartheid South Africa was an economic and educational success for its white population. A well-nurtured threat perception (the *swart* and *rooi gevaar*) created a sense of fear in the white community that, until the late 1980s, ensured their continuous support for the SADF in general and for conscription in particular. Its access to the best available manpower in South Africa ensured the development of the SADF into a professional, well-trained and well-led organization whose white manpower deficiencies were augmented by the use of white-led indigenous forces. A well-nurtured threat perception and the overwhelming support of the white population informed the professional outlook of the SADF. However, it was a military that was racially based and that excluded the largest part of the South African population from its ranks.

The need to finance operations, military changes and technology, more than any other factor, eventually led the SADF leadership into acceptance of the need to explore non-military avenues for peace in Angola, Southwest Africa/ Namibia and eventually South Africa. Howe is absolutely correct when he notes that the SADF's allegiance in the movement toward majority rule in South Africa "… revealed the force's ingrained sense of political loyalty to the state – despite the widespread personal opposition to de Klerk's reforms by many white SADF personnel."[28] Financial pressures and political realities eventually overrode the operational achievements of the SADF in the creation of the circumstances necessary for peace in Southern Africa in the early 1990s and the development of a "new" military for the country under the banner of the South African National Defence Force.

STRUCTURAL ARRANGEMENTS: 1994 AS A WATERSHED?

Few countries have experienced the kind of transformational change that the South African society has undergone since democratization in 1994. As a highly militarized state before 1994, the military was due to be an integral part of the transformation of the public sector in South Africa.[29] In post-1994 South Africa, the idea of transformation is closely related to the "national democratic revolution"[30] and often associated with the need to change the racial (and sometimes gender)[31] profile of both the public and private sectors.[32] Immediately after 1994, a process was initiated to demarcate the defence policy environment within which the newly created South African military, officially known as the SANDF, was to exist and operate. The process eventually led to the acceptance of the 1996 White Paper on Defence,[33] the 1998 Defence Review[34] and eventually also the 1999 White Paper on South African Participation in Peace Missions.[35] The development of these policy documents was extensive and very consultative. Views from the public, academics, think tanks, the government and the military were incorporated into a comprehensive policy that addressed a wide range of issues – from civil-military relations and broad policy issues to more structural issues such as force design options.[36]

These documents laid the structural foundation for the military professional development of the SANDF in a democratic South Africa. Chapter 11 of the South African Constitution makes provision for a defence force that must be structured and managed as a disciplined military force. The primary mission of the defence force is defined in terms of the need to defend and protect the Republic, its territorial integrity and its people in accordance with the Constitution and the principles of international law regulating the use of force. The White Paper on Defence, in a discussion titled "Military Professionalism", notes that stable civil-military relations depend to a great extent on the professionalism of the armed forces. The challenge, according to the White Paper, is to define and promote an approach to military professionalism which is consistent with democracy, the Constitution and international standards. Such an approach is described in terms of the following political, ethical and organizational features:

- Acceptance by military personnel of the principle of civil supremacy over the armed forces, and adherence to this principle.

- The maintenance of technical, managerial and organizational skills and resources, which enable the armed forces to perform their primary and secondary functions efficiently and effectively.

SOUTH AFRICA

- Strict adherence to the Constitution, national legislation and international law and treaties.

- Respect for the democratic political process, human rights and cultural diversity.

- The operation of the Defence Force according to established policies, procedures and rules in times of war and peace.

- A commitment to public service, chiefly in defence of the state and its citizens.

- Non-partisanship in relation to party politics.

- The building of a South African military ethic based on international standards of officership, loyalty and pride in the organization. This will serve as a basic unifying force that transcends cultural, racial and other potentially divisive factors.

The education and training programs of the SANDF are seen as the cardinal means of building and maintaining military professionalism "… to meet international standards of competence and professionalism." The overarching goal of the education and training programs is to establish an institution that is professional, efficient, effective and broadly representative of the South African population. Education and training are seen as the primary vehicles for the development of "… the political and ethical dimensions of military professionalism." The White Paper is very specific in terms of the subjects that the education and training programs should address: the key elements of the political process in a democracy, the constitutional provisions on fundamental rights and defence, the significance of the Constitution as supreme law, the principles of democratic civil-military relations, international law on armed conflict, respect for multi-cultural diversity and gender equality, and the normative dimensions of military professionalism. It is interesting to note that the White Paper specifically emphasizes the need for government to take into account the professional views of senior officers in the process of policy formulation and decision-making on defence through the Defence Staff Council, the Council on Defence and the structure of the Department of Defence.

Clearly, from a policy and structural perspective, the foundation for the development of a professional military force was laid through the constitution and the 1996 White Paper on Defence. Policy, though, is nothing more than an expression of intention. The question is, how were these provisions and stipulations implemented and what kind of force did the SANDF turn out to be?

MILITARY PROFESSIONALISM IN THE POST-1994 ERA: SOME REAL THREATS

After the forced marriage between the former SADF and the revolutionary forces that bore a child on 27 April 1994, the SANDF, the military was transformed from a conscript military into an all-volunteer force, which necessitated an "up-or-out" approach to the management of personnel. Of course, the integration (some would say absorption) of the non-statutory force armed wings of the different liberation movements into the statutory military (SADF) had a defining influence on the military professionalism of the SANDF.[37] Although some of these influences had a positive impact, there are also some real threats that emerged from this marriage, the first of which is a growing political-mindedness that originates from the revolutionary armies.

Growing Political-mindedness
Originating from Revolutionary Armies

Needless to say, revolutionary armies are the diametrical opposite of statutory armies. They differ in ethos, structure, doctrine and procedure. One of the most outstanding features of revolutionary armies is their unique non-western penetrative model of civil-military interface, with a deliberate fusion of the military and political dimensions of the revolutionary struggle. Politics are an integral part of revolutionary armies. Whereas the western conception of military professionalism *consciously de-politicized* military personnel, revolutionary armies deliberately politicized their members through political indoctrination and the use of political commissars to ensure individual soldiers and units remained politically dutiful. Thus, the soldiers from the armed wings of the revolutionary movements were highly politically-minded. The bulk of the top officers also retained their membership in and identification with the reigning party, restricting loyalty to the ruler rather than the state.[38] Mixing the (apolitical) tactically- and operationally-minded view of military professionalism from the SADF with the politically-minded soldiers from the revolutionary armies had a defining influence on military professionalism in the SANDF. The SANDF, for example, saw an immediate outflow of ex-SADF members who felt themselves professionally out of place. This not only helped the process of downsizing and affirmative action to ensure representativeness in the SANDF, it also led to growth in the private military and security industry in Africa and elsewhere. The downside, of course, was a loss of warfighting experience from the military in a very short time and an accompanying politicizing of the military. It was transformed from a tactically- and operationally-minded force into one that, at times, tended to be too politically inclined. This has led to a situation where the members' loyalty towards the state (ongoing) and the regime (temporary) was and is questioned.[39] This questions whether the values and the interests of the state, including the military, claim precedence over those of any other temporarily powerful group or leader. The potential threat this holds for military professionalism is further strengthened by the absence of a broad debate on societal security and defence.

Absence of a Broad Debate on Societal Security and Defence

As in the case of the SADF, the policy environment influences the professional military ethos in the SANDF and subsequently has an effect on military professionalism. One of the outstanding features of the post-apartheid South African security and defence landscape is the general absence of a broad debate on societal security in general and defence in particular.[40] No explicitly formulated security policy documents have been published since the 1994 White Paper on Defence and the 1998 Defence Review. More specifically, there is no defence debate in South Africa at the conceptual level of defence and there is no in-depth, independent and critical questioning and scrutiny of defence or of defence and strategy policy documents and their impact on military professionalism. The lack of debate, Greg Mills argues, is also a reflection of a disregard for consultative and parliamentary processes, vested interests in procurement decisions and the weakened and politically emasculated nature of civil society.[41] The lack of debate is underpinned by a general lack of knowledge of defence and military-related issues (also referring to military professionalism) inside and outside the military and political domains in South Africa. It creates the impression that defence, in general, and the military, in particular, is not a priority for the post-1994 South African government and leads to rising skepticism with regard to current approaches to National Security. Hence, no further conceptualisation or reinforcement of military professionalism occurs. The issue is further challenged by the current ruling party and the SANDF's adverse relations with the media, especially when it comes to military-related issues.

Adverse Relations with the Media

In most modern democracies, the public and media play an indispensable role in shaping the nature of the armed forces and the nature and content of the defence debate. The SANDF's approach in dealing with the media is often rooted in the need to prevent the spread of information that may harm or embarrass the government and its military. It is a known fact that nobody in the military is allowed to engage the media without explicit authorization from the Office of the Minister of Defence. Thus, the media frequently rely on rumours and unofficial discussions with military personnel. Defence-related issues that are reported on and come into the public domain are often sensational. Stated differently, media reporting on South African military-related issues is mostly sensational in nature because of the military's failure to respond to media enquiries and the absence of a formal relationship between the media and the military. Since the public is not well-informed about the military and the military is more often than not portrayed negatively in the media, many see the military as dysfunctional. Thus, from a cultural perspective, the SANDF has become a peripheral societal entity, isolated from society in general, and there is a growing civil-military gap.[42] The role of the media in particular is also questioned. The lack of a public defence debate is to a large extent reflected in the dreadful nature of military-media relations in South Africa and the very superficial reporting on all military matters in the media.

Disabling Bureaucracy

The near absence of a broad societal debate on defence that is aggravated by adverse relations with the media is further complicated by inward-looking bureaucratization of the defence debate by the South African military. Stated differently, the defence debate is mostly a bureaucratic debate. The defence agenda is the result of a military bureaucratic process and the defence debate within the military is formal, but not necessarily well-structured. To a large extent, the Ministry of Defence, the Defence Secretariat and the military command structure dictate the underlying approach to the defence debate in South Africa.[43] Therefore, one of the key challenges/threats confronting military professionalism in the SANDF is a disabling bureaucracy. A strong bureaucracy is something that was inherited from the SADF. However, the apartheid military was staffed by skilled and efficient bureaucrats with a nuanced understanding of the need to keep the military operationally effective at all times. This does not necessarily seem to be the case at present with the SANDF and its bureaucracy. A working, enabling bureaucracy is an indispensable part of military effectiveness. However, from a more critical and theoretical perspective, bureaucracy is something that may be used in defence of everything or that may serve as an excuse for anything. Bureaucracy is a tool that may be used to cover up inactivity, incapacity and incompetence and to escape accountability and responsibility. In a bureaucratized institutional environment it is very difficult to determine who made a decision and when and where it was made. A disabling bureaucracy suffocates all forms of initiative and undermines operational effectiveness. One of the key problems of a bureaucratized military is its organizational centralization of decision-making – making a mockery of the military operational need for *aufstrag-staktik* or mission command. It would not be wrong to argue that military professionalism in the SANDF is suffocated through a process of increased bureaucratization. This leads to the next threat to military professionalism, viz. lack of military-mindedness among the ruling party.

Lack of Military-mindedness Among the Ruling Party

There is reason to question political expertise on defence-related issues within the ruling African National Congress (ANC) government. Politicians in general, and those from the ruling ANC in particular, are not necessarily military-minded in their approach. Many ANC politicians approach defence-related issues with a conflicted mindset. The ANC as a ruling party does not necessarily draw a very clear line of demarcation between the notions of "a military for a political party (ANC)" and "a military for the country." Moreover, since *Umkhonto we Sizwe* (or MK), translated as "Spear of the Nation", which was the armed wing of the ANC, and its structures were never closed down after 1994, it is still a military in the ANC barracks. MK cadres are still often seen at ANC party gatherings. This threatens the standing of the military as a legitimate profession owing to its members' dabbling in partisan politics[44] and not accepting that there should be a distinction between the state (ongoing) and the regime (temporary).[45] The ruling party is not acting against members of the SANDF that transgress on this issue and the SANDF is thus losing credibility as a neutral political instrument. Because of not knowing what can be expected from defence, the political debate on defence and military issues is very often very superficial. The role of the opposition parties, which sometimes have a good grasp of defence-related issues, is often seen as destructive by the ruling ANC government. It is therefore very difficult to achieve or reach some form of consensus on defence and defence-related issues in the political domain.[46] Thus, very much like the apartheid defence debate, the post-1994 defence debate is highly bureaucratic, while the governing party tends to exclude both the opposition parties and the public at large from all things military. This contributes to the absence of a broad debate on societal security defence and the sociopolitical environment in which the SANDF functions, as well as to certain fears and a consequential neglect to publish updated defence policy papers.

Fears and Neglect to Publish Updated Defence Policy Papers

From the professional military side, the defence debate is often driven by a number of fears. The most prominent in this regard is the fear that it may lose its conventional warfighting capability. At the political level, the ANC government is not necessarily interested in the publication of formal security and updated defence policy papers. The 1995 White Paper on Defence and the 1998 Defence Review are outdated. These fears and neglect to publish formal policy documents may be rooted in the reality that these policies will highlight the disequilibrium in the South African defence domain – that the military in general does not really need the equipment that was and still is on the procurement list.[47] Laurie Nathan, the Director of the Centre of Mediation at the University of Pretoria, illustrates this concern when he states that the South African Parliamentary Defence Committee, for example, accepted the logic of non-offensive defence as a matter of policy, but in contrast it accepted the recommendations of military officers on an offensive force design.[48] This caused tension and adversarial relations between the parliamentarians and the politicians.

Lack of Academic Interest in Defence-related Issues

The shift toward a more human security-oriented paradigm in the 1990s was accompanied by waning interest in the (mostly civilian) academic community in defence-related issues. South African academics, in many instances, are simply not interested in defence-related research. It is interesting to note, for example, that since 1994, the Department of Strategic Studies at the University of South Africa (UNISA) and the Strategic Studies Institute at the University of Pretoria (UP) have either been closed down or amalgamated with other departments and institutes, contributing to a further lack of public debate and education on matters related to military professionalism.

Lack of a Clearly Defined External Threat and Contemporaneous Decline in the Defence Budget

The military professional ethos of the SANDF is hamstrung by a disconnection between funding, missions and expectations. The lack of a clearly defined external threat and the contemporaneous decline of the defence budget since the early 1990s are realities. At the same time, the military is often confronted with policy directions that are not necessarily in line with its capacity. This strategic planning gap is underpinned by policy decisions that are often shaped by non-military considerations that are not necessarily well thought through, lack a sense of military purpose and do not always have South Africa's best interests at heart.[49] The human security paradigm,[50] for example, features very prominently as a South African government policy stance that contributes to a variety of complex and difficult issues arising from the domestic and international environments. There is, however, a divide between the idea of human security as a policy paradigm and the manner and method of employing the South African military. More specifically, the SANDF never embraced the notion of human security in organizational structure, doctrine and equipment. In the end, human security is not what armies are about and very few South African military programs can be considered human security-related. On a political level the notion of human security has contributed to the marginalization of the military in society. It also influenced the military organizational ethos in ways that were not always conducive to professional military development. It is possible to argue, for example, that the creation of military unions and many of the military disciplinary challenges that have dramatically affected the professional ethos of the SANDF since 1994 have their roots in the idealistic notions of the human security paradigm.

Unionization of the SANDF

The military professional ethos of the SANDF is affected by a host of command, control and management challenges. There is without doubt a Congress of South African Trade Unions (COSATU)[51] unionist and occupational mindset in the South African military at present.[52] It is an approach to command that is characterized by management through consensus in which there is no tradition of clear-cut decision-making. An occupational approach to command is characterized by a high level of centralization. The chain of command of the South African military was profoundly influenced by the business-driven structural transformation of the military in the 1990s.[53] A variety of historical and other influences affect the military command culture of the SANDF. This includes the ethnical background and the pre-1994 service culture of military personnel. Many of the white leadership, for example, have become intimidated and most white officers serve with a retirement mentality: they do not want to cause a stir, rock the boat or take decisions and stances that may have a ripple effect and harm their careers. At the same time, many black soldiers still tend to see themselves as freedom fighters or serve with a "freedom fighting" mentality in the SANDF.[54]

Populist tendencies and a unionist mindset impinge on discipline and military professionalism in the SANDF. Since 1994, South African military personnel have had the choice of belonging to a military union. There is a widespread belief that the unions are undermining the military professional ethos of the SANDF. Union membership limits the capacity of the military and the willingness of its members to deploy and leads to a lack of discipline in the training environment. The unionized nature of the military is closely tied to its command culture and quality of internal communications.[55] The unions create the opportunity for soldiers to disobey orders and to undermine the command structure. Whether the military and the military unions understand their respective roles in interacting with each other in the context of the constitution is unclear.[56] The unionist mindset affects the way soldiers view their own military careers as "just another job" and it is contrary to the military sociologist Charles Moskos' view that soldiers should have "institutional" motives for military service, suggesting patriotism, love of service and dedication, as opposed to the more "occupational" considerations that have more to do with material rewards and career advancement.[57]

Government Policies to "Correct the Wrongs of the Past"

Government policies of affirmative action and equal opportunities have had to be enforced since 1994. Although affirmative action does have merit *per se,* many individuals from disadvantaged groups were awarded promotions and appointments without necessarily complying with the minimum requirements in terms of competencies and standards for admission. Frequently, no questions were or are being asked about the suitability of candidates for particular positions or appointments. Appointments often seem to reflect "a body in a post" approach. Considerations such as political influence, race and gender – rather than merit – often drive the appointment procedures and lead to compromising "corporateness"[58] a term coined by the American political scientist Samuel P. Huntington.[59] Emphasis on race is exclusive. Diversity, in contrast, promotes inclusivity.[60] The result is that mediocrity is often tolerated rather than the appointment of personnel from the "wrong" race group.

This is augmented by perceptions about the acceptance of mediocrity and the lack of a disciplined work ethos in the SANDF. Soldiers, in general, and officers, in particular, often seem to be promoted in spite of involvement in situations that border on criminality.[61]

The Notion that Military Culture Should Mirror Societal Culture

Since 1994, the South African policy domain has assumed that the military culture needs to mirror the societal culture. This is rooted, to a large extent, in the perception that everything the pre-1994 South African military did was wrong and ought to be changed, leading to the need to "democratize" and "civilianize" the South African military since 1994.[62] This need for change was rooted in lack of understanding of the uniqueness of military culture and the need for a unique military culture (i.e., the military's right to be different).[63] Thus, the cultural ethos of the SANDF was dramatically influenced by government policies to address inequalities and structural challenges in South African society. The issue of gender is a good example in this regard. There is obvious tension between government policies on gender equality and military necessities, in general, and the demands of the warfighting domain, in particular.[64] Militaries around the globe give recognition to the fact that women are physically better suited for certain military jobs.[65] The SANDF was required to open all appointments in the military to women. That does not mean that women are necessarily physically and otherwise suitable for certain roles. Thus, the presence of women in the warfighting environment, and more specifically their effect on the ability of the military in this environment, dramatically affected the ethos of the military. More specifically, it did not necessarily contribute to a more positive view of women in the SANDF and their position in society, in general, contributing yet again to a lack of "corporateness" among military professionals.

CONCLUSION

The pre-1994 South African armed forces were described as an anomaly in Africa.[66] The SADF adhered to the typical western outlook on military professionalism with an emphasis on the need to depoliticize and militarize the armed forces to allow for an autonomous environment of military practicalities. This view on military professionalism is not in line with what has unfolded in Africa since decolonization in the 1960s. The growing political-mindedness of the post-1994 SANDF, together with a dramatic change in the operational tasks of the military, had a defining influence on professionalism in the South African military. More specifically, African military professionalism seems to be informed by the immaturity of the political structures and traditions and the nature of their societies in general. Military professionalism in African armed forces is affected by dysfunctionalities with regard to recruitment, deployment, operational tempo, defence management and the creation of parallel military forces. Since democratization in 1994, the South African armed forces have gone through a deliberate process of Africanization and many of the typical characteristics of African militaries have made their appearance in the SANDF.

As a matter of irony though, the declared policy framework for the SANDF is typically Huntingtonian in nature. There thus seems to be tension between the structural provisions for military professionalism and civil-military relations on the one hand and the current South African government's interpretation and operationalization thereof. Since 1994, the SANDF has been transformed from a conscript to an all-volunteer army, but has not been able to implement an up-or-out personnel management system because of the stringent South African labour laws. The transformation process was primarily driven by the integration of the politically minded soldiers of the former revolutionary movements. The SANDF thus became a highly politically minded force.

The SANDF is faced with a growing civil-military gap and inward-looking bureaucratization of defence and the defence debate. As is the case in many African countries, South African civilian officials seem to lack deep-rooted understanding of military and security issues and institutions. This is accompanied by a tendency to approach all things military with a struggle or revolutionary mind-set and an inability to draw a clear line of demarcation between the military, the party and the state.

On an operational level, the military is over-extended with a defence budget that is continuing its decline in real terms. The defence budget, indeed, reflects the human security stance of government. The practical use of the military, though, is rooted in the hard reality of *realpolitik* where the military, as a potential source of power, is used in the diplomatic context in a coercive manner. There is thus a strong argument that the South African government and its military is not "walking the talk" through operationalization of the human security paradigm. And the military is paying the price in terms of professionalism, underfunding and organizational overextension.

Organizationally, the SANDF is caught up in a unionist occupational mindset with a high level of centralization and management through consensus. The military is highly bureaucratized, partly because of the government's inability to understand its need to be different from society. Thus, just like the rest of the South African government bureaucracy, the SANDF enhances mediocrity through emphasis on political influence, race, and gender – rather than merit.

There is no doubt that the SANDF is still one of the better militaries in Africa. However, in response to politization, bureaucratization and continued underfunding, its professional ethos is in serious decline and there are red lights coming on all across the spectrum. From a technological and organizational perspective, the Army in particular is faced with serious military professional shortfalls. If these issues are not addressed as a matter of urgency, lack of military professionalism may become an unexploded Improvised Explosive Device (IED) in South African society!

ENDNOTES

1. Emphasis added.

2. Lloyd J. Mathews, *The Future of the Army Profession* (Boston: McGraw-Hill, 2002). Don M. Snider and Gayle L. Watkins were the project directors for this publication.

3. James Burk, "Expertise, Jurisdiction, and Legitimacy of the Military Profession" in Lloyd J. Mathews, ed., *The Future of the Army Profession* (Boston: McGraw-Hill, 2002), 32.

4. Don M. Snider, "Officership: The Professional Practice", *Military Review* (January-February 2003), 4.

5. See Don M. Snider, "Once Again, The Challenge to the US Army During a Defence Reduction: To Remain a Military Profession", *Professional Military Ethics Monograph Series* (Center for the Army Profession and Ethic, Strategic Studies Institute, US Army War College, 2008).

6. Joseph Soeters, Donna J. Winslow and Alise Weibull, "'Military Culture' in Giuseppe." Caforio, ed., *Handbook of the Sociology of the Military* (New York, NY: Kluwer Academic/ Plenum Publishers, 2003), 246.

SOUTH AFRICA

7. Snider, 2003.

8. Mathurin C. Houngnikpo, "Africa's Militaries: A Missing Link in Democratic Transitions", *African Security Brief*, No. 17 (January 2012), 2.

9. See chapter 2 of Herbert M. Howe, *Ambiguous Order: Military Forces in African States* (London: Lynne Reinner, 2001).

10. Ibid., 47.

11. Ibid., 44.

12. Roger S. Boulter, "Afrikaner nationalism in action: F.C. Erasmus and South Africa's Defence Forces, 1948-1959", *Nations and Nationalism*, Vol. 6, No. 3 (2000), 438.

13. Ibid., 443 and 450.

14. The words *totale strategie* (total strategy) were used for the first time in official policy documents in the White Paper on Defence and Armament Production, 1973, laid before parliament by the Minister of Defence, Mr. P.W. Botha. See Republic of South Africa, Department of Defence, *White Paper on Defence and Armament Production* (1973), Preface, 1.

15. See, for example, Andre Beaufre, *Introduction to Strategy* (London: Faber & Faber), 1965.

16. Magnus Malan, *My Lewe Saam met die SA Weermag*, (Pretoria: Protea Boekhuis, 2006). Malan provides a good example of the threat perception that came to dominate SADF thinking.

17. Howe, 2001, 44.

18. Philip H. Frankel, *Pretoria's Praetorians: Civil-Military Relations in South Africa* (Cambridge: Cambridge University Press, 1984), xvi.

19. Republic of South Africa, *Briefing on the Organisation and Functions of the South African Defence Force and the Armaments Corporation of South Africa LTD* (Cape Town: SA Naval printing press, June 1987), 6.

20. Howe, 2001, 52.

21. Abel J. Esterhuyse and Evert Jordaan, "The South African Defence Force and Counterinsurgency, 1966-1990", in Deane-Peter Baker and Evert Jordaan, eds., *South Africa and Contemporary Counterinsurgency: Roots, Practices, Prospects* (Claremont: UCT Press, 2010), 159-190.

22. Republiek van Suid-Afrika, *Oorsig oor Verdediging en Krygstuigproduksie: Tydperk 1960-1970* (Pretoria: Verdedigingshoofkwartier, April 1971), 9.

23. Stephen Biddle, *Military Power: Explaining Victory and Defeat in Modern Battle* (Princeton: Princeton University Press, 2004), 28.

24. Geoffrey Parker, *The Cambridge Illustrated History of Warfare: The Triumph of the West* (Cambridge: Cambridge University Press, 2005), 1-11.

25. Biddle, 2004, 48-51.

26. Howe, 2001, 51.

27. See, for example, the discussion of South African military exploits in the 1980s in: Paul L. Moorcraft, *African Nemesis: War and Revolution in Southern Africa, 1945-2010* (London: Brassey's, 1990).

28. Howe, 2001, 52.

29. Jakkie Cilliers, "Introduction", in Jakkie Cilliers, ed., *Continuity and Change: The SA Army in Transition*, *ISS Monograph* 26 (August 1998).

30. The idea of a national democratic revolution is often used by the ANC, South Africa's ruling party, and the South African Communist Party (SACP) in the context of transformation. See, for example, the notes of the ANC National Working Committee to an SACP Central Committee discussion in: Anon, "Managing National Democratic Transformation", *Bua Komanisi*, Vol. 5, No. 1 (May 2006), retrieved on 21 May 2009 from <http://www.anc.org.za/ancdocs/misc/2006/anc_sacp.html>. Also see the differences and political infighting for control over the so-called national democratic revolution in: Aubrey Matshiqi, "Zuma must Heal our Intelligence Services", *Business Day* (14 August 2009), retrieved on 20 March 2012 from <http://www.businessday.co.za/articles/Content.aspx?id=78542>.

31. Anon, "SA Leading Way on Woman in Military in Africa", *DefenceWeb* (9 August 2009), retrieved on 20 March 2012 from <http://www.defenceweb.co.za/index.php?option=com_content&task=view&id=3536&Itemid=379>.

32. In South Africa at present, the idea of "transformation" is closely linked to the notion of affirmative action and "representivity" at all level and sectors of society. An overview of the published articles of the South African academic journal *Transformation* reflects either an implicit or explicit acceptance of race as the basis of transformation in the South African context. The journal is available at: <http://www.transformation.ukzn.ac.za/>, accessed on 20 March 2011. This is a rather limited approach, as it measures one's performance and effectiveness on only one level. A more comprehensive approach is needed. It is also interesting to note that transformation in South Africa is seen by some as an ideologically driven government policy to become more conformant with socialist and African nationalist group thinking. For example, see the definitions of South African political transformation at the following sites, retrieved on 20 March 2012 from <http://www.sanakirja.org/search.php?id=141385&l2=15>, <http://www.tfode.com/transformation> and <http://tinydict.com/Transformation>.

33. South African Government Information, Department of Defence, "Defence in a Democracy", *White Paper on National Defence for the Republic of South Africa* (1996), retrieved on 20 March 2012 from <http://www.info.gov.za/whitepapers/1996/defencwp.htm>.

34. South African Department of Defence, *South African Defence Review* (Pretoria: 1 Military Printing Unit 1998), retrieved on 20 March 2012 from <http://www.dod.mil.za/documents/defencereview/defence%20review1998.pdf>.

35. South African Government Information, South African Department of Foreign Affairs, *White Paper on South African Participation in Peace Missions* (24 February 1999), retrieved on 20 March 2012 from <http://www.info.gov.za/whitepapers/1999/peacemissions.pdf>.

36. Laurie Nathan, "South African Case Study: Inclusive SSR Design and the White Paper on Defence" in Laurie Nathan, *No Ownership, No Commitment: A Guide to Local Ownership of Security Sector Reform* (University of Birmingham, UK: Paper commissioned by the Security Sector Reform Strategy of the UK Government's Global Conflict Prevention Pool, October 2007), 94-99, retrieved on 20 March 2012 from <http://www.ssrnetwork.net/documents/Publications/No_Ownership_No_Commitment_v2.pdf>.

37. The SANDF was formed through a process of integration and amalgamation of the former South African Defence Force, the defence forces of the former black homelands of Transkei, Bophuthatswana, Venda and Ciskei (TBVC), and the former armed wings of the African National Congress, known as Umkhonto we Sizwe (MK), and the Pan African Congress, known as the Azanian People's Liberation Army (APLA). Two thousand members of

SOUTH AFRICA

the KwaZulu-Natal Self-protection Force (KZSPF) were also brought into the SANDF. It is interesting to note that both MK and APLA have been integrated into the SANDF, but that they are still seen in their uniforms – very often at funerals of former comrades, public rallies and COSATU-organized strikes.

38. Howe, 2001, 11.

39. Howe, 2001, 9.

40. Recognition should be given to the fact that social issues, such as crime and joblessness, as security concerns, are dominating the South African security agenda. The security agenda, though, does not necessarily imply an in-depth security debate about the issues on the agenda.

41. Greg Mills, *An Option of Difficulties? A 21ˢᵗ Century South African Defence Review. The Brenthurst Foundation, Discussion Paper 2011/7* (August 2011), 5.

42. Lindy Heinecken, "Defence, Democracy and South Africa's Civil-Military Gap", *Scientia Militaria*, Vol. 33, No. 1 (2005), 119-140.

43. Recognition should be given to the fact that the Minister of Defence recently appointed a four-person committee to conduct a Defence Review with recommendations to be made to the Minister by November 2011. The review was done without any participation or input from the broad South African society.

44. Richard Swain, *The Obligations of Military Professionalism*. (National Defence University's Institute for National Security, Ethics and Leadership, December 2010), 7.

45. Ibid., 9.

46. Peter Du Toit, "Verdedigingskomitee 'Hoort onder Administrasie'" (Vrydag: Die Burger, 1 July 2011), 2.

47. See the arguments by Greg Mills in this regard in Mills, 2011.

48. Laurie Nathan, "Obstacles to Security Reform in New Democracies", in Clem McCartney, Martina Fischer and Oliver Wils, eds., *Security Sector Reform: Potentials and Challenges for Conflict Transformation* (Berlin: Berghof Handbook Dialogue Series No 2, Berghof Research Center for Constructive Conflict Management, 2004), 3, retreived on 18 January 2012 from <http://www.berghof-handbook.net/documents/publications/dialogue2_ssr_complete.pdf>.

49. A good example in this regard is the ANC government's outright refusal to work with the US Africa Command in Africa on matters where a clear confluence of South African and US interests is obvious. At the ANC's December 2007 Polokwane conference the ANC accepted a notion in which "the conference urged Africa to remain united and resolute in the rejection of the Africa Command Centre (sic) (AFRICOM)". The resolution was retrieved on 20 March 2012 from <http://www.anc.org.za/docs/misc/2007/abstracto.pdf>.

50. Tim Murithi and Angela Ndinga-Muvumba that security is no longer an issue that is confined to the demands and requirements of nation states, but increasingly people have to be placed at the centre of efforts to achieve security. This is a transition to a less state-centric conceptualisation of security but seeks to be more holistic to include aspects such as economic, food, health, environmental, personal, community and politica security. Hence, the reason why the notion of people-centred "human security" has taken on greater prominence in Africa. states See: John Akokpari, Angela Ndinga-Muvumba and Tim Murithi, eds., *The African Union and Its Institutions* (Auckland Park, South Africa: Jacana Media (Pty) Ltd, 2008), 7 and 10.

51. Congress of South African Trade Unions.

52. Erika Gibson, "Soldate basisse Verbied na Optog-skorsing", *Beeld*, Friday 3 December 2010, 10.

53. Deane-Peter Baker, "New Partnerships for a New South African Army's Stabilization Role in Africa", *Strategic Studies Institute Monograph*, (US Army War College: June 2009), 5, retrieved on 20 March 2012 from <http://www.strategicstudiesinstitute.army.mil/pubs/display.cfm?pubID=928>.

54. Erika Gibson, "Hoë in Weermag 'sal Wittes Wegjaag'", *Die Burger*, 10 December 2010, 12.

55. Michael Kaplan, "They're Soldiers at Work, but not at Heart: Life in the SANDF, 17 Years after the Revolution", *Cape Town News*, 30 May 2011, 7.

56. See this front-page article for a detailed exposition of this issue: Dianne Hawker, "Army Unions Forced to Soldier on", *The Sunday Independent Dispatches*, 12 December 2010, 15.

57. Cited by John Allen Williams, "The International Image of the Military Professional", *African Security Review*. Vol. 4, No. 5 (1995), retrieved on 23 November 2011 from <www.iss.co.za/pubs/asr/4No5/Williams.html>.

58. Corporateness is a sense among professionals that they are a profession with certain standards for admission to their ranks and a set of competencies that should be exhibited by those members.

59. Cited in Williams, 1995.

60. Heidi Swart, "Haemorrhage of Skills at Overstretched Army", *The Sunday Independent News*, 24 October 2010, 6.

61. Michael Kaplan, "Crisis in the Defence Force", *Cape Times*, Monday 30 May 2011, 1.

62. The need to democratize defence and to civilianize by means of, for example, the appointment of a civilian Secretary of Defence, was one of the underlying messages of the 1995 White Paper on Defence. Retrieved on 20 March 2012 from <http://www.info.gov.za/whitepapers/1996/defencwp.htm#foreword>.

63. Patrick Mileham, "Military virtues 1: The right to be different", *Defence Analysis*, Vol. 14, No. 2 (1998), 169-190.

64. Heidi Swart, "Soldiers and Sex: SANDF and UN Clash", *The Sunday Independent News*, 24 October 2010, 6.

65. Please note that this does not exclude them from the warfighting domain. It reflects the recognition that they may be biologically better suited, for example, to flying attack helicopters than to loading heavy tank rounds. See Martin Van Creveld, *Men, Women & War* (London: Cassell, 2001) for an exposition in this regard.

66. Howe, 2001, 51.

CHAPTER 2

Threats to Professionalism in the United States Military

Lieutenant-Colonel Douglas R. Lindsay, PhD
R. Jeffrey Jackson, PhD
Lieutenant-Colonel Daniel J. Watola, PhD
Craig A. Foster, PhD
*Lieutenant-Colonel Richard T. Ramsey**

Today's military environment is complex and in the midst of unprecedented fluctuation. So pervasive is this situation, that even a cursory view of the literature on military matters will reveal that virtually every article begins with some semblance of this statement. While different authors have varying perspectives as to why this is the case, it is nonetheless, a present day military reality. This "new" reality has both positive and negative manifestations. As an example, suicides in the military have risen in recent years, almost doubling in the Army from 2001 to 2008.[1] Interestingly, although not surprisingly, this time frame coincides with ongoing military operations in Afghanistan and Iraq. While the evidence is still coming in on the direct causes of such adverse consequences of war, it is clear that the ongoing operational tempo of today's military forces is having a powerful and often negative impact on soldiers. It is at this point of impact that the current chapter is aimed. If we know that such a tempo and operational complexity are the new norm in the military, what threats do they have on the professionalism of military forces? How do they impact the military's ability to carry out their missions?

Before examining these questions further, it is important to clarify the concept of professionalism. One definition states that professionalism is "the conduct, aims, or qualities that characterize or mark a profession or a professional person."[2] Put another way, it is "the competence or skill expected of a professional."[3] Consistent with these two definitions is the idea that there are skills and expectations that we have for professionals which vary based on the particular vocation. Medical practioners Sylvia and Richard Cruess[4] who have devoted considerable effort to the study of professionalism within the medical field, expand this expectation further, identifying professionals as:

---

* The views expressed in this chapter are those of the authors and do not necessarily reflect those of the United States Air Force Academy or the United States Department of Defense.

1. possessing a discrete body of knowledge and skills;

2. obtained through a long period of education and training;

3. that provide service to the public via their expertise;

4. with members held to ethical and technical standards that are;

5. higher than expectations of non-professionals.

When we consider the profession of arms, we certainly have high expectations of our military members. This is an obvious statement, but one that is often lost in the tempo of military operations. The military is like no other occupation in terms of its structure and intent. Military forces serve the public (and more specifically, their governments), by providing the strength behind political structures. The military not only offers a realistic deterrent to opposing governments and organizations, but also has the potential to wield an unprecedented level of force and lethality. When examined with this understanding, everyone expects that the wielding of such lethality would rest in the hands of trained and disciplined professionals. In the United States, a significant amount of resources are spent to make sure that this training is effective, efficient, and appropriate.

A challenge that we see today is that current warfare, typically referred to as full-spectrum warfare,[5] is not as straightforward as in the past. Today's military member is called on to wage war in various ways. In fact, during a single combat tour, a soldier could engage in kinetic operations, mentoring of foreign officers, rescue operations, and civil affairs. So common is this notion that terms such as the "Strategic Corporal"[6] have entered our lexicon. This creates a very different environment for the training of our military forces. Of the four examples listed above, which one should you train first? To take a traditional approach, one would focus on kinetic operations due to their serious ramifications. This entails such skills as hand-to-hand combat, marksmanship, and land navigation. To take a more cultural perspective, one would focus on cultural understanding, relationship building, and language proficiency. A compounding challenge is that we must not only prepare our soldiers for the war of today, but also the war of tomorrow. If recent history is any guide, the nature of future wars will shift depending on which hemisphere, time zone, country, and culture we find ourselves. Certainly, this creates challenges to our military professionals who are trying to expand and sharpen their skills and stay current knowing they may never use the specific skills they have spent years honing. Therefore, when we talk about threats to professionalism, it should be obvious that a major challenge will be in acquiring the number, range, proficiency, and currency of knowledge and skills and to implement the right competency at the right time with the right magnitude in highly dynamic and complex environments. Put differently, as the bar for military expertise continues to be raised, more and more is required of military members to maintain the standards of professionalism.

With this understanding of professionalism and the context of current military operations, we would like to provide an example of the threats that US military forces are facing while deployed. While this is a fictional account, the information is based on the real experiences of the authors and other military comrades. This example will serve as the centrepiece for three major challenges to military professionalism: leadership, moral development, and cultural awareness.

DEPLOYMENT EXAMPLE

He was recruited and joined the military to be a warrior – to be part of something larger than himself. He enjoyed serving as part of a team. He felt like his leaders cared about him and his well-being and slowly, their interests became his interests. He viewed those that he worked with (young, impressionable, junior enlisted troops like himself) as his siblings, not mere coworkers. As a result of his own development and performance, having earned the trust of his leaders and with "the potential for even greater responsibility," he quickly earned his non-commissioned officer stripes. As a young sergeant, much of his first deployment involved kinetic action; his unit dealt with direct fire engagements, IEDs, and improvised rocket and insurgent attacks against their forward operating base (FOB) on an almost daily basis. He was competent in such engagements and as a warrior, he saw his mission during the deployment in narrow terms, to kill or be killed in the execution of his commander's intent. Early on, he witnessed the killing of a young soldier in his section and the severe wounding of others. The sergeant had some experience working with host-nation security forces, but generally felt they were incompetent, ill-prepared, and poorly led. He didn't have – and didn't believe he needed to have – any appreciation for the reasons that the security forces were in the state in which he found them when his unit arrived in theatre. The young leader had a few experiences meeting local leaders and had some non-confrontational interactions with the local people, but he mostly distrusted everyone. Because he couldn't easily tell who was friend and who was foe, he usually just assumed everyone was the enemy. His leaders never explained why they went to such lengths to interact with the locals, and he didn't much care since it didn't seem to matter.

USA

When he returned home after this first twelve-month deployment, he felt welcomed and embraced by friends and family. However, he sensed a slight detachment from society. To him, the broader world possessed little to no knowledge about what he had experienced while deployed, and certainly wouldn't have comprehended the stress of being fired on and having to make life and death decisions. Some of the firefights in which the young sergeant had found himself during his trip to the Middle East resulted in death – on both sides. But with more time and distance, he began to have trouble reconciling those deaths. The people he saw at the other end of the optics on his weapon were not uniformed enemy. In fact, most of them looked much like the local leaders he saw on occasion, and aside from the attire, he saw similar faces within his local community. Did he kill the right people? Did he tell the members of his squad to shoot the right targets? Again and again, he found himself wondering if he was missing the big picture and why the people he killed looked like the same people he drank tea with on more than one occasion. Although he was pretty confident he was a good leader at the junior level, he wasn't sure about the true objective of the mission. While he was raising these questions in his mind, he wasn't really wondering how his subordinates were dealing with similar deployment experiences.

As time marched on, he knew his unit was on tap to deploy again in about a year. He had been promoted and was now a mid-level Non-Commissioned officer with more responsibility – to include direct leadership of more people. He repeatedly said his primary responsibility was to train his people and bring them all home, alive and in one piece. His lieutenant had a similar view and was very capable; he seemed to know his stuff when it came to technical and tactical skills and had a strong command presence in the unit, but didn't seem like he really had any idea about the people, culture, or history of the country to which they were preparing to deploy. The lieutenant also did not seem motivated to heed Sun Tzu's advice to "know thy enemy," so there was not a great impetus for the rest of the unit to pay attention to such matters. To this seasoned veteran, this did not seem altogether different from how his leaders approached preparation for his first deployment. Thus, the military mission seemed rather narrow and focused: identify and eradicate the enemy.

When the time came to deploy, the unit was well trained – technically and tactically – and incredibly cohesive, exactly what the lieutenant and his own supervisors expected the unit to be. They even developed a rudimentary understanding of the culture and history of the country to which they were deploying. The unit arrived in country without incident and conducted a relief in place – transfer of authority (RIP-TOA) with the outgoing unit. All went well. During the RIP-TOA, as the incoming and outgoing units conducted operations together, neither experienced any kinetic actions and all seemed relatively calm in the area of operations. For the sergeant and his people, the area seemed especially peaceful compared to their previous deployment.

As the unit assumed control and the operations tempo increased, the unit continued to be involved in very few kinetic operations. A reactive, but legitimate "combat patrol" during which the team anticipated direct fire contact typically followed the rare, inaccurate improvised rocket or mortar attack against the FOB. However, these patrols infrequently resulted in anything but unanswered questions and frustrating engagements with the local population near the firing point of origin. His irritation grew, but he had come to understand their mission was to protect and serve the local people and help them develop their civil capacity, which meant engaging them with words rather than weapons.

He thought that his unit might spend more time engaging the local population with, as his leaders espoused "money as a weapon system" instead of more traditional military weapons systems. However, he was still unsure about this approach and he was uncomfortable in his ability or the ability of his immediate superiors to establish any valuable alliances with the locals. While very few of the enemy seemed interested in engaging the friendly forces in a direct fire fight or with IEDs and explosively formed projectiles (EFPs), he still felt constantly on edge. The unit spent a significant amount of time meeting with local leaders and conversing with the local population. Short of a few kinetic moments, there were no other significant events except for some intermittent indirect fire on the FOB for the remainder of the deployment.

This time when the sergeant returned home, life seemed more difficult than it had after his first deployment. He had trouble sleeping, he couldn't adapt to his old routines, and his relationships seemed distant. In addition, he also had trouble knowing who he could trust. While he initially felt compelled to say something about his adjustment issues to someone in his chain of command, it seemed like everyone else was doing okay and he didn't want to look like the "weak" one in the unit by admitting his troubles. After being back for six months, everything seemed too complicated, distorted, and isolating.

As stated previously, this example is an amalgam of sorts. It is the combination of many different experiences that our military forces are facing. While hypothetical in this specific case, it is not atypical for a soldier to face vastly different missions and experiences on successive deployments or even within the same deployment. That said, this example gives us a backdrop to examine three threats to professionalism that are potentially compromising our military forces. Specifically, leadership is often effective, but there are barriers preventing it from being more effective. Moral reasoning tends to be varied and generally assists with the obedience of military members, but does not fully prepare them for asymmetric warfare. Finally, cultural awareness is becoming a new centre of gravity that is under-developed in comparison to pure combat skills. While there are certainly other threats and impediments that could be examined, these are three that seem to be the most pernicious based on the authors' experiences.

LEADERSHIP

Leadership is an avenue for both describing and addressing these threats. Considering the hierarchical, structured nature of military organizations, direct supervisors are given tremendous responsibility for controlling the effectiveness and well-being of their followers, to include preparation for a deployment. Accordingly, it seems easy to argue that a change in leader behaviour is the only method that will create any substantial defence against the threats that beleaguer military professionalism today. In support of this view, we address key points regarding leadership, the limiting factors of human nature, and leader development. We then provide some related recommendations.

First, leadership matters, and military leadership often matters more due to the dire consequences attached to success and failure. The evidence supporting the link between leadership and performance is consistent across both civilian and military sectors. Indeed, in a recent meta-analysis, transformational leadership had strong positive effects in business, public sector, and military settings.[7] Further, the transformational leadership style had significant relationships with follower motivation, follower satisfaction with leaders, and correspondingly, follower perceptions of leader effectiveness. Within the civilian sector, the relationship between transformational leadership and positive outcomes appears to be internationally robust; Researchers Hsu and Chen[8] identified a similar finding with employee satisfaction in China and Rukmani and Jayakrishnan[9] found that leadership predicted perceived leader effectiveness in India. Psychologists Kaiser, Hogan, and Craig[10] quantified the impact of senior leadership on team and organizational performance, noting that the Chief Executive Officer (CEO) accounts for between 14 and 45% of the overall performance of the organization. In terms of a primary objective within the private/corporate sector, in small businesses effective leadership was strongly linked to profitability.[11] Taken as a whole, there is consistent evidence that good leadership predicts positive organizational outcomes.

The positive relationship between leadership and performance is supported further by research conducted in a military context. Such research demonstrates the positive influence of transformational leadership in military training,[12] leadership style in garrison and during an exercise,[13] leader trustworthiness in the deployed environment,[14] and the influence of leadership on operational readiness.[15] Military-based research also promotes concerns in terms of developing effective leadership for dangerous contexts[16] and comprehensive soldier fitness.[17] To summarize, the common theme in this research is that effective leadership generates positive outcomes, which reflect professionalism. Professionals live up to and achieve a high standard. These high standards should be particularly attractive for the military as an organization that values both leadership and professionalism.

Second, many military leaders need to be more effective. While we admire the arduous roles that military leaders undertake, it seems clear that many military leaders have important areas in which they must improve. As suggested by the example where the NCO is disengaged from his leaders and doesn't give much thought to his subordinates, it might be dangerous and naïve to suggest otherwise. Consider the evidence culled primarily from the civilian world. The base rate for leadership incompetence is reported to be around 50 percent; thus, as many leaders are regarded as ineffective as effective.[18] Further, the vast majority of subordinates report that the most stressful aspect of their work is their supervisor.[19] While it is unlikely that any leader endeavours to be toxic, destructive, tyrannical, passive-avoidant, ineffective or even just adequate, the evidence suggests that many leaders are.

Military leaders might be tempted to think that this research does not pertain to them because they are better at leading than their civilian counterparts. While there are certainly military leaders who are quite effective, it is clear that military leaders are not exempt from ineffective or downright poor leadership. In several studies, researcher and retired Colonel George Reed and colleagues[20] found that every member of their military sample had experienced at least one episode of destructive leadership from a supervisor. The most common forms ranged from playing favourites to being rigid and heavy handed to losing their temper. Moreover, consistent with the aforementioned notion that leadership matters, these destructive displays were strongly related to increased follower dissatisfaction and likelihood of leaving the service. Similarly, those who experienced abusive supervision in another research study were less likely to participate in behaviours that would actually be useful to the organization.[21]

USA

To the extent that leaders are unaware of these negative tendencies, they are unlikely to address them and unlikely to produce optimal results. This should be intolerable in the military context, particularly in the current combat environment where the discrepancy between subordinate perceived incompetence and leader perceived effectiveness can erode trust, morale, coordination, and unit cohesiveness. These conditions may not entirely lead to mission failure, but can easily contribute to inefficiencies. Ultimately, these inefficiencies can literally have life or death consequences in the short-term and problems of readiness and retention in the long-term. To state the obvious, inaccurate perceptions of leadership effectiveness are a serious threat to professionalism.

Third, many military leaders, and leaders more generally, may not self-correct through experience. The major roadblock to self-correction is that military leaders often do not know what they are doing wrong. In the case of the current example, the lieutenant was not aware that he needed to prepare his soldiers with respect to cultural understanding to better accomplish their mission. This begins with a self-enhancement bias in which people tend to process social information in a way that is favourable to their self-concept.[22] For example, most leaders will tend to overestimate the degree to which mission success was due to their leadership, but overestimate the role of external factors, like the quality of their followers, when the mission fails.[23] One outcome of this self-enhancement bias is that individuals will typically maintain a number of positive illusions, which include a tendency to overestimate personal abilities in a several areas.[24] This occurs across many dimensions of human performance; most people think they are better drivers, lovers, students, leaders, and so on compared to the average person. Positive illusions are likely to be rampant in the area of leadership. Leadership is a broad skill that largely measures how well one can work with and get along with other people. As such, it is psychologically difficult for leaders to admit to being average or below average on this characteristic. To make matters worse, leadership is notoriously difficult to measure, and the real world rarely, if ever, presents two completely comparable leadership roles. Thus, leaders can point to nebulous situational factors to dismiss evidence suggesting that their leadership was lackluster. To be fair to leaders, these "justifications" are sometimes accurate. Leaders obviously experience challenges that are difficult to overcome. The problem is that these justifications are sometimes inaccurate, and self-enhancing biases can cause leaders to miss opportunities to develop corresponding self-awareness.

The propensity for individuals to overestimate their leadership abilities works in concert with many organizational dynamics. In particular, leaders have difficulty getting useful feedback due to several barriers limiting its accuracy. For starters, people often avoid direct or seemingly negative feedback because they do not wish to hurt another person emotionally or they do not wish to be viewed negatively as a consequence of providing the feedback. The challenge of providing honest feedback is likely even greater within a military organization, which maintains a hierarchical culture with relatively high power distances between supervisors and followers. In essence, the rank structure and power dynamic can inhibit upward feedback to leaders. As one US Air Force General stated, "When I got my fourth star, I knew I would never again hear the truth."[25] In the business community, this gap in feedback is referred to as "CEO disease."[26] A second limitation is the heavy reliance on the official annual performance appraisal which exacerbates positively biased feedback. Although these reports reflect many of the duties and activities of officers and enlisted members, there is widespread agreement that they are also inflated. While the inflation of performance reports appears to be an administrative necessity to provide subordinates with an equitable chance in the promotion process, the glowing reports provide material for inaccurate positive self-perceptions of leadership ability. Third, the military uses a single rater who provides a top-down evaluation. Fundamental to such a rating system is the direct absence of subordinate input. This process can cause supervisors to provide positive assessments to those leaders who "get results" while possibly undervaluing the degree to which those same leaders are truly exhibiting leadership skills with their peers and subordinates.

The positive bias inherent in organizational feedback might be further enhanced by the tendency to promote based on technical competence rather than leadership skill. This is most apparent in the progression from the individual contributor level to the front-line supervisor, but is an issue at subsequent levels of leadership as well. Oftentimes, success or effectiveness is measured in terms of individual effort, dedicated time spent in duty performance, capability in a particular skill area, capacity to simply complete a lot of work, or some combination of these factors. These factors do not truly reflect leadership in the sense of building a team or getting results through others. Nonetheless, this performance evaluation is taken as an indicator of "having the potential to serve in the higher grade." A limitation, of course, is that this assessment of potential is based on how one performed in the last job, not necessarily how they will perform in the following job, which should entail greater complexity in leadership requirements.[27] In this respect, promotions can serve as false feedback about leadership effectiveness – "keep doing what you've been doing!"

USA

Before we provide recommendations to address these pervasive psychological and organizational impediments to leader development, it is important to be fair to the military and to commend the military for being concerned about threats to professionalism. One type of fairness is to make sure that the military is not singled out in terms of these limitations or barriers. Indeed, any organization is vulnerable to and experiences the same dynamics. The psychological issues are certainly inherent in western culture and the organizational issues are representative of most traditional organizations. That said, this "misery loves company" position offers little consolation for an organization identifying itself as the profession of arms. A second point of fairness is that many leaders urgently strive to overcome these typical barriers and there are systems in place that, at a minimum, offer some structure for support. Thus, many leaders solicit feedback and create the kind of environment where they can collect information about their leadership style and its impact. Similarly, many leaders work hard to accelerate the learning curve to develop competency at the next level of leadership. Support mechanisms in the form of mentoring and climate surveys are also available for use. These are certainly noteworthy, but are not necessarily uniform nor consistently supported by data.

Our first recommendation is that self-awareness, or at least leader awareness, should be a primary target of development and should be a part of the curriculum in every professional military leadership school and program. Self-awareness is seen as a common and core ability in most leadership competency models. There can be great value in preparing leaders to be more effective by increasing their self-awareness, identifying strengths and development opportunities, and supporting the closure of leadership gaps at one's current and next level of leadership. There are multiple methods for developing these kinds of human and social capital. Leadership scholar David Day[28] outlines an assortment of strategies that can be implemented, to include coaching and mentoring, 360-degree feedback, and action learning. There is also an argument to be made that some competencies can be activated through training and education before being hired into a job.[29] Given some of the difficulties in giving and receiving feedback in these relationships, let alone finding and developing such relationships, it may be more useful to systematically include self-awareness development in training programs. The use of personal assessments, such as common personality measures, help leaders understand their style and tendencies as well as the strengths and weaknesses associated with them. Moreover, in a group experience leaders gain firsthand experience about differences in styles, exposing them to the idea that leadership can take different forms and that there is a distribution of personality styles (i.e., "not everyone is like me"). One caution in creating self-awareness is to not undermine a leader's confidence, a variable that also appears critical to leader success. Thus, self-awareness related training should protect leaders' confidence and optimism by showing how self-awareness can improve long-term leader success.

The second recommendation is to extend the culture of providing specific military performance feedback to the broader area of leadership performance. Typically, military organizations are very effective in providing very candid feedback about marksmanship, flying proficiency, bombs on target and other forms of specific skill performance. Feedback for these matters is generally face-to-face, direct, and oriented toward performance and behavioural improvement. This type of feedback is far less commonplace for leadership skills, although many of the same methods for military improvement could be applied to leaders. Leaders who embrace the value of self-awareness, and recognize the common tendency toward self-enhancement, should be more receptive to this kind of feedback.

Related, the third recommendation is to better support the formal and informal use of 360-degree feedback or multi-rater feedback.[30] This is not a new recommendation in general, or specifically within the military. However, this single process has the potential to significantly mitigate many of the vulnerabilities encountered currently. Done correctly, 360-degree assessments overcome the limitations of no feedback, limited feedback, or false feedback. It directly challenges the inclination toward self-enhancement. This evaluation system should identify skills that need to be developed and practiced as well as those that are appropriately used and applied. Although 360-degree assessments draw some criticism, this application nonetheless improves the reliability and validity limitations of the current system. Moreover, the robust and sincere implementation of such a system could shift military culture to a more transparent process. As noted, currently there is objective skill-based information regarding the ability to hit targets with bullets, missiles, and bombs that provides crucial developmental information for being a skilled warrior. This same kind of information is needed for developing skilled and professional leaders.

In summary, effective military leaders ameliorate the existing threats to the US military by:

1. being more likely to successfully complete their respective missions;

2. enhancing the current and ongoing well-being of their troops; and

3. leaving the organization better prepared for its future endeavours.

USA

It is also important, however, to note that in the milieu of modern warfare, the enhanced effectiveness of military leaders has unique opportunities to create a greater moral good as well. In the context of traditional symmetric warfare, effective leadership on one side would frequently involve by definition, more harm and death on the other side (e.g., the better General Patton did the more the Mussolini's Italian army suffered). However, effective military leadership in the context of asymmetric and joint warfare can protect not only the well-being of all warfighters, but also the well-being of local populaces. When alliances with local populations are seen as more effective than defeating the same populations, effective leadership enhances the possibility of a win-win, benefitting both sides rather than a win-lose outcome that lies at the nature of direct, traditional combat.

MORAL REASONING

The sergeant's difficulty in distinguishing between the local leaders he drank tea with while nation building and the enemy he engaged during kinetic operations suggests another serious threat to military professionalism: the potential for immoral or illegal behaviour when faced with the ongoing combat stress of counter-insurgency warfare. The results of an incorrect or improper tactical decision can have strategic consequences, as demonstrated by the prisoner abuses witnessed at Abu Ghraib, the killing of civilians in Haditha, or the more recent killing of civilians in Kandahar. As the nature of modern warfare grows increasingly unconventional, retired Marine General Krulak's[31] "Strategic Corporal" may have difficulty making moral decisions due to outdated military training and the heightened exposure to combat stress that is characteristic of irregular warfare. In fact, the selection and initial training practices employed by the US military may not support a soldier's ability to make prompt, moral decisions on these new urban battlefields.

Selection Practices

The US military recruitment system is designed to attract and recruit young men and women. Military historian Gwynne Dyer[32] suggests young adults are favoured for a number of reasons as they:

1. seek independence from their parents or sponsors;

2. are generally unencumbered by the obligations of spouses or dependent children;

3. are prepared to enter the workforce to earn a paycheque;

4. are eager to develop their own adult identity;

5. are attracted to the instant respect and validation of adulthood the military confers on its members; and,

6. they feel the need to belong to a group such as a "band of brothers."

While young men and women provide the military with a strong, healthy, and malleable resource for warrior development, the young may also be deficient in terms of their worldly experience and moral development. Most young adults demonstrate only a middle range of moral development, which may inadequately support the moral reasoning required of them to be successful in today's wars.

Moral reasoning is the process by which people make ethical (or unethical) decisions, and the quality of moral reasoning reflects the state of one's moral development. Renowned psychologist Lawrence Kohlberg[33] theorized that people progress through six stages of moral development, where successive stages are characterized by increasingly complex methods of analyzing moral situations. The six stages are divided equally into three levels: the preconventional, conventional, and post-conventional. People operating at the preconventional level (predominantly children) make moral decisions based primarily on self-interest. Therefore, their decisions often reflect their obedience to authority in order to obtain rewards or avoid punishment. Those operating at the conventional level (primarily late adolescents and adults) make moral decisions to obtain the approval of others. As a result, they follow rules or laws and do their duty consistent with the missions they have internalized. Finally, few adults ever reach the post-conventional level where moral decisions are based on abstract, universal principles that transcend societal or national boundaries.

Based on this framework, it is clear the military actively recruits young adults operating principally at the conventional level of moral development. This benefits the military given the premium it places on obedience to authority and doing one's duty. However, it also suggests that its youngest recruits, and those most likely to make split-second tactical decisions, may be incapable of post-conventional reasoning. One consequence of the specific application of duty might be neglect of collateral damage incurred in the performance of duty. It is this level of moral development, as demonstrated by the ability to understand and apply moral principles to all peoples that would benefit soldiers most when performing counter-insurgency missions. A lack of such development is a threat to professionalism.

USA

Training Practices

The US military's basic training system that is very successful in socializing civilians into soldiers, may very well handicap these soldiers by biasing them toward a "shoot first" and "reason later" decision process. Dyer[34] claims that military institutions require the obedience of its members even unto death and the killing of others; however, the military's authority ultimately requires the consent of its members. Basic training extracts this consent from members through carefully orchestrated techniques and practices. For example, the conduct of hygiene, uniform, or weapons inspections involves a soldier's unquestioned submission to authority. During an inspection, a soldier stands still (e.g., at rigid attention with eyes staring straight ahead), while somebody painstakingly examines the soldier for the most trivial of faults. Similarly, military members typically learn close order drill (marching in formation) during basic training, even though it has been over one-hundred years since mass formations were tactically used on the battlefield. What practical purpose does this serve? Dyer suggests the act of moving in concert with others teaches two things: you are no longer an individual but part of a group, and orders have to be obeyed automatically and instantly. Thus, basic training encourages doing one's duty and instant obedience to superiors. These habits may be well suited to the clear-cut rules of regular warfare, but may be incompatible with the ambiguity of today's counter-insurgency missions.

In addition to obedience and duty, basic training also engenders another major outcome: the capacity to kill on command. Former US Army Ranger Lieutenant-Colonel Grossman[35] suggests that only recently have we learned that this capacity is difficult to develop in soldiers. Specifically, US Army Colonel S.L.A. Marshall studied soldiers' combat performance in the Second World War and found that only 15 percent of trained riflemen fired their weapons when in contact with the enemy, even when their positions were under attack and their lives were in immediate danger. In response, the army modified its basic training program by incorporating forms of classical and operant conditioning to elicit the appropriate lethal response.[36] Dyer suggested that persuading soldiers to kill the enemy is now a central part of the training process, as the bull's eye targets at the end of long, grassy fields have been replaced by human silhouettes that pop-up briefly and require an immediate response from the soldier. Such weapons training is designed to establish "reflex pathways that bypass the moral censor."[37] To Grossman, shooting human targets in combat scenarios amounts to a program of desensitization, conditioning, and denial as a defence mechanism. Dyer reported that when Marshall reinvestigated shooting rates during the Korean War in the early 1950s, he found that 50 percent of infantrymen were firing their weapons. As these training modifications continued, between 80 and 95 percent of American soldiers were reported to be shooting to kill by the Vietnam War.[38]

To take young adults who have spent much of their lives hearing that killing is wrong, and turn them into soldiers who will kill instantly on command is no easy task, but the military does this routinely in as little as six weeks during basic training. This is possible, in part, due to the conditioning described in the preceding paragraph, but more specifically by applying methods of moral disengagement. Psychologist Albert Bandura[39] suggests there is ample support for the power of moral disengagement practices to encourage seemingly immoral behaviours once activated,[40] especially in periods of strife and tyranny.[41] He goes on to state "the conversion of socialized people into combatants dedicated to killing foes is achieved not by altering their personality structures, aggressive drives, or moral standard…rather it is accompanied by restructuring the morality of lethal means so they can be free from self-censure." These methods include moral justification (e.g., fighting ruthless oppressors), euphemistic labeling (e.g., "servicing" a target), advantageous comparison (e.g., bombing Vietnam to save it from communist oppression), displacement of responsibility (e.g., "I was just following orders"), diffusion of responsibility (e.g., performing a small, but key role in a violent act), disregard or distortion of consequences (e.g., employing stand-off or remotely-controlled weapons), and dehumanization (e.g., referring to the enemy as sub-human or demonic).

The preceding methods of moral disengagement are effectively employed to socialize soldiers in basic training, and they are also critical to arouse a nation as it prepares for war. McAlister, Bandura, and Owen[42] studied the relationship between moral disengagement and support for military force immediately following the attack on the World Trade Center on September 11, 2001. They found that moral disengagement completely mediated the effect of the terrorist attack on public support for the use of force against terrorists, leading them to conclude when a nation goes to war, it must "create conditions that enable soldiers to inflict death, destruction and suffering without exacting a heavy personal toll of chronic stress, guilt and anguish…through the various mechanisms of moral disengagement." After being exposed to these methods of moral disengagement in basic training, they are likely to continue to affect soldiers' behaviour while deployed. Our intent here is not to say that the training that occurs during basic training is inappropriate. Rather, it is to point out that by creating such conditions, there could be predictable consequences when a soldier is put under stress in a wartime environment (or even upon redeployment). Again, it a potential threat to the professionalism of our military forces that is governed by the Laws of Armed Conflict and readily visible and judged by a media-rich public.

Combat Stress

One final characteristic of counter-insurgency (commonly referred to as COIN) warfare, combat stress, may also serve to diminish a soldier's moral reasoning. Brigadier-General Herbert McMaster[43] asserts that it is often combat stress, not a lack of ethics, that leads to unprofessional, unethical, or immoral behaviour on the battlefield. COIN environments are characterized by violence, immorality, distrust and deceit. When uncertainty is combined with persistent danger, the resulting stress erodes military professionalism and the moral character of soldiers and units.[44] Researchers John Taylor and Stanley Baker[45] found some evidence for this in their study of moral development in combat veterans. Specifically, they found that post-traumatic stress disorder-diagnosed veterans demonstrated lower moral development as measured by Rest's[46] Defining Issues Test than non-diagnosed veterans. When combat stress arrests soldiers' moral reasoning abilities, then the potential for immoral action (e.g., prisoner abuse or the killing of civilians) increases. Such actions serve to undermine the COIN effort when insurgents use these negative examples to portray the opposition as unethical as judged by the opposition's own standards of behavior.[47] For this reason, military leaders must ensure soldiers take the moral high ground despite the perceived depravity of the enemy.

Collectively, the military's selection system and training practices take a population whose moral development level is mid-level and whose moral reasoning is focused on the concepts of obedience and duty, and then instills them with a preference toward kinetic solutions by applying moral disengagement techniques in order to facilitate violent action against the enemy in the pursuit of national objectives. While understandable in a traditional military environment, these practices, however, may fail to prepare soldiers for the moral reasoning demands of the COIN battlefield. Simultaneously, the enhanced combat stress that is characteristic of irregular warfare serves to exacerbate the problem by diminishing the soldier's capacity for moral reasoning. Put simply, without continuous moral development training and combat stress reduction programs,[48] the US military may be setting itself up for a threat to the professionalism of their soldiers.

CULTURAL AWARENESS

A third threat to professionalism that is highlighted in the example is the failure to understand the role of culture and having cultural awareness in conducting military operations. As has been seen in recent history (especially in those conflicts that the United States has been involved in such as Operation Iraqi Freedom and Operation Enduring Freedom), COIN operations have become the norm. This type of warfare was emphasized by General David Petraeus during his time in command in both Iraq and Afghanistan. This is an asymmetrical type of warfare where there are not large standing armies fighting against each other, and where the goal is the eradication of the enemy, sometimes at a high cost to, or in spite of, the local population. In the traditional form of warfare, it is easy to spot the enemy as they are typically wearing a uniform and are firing at you. In an insurgency environment, however, these types of scenarios are non-existent. One side is outnumbered and as the asymmetric name applies, uses non-traditional tactics to gain an advantage on the superior force. This involves the use of such techniques as suicide bombs, IEDs, and rocket attacks. While the smaller force is no match for a direct offensive, insurgents effectively use these types of indirect attacks to keep the larger force off balance and have a significant, unsettling impact on the civilian population.

In a COIN operation, since there is no large, omnipresent military structure to focus on, the primary focus becomes the local civilian population. In military terms, this is often referred to as "winning the hearts and minds" of the local population. In order to win the hearts and minds of the local population, one must understand what is important to that population. This is where cultural awareness and understanding becomes critical. If one enters the dialogue with an ethnocentric position, this will necessarily impact the subsequent discourse. The failure to understand the other side represents a threat to professionalism along two primary factors.

The first of these factors has to do with understanding where one is. This is more than a geographic or physical understanding of the local terrain. It literally means understanding the context in which one is conducting military operations. A tenet of successful COIN operations is the power of the local population. In the case of Afghanistan, the local population is facing pressures from the Taliban as well as Coalition forces (e.g., International Security Assistance Forces or ISAF). This creates a push-pull relationship on the population. While there is the physical component to the struggle, the preeminent prize is the support and participation of the local population. From the Coalition's perspective, they would like to engage the population to oppose the Taliban and their practices. The challenge is that in order to engage them, Coalition forces must understand where they are and what is important to the local population. The issue must be more compelling than the Taliban presence, threat, or rhetoric or no positive movement will be made. Trying to use a solely western mindset in dialog with the Afghan population will be ineffective as it imposes a decision paradigm that is not consistent with Afghan processes. Therefore, military forces must have a basic understanding of the local population before any hearts or minds are "won." This understanding must happen early in a soldier's career since it is not something that can be gained overnight. This means that in order to combat this threat to professionalism, training must occur early and consistently and not just right before the soldier is ready to deploy.

One must also know the enemy. On the surface, this seems pretty basic. If one wants to defeat the enemy, one must understand their motivations, their training, their tactics, and so forth. Of course, militaries have been working on understanding each other for centuries and utilize tactics such as surveillance, reconnaissance, and unmanned aerial vehicles to gain an advantage on the enemy. What is noticeably different in a COIN environment is that it is difficult to distinguish the combatants from the local population. In fact, they are often one and the same. This makes it difficult when a patrol is under fire and has to make rapid fire/don't fire decisions. In such scenarios, there are often rules of engagement that must be followed which dictate what actions can be taken at what time. At the same time, we must understand the enemy's rules of engagement and understand that in a COIN environment, they are likely to be much different from our own (e.g., suicide bombs, IEDs., etc.). This concomitant understanding of both the host nation's population and the enemy's process make for a difficult battlefield and pose a threat to professionalism and the professional conduct of military forces.

The second factor that must be understood has to do with a relatively new mission that our military personnel face: mentoring of foreign forces. In fact, the United States alone has thousands of service men and women stationed in Iraq and Afghanistan in a purely mentorship role. Their job is to help develop and train their counterparts. From a technical perspective, it is easy to train someone on a task. However, when one considers the actual context in which they are operating, it becomes much more complicated. For example, in the United States (and in the majority of nations around the world), corruption is something that is not morally accepted. In fact, when it is discovered it is typically dealt with quickly and severely. However, in Afghanistan, corruption (i.e., bribes, payoffs, etc.), is not uncommon and is typically seen as a normal part of life. In many cases, it is literally a cost of doing business. The challenge is that when billions of dollars are entering Afghanistan every year, how is the issue of corruption managed? From the American taxpayer's standpoint, there is very little tolerance for taxes going to support a process that has even a hint of corruption, let alone an expectation of such. On the other hand, from a governmental perspective, it is just part of navigating the political process in the country.

From a practical perspective, in order to mentor effectively, one must understand not only the individual you are working in, but also the environment in which the individual works. This is the crux of the challenge. If mentors are advising their protégés without fully understanding their motivation and context, this level of benign ignorance can lead to a non-productive situation for both parties. In reference to the previous example, the mentor must understand the role of corruption in the country in order to mentor effectively within that context. That does not mean accepting the situation, but an understanding will aid in the development of a mentoring situation that will understand this fact, in order to work around it. Otherwise, one ends up with western judgements that create an ineffective situation and hurt the credibility and professionalism of all those involved.

DISCUSSION

Professionalism requires a high level of expertise and the ability to perform to high standards as well as stand up to the judgement of external evaluators. Each of the three targeted areas, leadership, moral reasoning, and cultural awareness are seen as critical and emerging components of professionalism in the armed forces. Competency in any one area is challenging, yet the requirement in modern warfare demands proficiency in all areas. Thus, significant threats to professionalism include the exponential increase in the requirements for the military, the lag in training and development and acquisition of a rudimentary level of expertise, the possibility of human limitations in acquiring high levels of proficiency across all required areas, and the belief among some military members that this higher level of competency is not vital in asymmetric warfare.

All of these threats can be addressed and some are currently receiving attention. In the American military, leadership training is required at multiple levels. As noted earlier, there are opportunities to improve this training and make it more robust. Further, it may be essential to provide booster training in leadership analogous to obtaining supplementary immunizations prior to deployment. Pre-deployment leadership training can emphasize core leadership skills and vulnerabilities that are very specific to the destination theater. Such training needs to complement technical skills and promote effectiveness in dealing with and supporting cohesiveness, self-efficacy, and well-being of the warfighters. This type of training can help leaders better understand when unilateral, authority-based decision-making is necessary and when collaborative decision-making is better.

Similar processes need to be done with moral reasoning. While the Law of Armed Conflict provides fundamental guidance, outside of the fog and friction of combat, it is valuable to examine moral reasoning from conventional and post-conventional levels. In dealing with civilians, prisoners, children as suicide bombers, an indistinguishable enemy and so on, perspectives that include the scope of duty and universal principles are valuable tools for preparing the moral battlefield in addition to the physical battlefield. This does not mean these decisions will be easier, but the ability to make better decisions might mean losing a tactical opportunity to gain a strategic victory.

Finally, more training can be used to acquire a broader perspective on culture and the customs of indigenous peoples. Moving from western or fundamental ethnocentrism to a more relative appreciation of cultural style fosters relationships and creates leverage points for military missions. As the centre of gravity shifts from lethal power to relational power, the ability to appreciate, connect, and relate creates an advantage that cannot be obtained via domination and alienation. Cultural intelligence promotes military intelligence and is vital to counter-insurgency operations.

One opportunity for thinking outside of the cultural box is to use the model of distributed learning or what has been called in groups, transactive memory. The basic idea here is that not everyone needs to have the highest levels of expertise, but someone does, and all should know who to go to when that expertise must be accessed. Thus, there is the possibility of deliberately designing and using specialty knowledge within military units. This is most easily illustrated in terms of cultural awareness, where a small component of the unit could represent the unit in terms of this expertise. This doesn't necessarily require that this group of people conduct all of the interface with the local population, but this group should be seen as the authority and guide for such engagements. In contrast, effective leadership skills and more highly developed moral reasoning should be distributed across the unit, but those in leadership roles should definitely be highly competent and should guide and influence the moral behaviour of the unit members. Clearly these are not small challenges to overcome, but responding to threats is something the military does well. This is another opportunity to demonstrate the professionalism of our military forces.

CONCLUSION

As the example illustrates, warfare today is vastly different than warfare of the past and these differences create certain threats to the professionalism of our military forces. While the concerns raised in this chapter pertain directly to the United States military, it is likely that most militaries are facing similar challenges. The key take away from this chapter is the fact that we need to fully understand and prepare our soldiers for the environment they will face in order for them to be effective. This speaks directly to the readiness of our forces and what we are doing to prepare them to operate effectively in a non-traditional warfare environment.

ENDNOTES

1. George Mastroianni and Wil Scott, "Reframing Suicide in the Military", *Parameters*, Vol. 41 (2011), 6-21.

2. Professionalism. in *Merriam-Webster.com*, retrieved 22 March 2012 from <http://www.merriam-webster.com/dictionary/professionalism>.

3. Professionalism. in *OxfordDictionaries.com*, retrieved 22 March 2012 from <http://oxforddictionaries.com/definition/professionalism?q=professionalism>.

4. Sylvia Cruess and Richard Cruess, "Professionalism Must Be Taught", *British Medical Journal,* Vol. 315 (1997), 1674-1677.

5. Craig Foster and Douglas Lindsay, "Generational Difference and the Future of the United States Military", in Julie Bélanger and Psalm Lew, eds., *Developing the Next Generation of Military Leaders* (Kingston, ON: Canadian Defence Academy Press, 2011).

6. Charles Krulak, "The Strategic Corporal: Leadership in the Three Block War", *Marines Magazine*, Vol. 28 (1999).

7. Timothy Judge and Ronald Piccolo, "Transformational and Transactional Leadership: A Meta-Analytic Test of Their Relative Validity", *Journal of Applied Psychology*, Vol. 89 (2004), 755-768.

8. Chia-Yuan Hsu and Wen-Yu Chen, "Subordinates' Perception of Managers' Transformational Leadership Style and Satisfaction: A Comparison of Electronic Manufacturing Companies in Mainland China and Taiwan", *International Journal of Human Resource Management*, Vol. 22 (2011), 3097-3108.

9. K Rukmani, M. Ramesh, and J. Jayakrishnan, "Effect of Leadership Styles on Organizational Effectiveness", *European Journal of Social Science*, Vol. 15, No.3 (2010), 365-370.

10. Robert Kaiser, Robert Hogan and Bartholomew Craig, "Leadership and the Fate of Organizations", *The American Psychologist*, Vol. 63 (2008), 96-110.

11. Glenn Valdiserri and John Wilson, "The Study of Leadership in Small Business Organizations: Impact on Profitability and Organizational Success", *Entrepreneurial Executive*, Vol. 15 (2010), 47-71.

12. Taly Dvir, Dov Eden, Bruce Avolio and Boas Shamir, "Impact of Transformational Leadership on Follower Development and Performance", *Academy of Management Journal*, Vol. 45 (2002), 735-744.

13. Bernard Bass, Bruce Avolio, Dong Jung and Yair Berson, "Predicting Unit Performance by Assessing Transformational and Transactional Leadership", *Journal of Applied Psychology*, Vol. 88 (2003), 207-218.

14. Patrick Sweeney, "Do Soldiers Reevaluate Trust in Their Leaders Prior to Combat Operations?", *Military Psychology*, Vol. 22 (2010), 70-88.

15. James Griffith, "Multilevel Analysis of Cohesion's Relation to Stress, Well-Being, Identification, Disintegration, and Perceived Combat Readiness", *Military Psychology*, Vol. 14 (2002), 217-239.

16. This is often referred to as in extremis leadership; Tom Kolditz, *In Extremis Leadership: Leading as if your Life Depended on it* (San Francisco, CA: Jossey-Bass, 2007).

17. Rhonda Cornum, Michael Matthews and Martin Seligman, "Comprehensive Soldier Fitness: Building Resilience in a Challenging Institutional Context," *The American Psychologist*, Vol. 66 (2011), 4-9.

18. Robert Hogan, Gordon Curphy and Joyce Hogan, "What We Know About Leadership: Effectiveness and Personality", *American Psychologist*, Vol. 49, (1994), 493-504; and, Robert Hogan and Robert Kaiser, "What We Know About Leadership", *Review of General Psychology*, Vol. 9 (2005), 169-180.

19. Robert Hogan, *Personality and the Fate of Organizations* (Hillsdale, NJ: Erlbaum, 2007); and, Robert Hogan and Robert Kaiser, 2005.

20. George Reed and Richard Olsen, "Toxic Leadership: Part Deux", *Military Review*, Vol. 90 (2010), 58-64; George Reed and Craig Bullis, "The Impact of Destructive Leadership on Senior Military Officers and Civilian Employees", *Armed Forces & Society*, Vol. 36 (2009), 5-18.

21. Kelly Zellars, Bennett Tepper and Michelle Duffy, "Abusive Supervision and Subordinates' Organizational Citizenship Behavior", *Journal of Applied Psychology*, Vol. 87 (2002), 1068-1076.

22. Constantine Sedikides and Aiden Gregg, "Self-Enhancement, Food for Thought", *Perspectives on Psychological Science*, Vol. 3 (2008), 102-116.

23. Keith Campbell and Constantine Sedikides, "Self-threat Magnifies the Self-serving Bias: A Meta-analytic Integration," *Review of General Psychology*, Vol. 3 (1997), 23-43.

24. Shelley Taylor and Jonathon Brown, "Illusion and Well-being: A Social Psychological Perspective on Mental Health", *Psychological Bulletin*, Vol. 103 (1988), 193-210.

25. Gen Stephen Lorenz, *Presentation to Air Officers Commanding*, (Colorado Springs, CO: United States Air Force Academy, 14 September 2010).

26. John Byrne, "CEO Disease", *Business Week*, April (1991), 52-59. "CEO Disease" is a term that describes a situation where subordinates are hesitant to share information with the leader, especially when that information is negative.

27. Stephen Drotter and Ram Charan, "Building Leaders at Every Level: A Leadership Pipeline", *Ivey Business Journal*, Vol. 65 (2001), 21-27.

28. David Day, "Leadership Development: A Review in Context", *Leadership Quarterly*, Vol. 11 (2000), 581-613.

29. Robert Jackson and Douglas Lindsay, "Lessons for Experience: Why Wait?", *Industrial and Organizational Psychology: Perspectives on Science and Practice*, Vol. 3 (2010), 48-51.

30. For a distinction between these types of feedback see Craig Foster and Melanie Law, "How Many Perspectives Provide a Compass? Differentiating 360-Degree and Multi-Source Feedback", *International Journal of Selection and Assessment*, Vol.14 (2006), 288-291.

31. Charles Krulak, 1999.

32. Gwynne Dyer, *War: The Lethal Custom* (New York, NY: Carroll & Graf, 2004).

33. Lawrence Kohlberg, "Stage and Sequence: The Cognitive-Developmental Approach to Socialization", in D. A. Goslin, ed., *Handbook of Socialization Theory and Research* (Chicago: Rand McNally, 1969), 347-480.

34. Gwynne Dyer, 2004.

35. Dave Grossman, *On Killing: The Psychological Cost of Learning to Kill in War and Society* (New York, NY: Back Bay Books, 1996).

36. Ibid.

37. Gwynne Dyer, 2004, 58.

38. Ibid; Dave Grossman, 1996.

39. Albert Bandura, "Moral Disengagement in the Perpetration of Inhumanities", *Personality and Social Psychology Review,* Vol. 3(1999), 193-209.

40. Albert Bandura, Bill Underwood and Michael Fromson, "Disinhibition of Aggression Through Diffusion of Responsibility and Dehumanization of Victims", *Journal of Research in Personality*, Vol. 9 (1975), 253-269.; Edward Diener, John Dineen, Karen Endresen, Arthur Beaman and Scott Fraser, "Effects of Altered Responsibility, Cognitive Set, and Modeling on Physical Aggression and Deindividuation", *Journal of Personality and Social Psychology*, Vol. 31 (1975), 328-337.; Stanley Milgram, *Obedience to Authority: An Experimental View* (New York: Harper & Row, 1974).; and, Philip Zimbardo, "The Human Choice: Individuation, Reason, and Order Versus Deindividuation, Impulse, and Chaos", in David Levine and William Arnold, eds., *Nebraska Symposium on Motivation* (Lincoln, NE: University of Nebraska Press, 1969), 237-309.

41. Burton Andrus, *The Infamous Nuremberg* (London: Fravin. 1969).; Albert Bandura, "The Role of Selective Moral Disengagement in Terrorism and Counterterrorism", in Fathali Mogahaddam and Anthony Marsella, eds., *Understanding Terrorism: Psychological Roots, Consequences and Interventions* (Washington, DC: American Psychological Association Press, 2004), 121-150.; Robert Ivie, "Images of Savagery in American Justifications for War", *Communication Monographs,* Vol. 47 (1980), 270-294.; Herbert Kelman and Lee Hamilton, *Crimes of Obedience: Toward a Social Psychology of authority and responsibility* (New Haven, CT: Yale University Press, 1989).; David Rapoport and Yonah Alexander, *The Morality of Terrorism: Religious and Secular Justification* (Elmsford, NY: Pergamon Press, 1982).; and, Walter Reich, *Origins of Terrorism: Psychologies, Ideologies, Theologies, States of Mind* (Cambridge, England: Cambridge University Press, 1990).

42. Alfred McAlister, Albert Bandura and Steven Owen, "Mechanisms of Moral Disengagement in Support of Military Force: The Impact of Sept. 11", *Journal of Social and Clinical Psychology*, Vol. 25 (2006), 141-165.

43. Herbert McMaster, "Preserving Soldiers' Moral Character in Counter-Insurgency Operation*"*, in Don Carrick, James Connelly and Paul Robinson, eds., *Ethics Education for Irregular Warfare* (Burlington, VT: Ashgate, 2009), 15-26.

44. Department of the Army, FM 100-5, *Operations* (Washington, DC: Department of the Army, 1976).

USA

45. John Taylor and Stanley Baker, "Psychosocial and Moral Development of PTSD-Diagnosed Combat Veterans", *Journal of Counseling & Development,* Vol. 85 (2007), 364-369.

46. James Rest, *Defining Issues Test Manual*, 3rd ed. (Minneapolis, MN: Center for the Study of Ethical Development, 1990).

47. Department of the Army, 1976.

48. McMaster, 2009.; Stefan Seiler, Andres Fischer and Yoon Ooi, "An Interactional Dual-Process Model of Moral Decision Making to Guide Military Training", *Military Psychology,* Vol. 22 (2010), 490-509.; and, Eva Wortel and Jolanda Bosch, "Strengthening Moral Competence: A 'Train the Trainer' Course on Military Ethics", *Journal of Military Ethics,* Vol. 10 (2011), 17-35.

CHAPTER 3

Higher Education and the Profession of Arms: Explaining the Logic

Dr. Bill Bentley
*Colonel Bernd Horn**

The question often arises amongst senior officers as to what the requirement for higher, or more accurately, graduate education is. Although few, if any, would deny the value of such an investment, the barrier is always time. For individuals who are exceptionally busy, the issue continues to be the trade-off between time spent on studies and time available to clear the ever present day-to-day workload. Many default to a position that time spent in an appointment or rank adequately prepares the individual for the challenges they encounter or will face in the future. Others argue that the failure of senior officers to pursue higher education becomes a danger to leadership and a threat to professionalism as they will be unprepared to steward the profession and navigate the institution through the complexity of the security environment. In fact, at the core of any profession is the requirement for higher education in order to master the theory-based body of abstract knowledge that underpins the profession itself. This is as true for the profession of arms as it is for medicine, law, engineering, and other widely recognized professions. The body of knowledge in question here is the General System of War and Conflict comprising tactics, operational art, strategy and policy.

So what exactly is the requirement for graduate education for senior officers? There is no "silver bullet" answer to the question; no quantifiable data that can categorically provide comprehensive proof. Rather, the response to the question lies in the logic – the argument for the critical importance of education for senior officers in the profession of arms. The starting point stems from the great Prussian theorist Carl von Clausewitz. He clearly identified that "If we pursue the demands that war makes on those who practice it we come to the realm of intellect."[1]

Simply stated, all members of the profession of arms in Canada must possess a deep and comprehensive understanding of the necessity, if we profess to truly

---

* The views expressed in this chapter are those of the authors and do not necessarily reflect those of the Canadian Forces.

CANADA

consider ourselves a profession in Western society, to possess a deep understanding and comprehension of a relevant body of knowledge. More exactly, as Eliot Freidson, a leading scholar on the subject of professionalism identifies, "A profession has a formal program that produces the qualifying credentials, which is controlled by the profession and associated with higher education."[2]

And, there is good reason. The failure to abide by this tenet could have serious repercussions as the institution discovered in the 1990s. By 1997, Doug Young, the Minister of National Defence (MND), General Maurice Baril, the Chief of the Defence Staff (CDS), and Louise Frechette, the Deputy Minister (DM), were all seriously concerned that the balance among the four pillars of professional development – training, education, experience and self-development – had become distorted and very problematic. Missing was an emphasis on education, particularly higher learning.[3] The MND confirmed, "Without higher education you're not tuned into what's happening in the larger society." He concluded, "That's where we lost the ball."[4]

As a result, Young, supported by monographs written by four eminent Canadian scholars – Jack Granatstein, Desmond Morton, Albert Legault and David Bercuson – oversaw the production of *The Defence Minister's Report to the Prime Minister on Leadership and Management in the Canadian Forces*.[5] The centre of gravity of this Report was the importance of higher education. Among the most important results were the stand-up of the Canadian Defence Academy, *Officership 2020*, *NCM Corps 2020* and the creation of the Applied Military Science Course and the National Security Studies Course at the Canadian Forces College (CFC). However, that was over a decade ago and predates the Canadian Force's (CF) involvement in Afghanistan, the Indian Ocean and Libya. If anything, today's security environment is much more challenging, complex and unpredictable than at the close of the 20th century. Arguably, the need for higher education is even greater today.

But the logic, or requirement for graduate education for senior officers goes beyond the failing of the past due to a lack of higher education or the more complex security environment. A second critical characteristic of any true profession is captured by scholar Andrew Abbott, another expert on the subject of professions. He observes that "In any profession practical skill grows out of an abstract system of knowledge, and control of the profession lies in control of the abstractions." Abbott asserts, "This characteristic of abstraction is the one that best identifies the professions." He explains, "Only a knowledge system governed by abstractions can redefine its problems and tasks, defend them against interlopers, and seize new problems."[6] For the Canadian Profession of Arms, this abstract system of theory based knowledge at the core of the profession is the General System of War and Conflict, illustrated below in Figure 3.1.

FORMAL EDUCATION

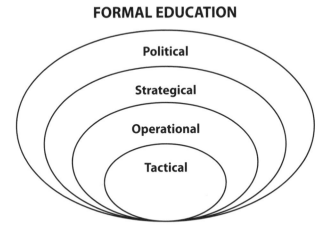

Figure 3.1: The General System of War and Conflict

This system must be understood as a complex adaptive system as described in complexity science. The system becomes less linear and more complex as one ascends from the tactical to the politico-strategic level. Formal education becomes the mechanism that allows and individual to better comprehend and understand the integrated, multifaceted, intricate and complex context of the military profession within the larger world it exists in. It is critical to mastering the necessary body of knowledge.

This requirement has long been understood by those studying the profession. Renowned strategist, Colin S. Gray identifies a key abstraction within the realm senior officers exist. He states, that "Strategy is virtual behaviour, it has no material existence." Gray explains, "Strategy is an abstraction, though it is vastly more difficult to illustrate visually than are other vital abstractions like love and fear."[7] Israeli strategist Shimon Naveh makes a similar, if more abstruse, point. He insists, "Military strategy evolves in a dynamic learning environment of praxis, which is a spatial reflection of the tensions between the ontological analysis of reality and the epistemological understanding of institutional knowledge, between conceptualization and application, theorizing and performance, institutionalization and change."[8]

Importantly, operational art, the playground of senior officers, is only slightly less abstract than strategy. Naveh asserts, "We can legitimately argue that the conceptualization of operational art transformed military science in a pattern resembling relativity and quantum mechanic."[9] He notes, "The development of operational art as a neoteric field of knowledge provided for the first time in the history of modern military thought an intermediate environment for discourse, which bridges harmoniously over the traditional cognitive gap between the conventional fields of military knowledge."[10]

The central point is that officers, particularly general officers, require knowledge and understanding at a higher level once they leave the tactical level of operations and staff appointments. They need a wider and deeper understanding of human behaviour, politics and the world around them, to mention just a few areas, in order to be able to operate effectively. Given this increasing complexity as one ascends the hierarchy in the General System of War and Conflict, higher education becomes a necessity. Military strategist Barry Watts underscores the requirement. He affirmed, "The cognitive skills exercised by combatants with tactical expertise differ fundamentally from those required of operational artists and competent strategists."[11] In fact, Watts identified a cognitive boundary as illustrated in Figure 3.2.

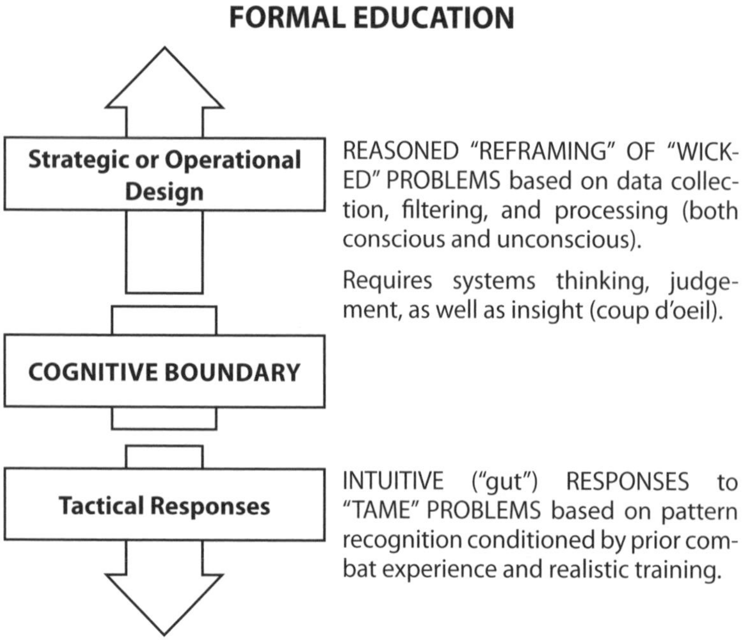

FORMAL EDUCATION

Strategic or Operational Design

REASONED "REFRAMING" OF "WICKED" PROBLEMS based on data collection, filtering, and processing (both conscious and unconscious).

Requires systems thinking, judgement, as well as insight (coup d'oeil).

COGNITIVE BOUNDARY

Tactical Responses

INTUITIVE ("gut") RESPONSES to "TAME" PROBLEMS based on pattern recognition conditioned by prior combat experience and realistic training.

Figure 3.2: Cognitive Boundary

In essence, the boundary is between the tactical level and the operational level. Therefore, crossing this boundary and operating as operational artists and military strategists requires advanced education, specifically graduate level education at either the Masters or PhD levels. Gray drives this point home persuasively. He argues, "Because strategy is uniquely difficult among the levels of war and conflict few, indeed, are the people able to shine in the role of strategist." He insists, "Their number can be increased by education though not by training, and not at all reliably by the experience of command and planning at warfare's operational and tactical levels."[12] Henry Yarger, yet another expert in the field, supports Gray's thesis. He points out that "strategy remains the domain of the strong intellect, the lifelong student and the dedicated professional."[13]

In short, senior officers of all ranks can never stop studying and learning if they are to lead and act as stewards of the profession into the future. Moreover, the General System of War and Conflict discussed above always takes place in a real world, within a contemporary context that is ever changing and evolving. Importantly, this context is accessed, created and understood through the study of conventional academic disciplines such as Geo-Politics, International Relations, History, Sociology, Anthropology, Economics and Science and Technology. Given the nature of the abstract theory-based body of knowledge at the core of the profession of arms, the old paradigm that is based on the concept that successful tactical command equals promotion, must be rejected. The new paradigm for the 21st century quite simply is : successful tactical command, plus higher education, equals promotion.

Respected American commander and warfighter, and current Director of the US Central Intelligence Agency, General David Petraeus, confirmed the need of graduate level education for senior commanders. He believes "Such experiences are critical to the development of the flexible, adaptable, creative thinkers who are so important to operations in places like Iraq and Afghanistan." Moreover, he concluded that graduate studies "provide a fair amount of general intellectual capital and often provides specific skills and knowledge on which an officer may draw during his or her career." Importantly, Petraeus insisted, "graduate school inevitably helps U.S. military officers improve their critical thinking skills."[14] It is no different for Canadian officers.

And so, a summary of the logic for higher education for CF officers is as follows:

- All officers need an undergraduate degree.[15]

CANADA

- All lieutenant-colonels and colonels employed at the operational or strategic levels need a graduate degree(s) from as wide a selection of universities as possible.

- All general officers / flag officers (GO/FO) require a graduate degree.

- A PhD is desirable (but not mandatory) for a GO/FO but it should be acquired prior to promotion to Flag rank.

- All GO/FOs should be involved in a comprehensive program of secondments, seminars, two-week courses, three-, six- and twelve-month programs, fellowships, etc. This program could be administered by the Canadian Defence Academy but must be directed by the CDS as the Head of the Profession of Arms in Canada.

The investment in graduate and post-graduate education in both time and resources is undisputedly high. However, the responsibility of senior officers to navigate the institution through an often ambiguous, perpetually changing, and always complex and dangerous world, imposes the obligation on its stewards. After all, those who claim the title of professional, and who society has entrusted with the safety of the nation and the lives of its sons and daughters, are obliged to ensure they are as prepared as possible to provide advice to the government and lead the nation in harm's way. Failure to do so, arguably, becomes a threat to leadership and professionalism.

ENDNOTES

1. Carl von Clausewitz, *On War*, in Michael Howard and Peter Paret, ed. (Princeton, NJ: Princeton University Press, 1976) 135.

2. Eliot Freidson, *Professionalism* (Chicago: Chicago University Press, 2001), 127.

3. Only 53.3 percent of officers had a Bachelor's degree and only 6.8 percent had graduate level education at the time.

4. Vice-Admiral Larry Murray, interview with Dr. Bill Bentley and Colonel Bernd Horn, PhD, 6 October 2010.

5. Doug Young, MND, *Report to the Prime Minister on the Leadership and Management of the Canadian Armed Forces* (Ottawa, ON: DND, 1997).

6. Andrew Abbott, *The System of Professions* (Chicago: Chicago University Press, 1988), 9.

7. Colin S. Gray, *The Strategy Bridge: Theory for Practice* (Oxford: Oxford University Press, 2011), 61.

8. Shimon Naveh, *Discursive Command – Operators – Systemic Operational Design: A New Framework for Strategic Epistemology*, (2005), 1, retrieved on 10 October 2011from <http://home.no.net/tacops/taktikk/kadettarbeld/hovan.htm.2005>.

9. Ibid., 2.

10. Ibid., 2.

11. Barry Watts, *US Combat Training, Operational Art and Strategic Competence* (Washington, D.C.: Center for Strategic and Budgetary Assessments, 2008), 52.

12. Gray, 2011.

13. Henry Yarger, *Strategic Theory for the 21st Century* (Carlisle, PA: Strategic Studies Institute, US Army War College, 2006), 8.

14. Ibid., 18.

15. This was mandated by the MND in 1997. However, see Bernd Horn, "A Rejection of the Need for Warrior Scholars?", *Canadian Military Journal*, Vol. 11, No. 2 (Spring 2011), 48-53, for an explanation of why education is essential for officers.

CHAPTER 4

Military Professionalism – An Organizational Challenge by Itself

Miriam C. de Graaff, MSc
Marc J. van Gils, MSc*

INTRODUCTION

Terms like "profession", "professional" and "professionalization" are common in daily use, however, they often are ill-defined and multi-interpretable (ambiguous). Within military organizations, the term "professionalism" is also commonly used. Military professionalism has generally been addressed using a historic perspective by describing military professionalism within the context of societies of late-medieval and early-modern Europe and by examining both the theory and practice of war, using literary, archival and artistic evidence.[1] In this chapter, however, we address military professionalism using an organizational/psychological perspective.

Military professionalism broadly refers to the construction of vocational or occupational identities and structures within the armed forces. However, more practically, military professionalism has been approached in different ways over the past years. Some regard commercial aspects such as efficiency and quality as the main issues at stake in a professional attitude whereas others focus upon a professional attitude in interactions with those around (enemy or not); the so-called *"chivalry,"* which refers to certain attributes and military values such as courage, heroism and honour.[2] In this chapter, we reflect upon this dualistic and ambiguous nature of military professionalism within the Royal Netherlands Armed Forces. Our goal is to demonstrate that since there is no agreed upon definition of military professionalism, it is military professionalism itself that causes organizational challenges within the Netherlands defence organization. It is argued that these challenges mainly arise from the lack of a clear and uniform understanding of the relationship between the domain of the leader (i.e., what constitutes the specific domains of both the officer and of the non-commissioned officer) and the complexity and unpredictability of the military context and its organizational and operational settings. In this chapter, attention is first directed to the origin and

---

*   The views expressed in this chapter are those of the authors and do not necessarily reflect those of the Royal Netherlands Armed Forces.

meaning of professionalism by focusing on professions and professionaliza-tion. Discussion will then shift to the organizational challenge instigated by the way military professionalism is operationalized within the Royal Neth-erlands Armed Forces. Finally, this chapter offers a proposal for dealing with this organizational challenge.

PROFESSION AS THE ORIGIN OF PROFESSIONALISM

Before we go further into military professionalism, it is necessary to take a look at the background of this concept. We will focus on the term "profes-sion" as its foundation and on two terms that are closely related to profes-sionalism: "professional" and "professionalization".

A profession is widely considered to be an occupation that finds its founda-tion in socially accepted values and is considered valuable for the continuity of society as a whole.[3] Medical occupations, as they serve society and stand for (amongst others) humaneness, responsibility and altruism, are consid-ered professions. As such, the military can also be considered a profession. After all, the core values of contemporary military organizations are safety, security and peace, all of which are social values necessary for the existence of the human species.[4]

However, being value-driven is not the only characteristic an occupation needs in order to claim status as a profession. A second characteristic is its reflective nature.[5] A profession distinguishes itself from a non-profession by the ability to continually adapt by using new knowledge and insights in order to better meet the needs of clients, employees and society.[6] A third character-istic includes the way in which employees are motivated. When it comes to motivating employees, an employee working in a profession focuses more on inspirational and intrinsic factors (such as the honour to work for a certain organization and the meaningfulness of the activities for society), whereas an employee working in a non-profession is motivated by more extrinsic factors such as salary and benefits.[7]

According to History professor David J.B. Trim, a profession can be charac-terized by seven qualities; a discrete occupational identity, formal hierarchy, permanence, a formal pay system, a distinctive expertise and means of edu-cation therein, efficiency in execution of expertise and finally, a distinctive self-conceptualization.[8] Several of these elements seem to be important in making the distinction between a profession and a non-profession. Some of the most important elements have to do with the individuals shaping the profession: the professionals.

A professional can be characterized as an individual with a considerable degree of discretion and professional autonomy due to his/her expertise and knowledge in the relevant domain.[9] Professionals are individuals that perform well when the organization offers them the liberty of action vice creating barriers for their actions by means of control mechanisms and rules.[10] According to these researchers, professionals set a profession apart from other occupations in a way that they are more loyal to their profession than to the organization they are working for. This means, for example, that medical doctors will be prone to be loyal to the values of their profession (such as humaneness), much more than showing loyalty to the actual organization they are employed in, particularly in situations when the professional (and as such, for society) values are defiled.

Professionalization is like professionalism, an ambiguous and ill-defined concept. Nowadays, it is used in many ways and is mostly understood to have something to do with making the organization more businesslike. What this exactly means often remains unclear. Terms like "cut-backs", "reorganization", "budget reductions", "efficiency" and "quality" are often associated with the concept of professionalization. In our vision, however, professionalization has much more to do with the organizational efforts to make employees more aware of their own values, motives and convictions of stakeholders. In our opinion, a true professional has the capacity and the will to proactively take these values and the way they influence behaviour into account when performing within the context of the organization. Of course, there is also the aspect of development of the content of the profession itself, such as financial or logistical skills and knowledge. In our vision, however, being fully developed in this sense doesn't necessarily make an employee a professional, at least not within the Dutch Armed Forces.

MILITARY PROFESSIONALISM – DUALISTIC BY NATURE?

In this section, we will go into the dualistic nature of military professionalism within the Dutch defence organization. Examples of the ambiguous (and sometimes even double binding) attitude toward professionalism are provided. This will be accomplished by discussing professionalism by referring to two "contrasts": 1) the individual versus the organization, and 2) traditional versus managerial approaches.

The Organization vs. the Individual

Within the Dutch Forces, professionalism receives considerable attention on two levels, namely the individual and the organizational level. First, we will briefly address the individual level, since within the Dutch Forces, the servicemen themselves receive most of the attention when it comes to professionalism. We see this for example, in leadership development programs in which the (future) leaders are trained to act and lead in a professional manner. Within this training, three elements are considered key elements in leadership (development): self-leadership, moral professionalism and ownership.

First, self-leadership is defined as the ability to effectively manage one's own behaviour through awareness of underlying personal values and motives. The premise of self-leadership is that without being aware of the source of one's own behaviour, it becomes arbitrary and as such, may easily lead into unintentional and even undesirable effects.

Secondly, another example of the perceived importance of professionalism is the increasing importance of the so-called moral professionalism within the Dutch military. Courses in ethics for example, are designed to increase moral professionalism, aiming to enhance moral development and moral awareness. The concept of moral professionalism, introduced within the Dutch Armed Forces by Verweij, Professor in leadership and ethics at the Dutch Military Academy, presumes that acting in a morally professional manner not only implies an awareness of the moral dimensions of situations (the values at stake), but also comprises judgement, communication and (behavioural) reaction, in addition to taking full responsibility for the decision and its consequences.[11] The organization uses two management strategies in order to give rise to morally responsible behaviour: a normative strategy by means of behavioural codes or codes of conduct and a stimulating strategy in which military personnel are educated in critical thinking instead of just obeying orders and following rules without reflection upon the moral dimensions of the situation.[12]

Third, ownership refers to the ability of an individual to acknowledge the fact that they are responsible for their thoughts, feelings and personal development. The basic assumption is that all thoughts and feelings originate within an individual. The external world can at most be a trigger, but can never be the origin of cognitive and emotional processes that take place within.[13] This implies that everything a person perceives through his/her senses can be considered feedback about their assumptions about the world and the way he/she relates to it. When an individual acknowledges and internalizes this fact, the received feedback becomes a powerful tool in his/her professional and personal development. For example, when an individual becomes aware of the effects of his/her communication on others through feedback received, and it turns out to have undesirable effects, he/she can choose to change their communication approach to a more effective style. Moreover, if the individual also becomes aware of the underlying internal assumptions and reasons which make him/her communicate in an ineffective way in the first place, this awareness provides the power to change the entire communication pattern into a more effective one.

As it becomes clear, the distinction between "personal" professionalism on the one hand and job content on the other hand is relevant. We mentioned at the beginning of this chapter that the process of professionalization addresses both the individual and organizational levels (the organization as the system in which the individual operates). Even though the balance shows more focus on the individual than the organization, some initiatives also take place at the organizational level. For example, in the field of integrity, an institute has been tasked to address integrity issues within the organization (the so-called *Centrale Organisatie Integriteit Defensie*, the central organization for integrity issues in the defence organization). This institute focuses not only on controlling the activities of individual employees but also the context in which behaviour is shown and the boundary conditions the organization imposes on its employees.

Even though there are some small initiatives that address the organization as a whole, professionalism is mostly considered to be personal effectiveness resulting from the balance between personal and organizational values. So, what makes a military person a professional depends on the extent to which he/she is able to 1) recognize and appreciate personal and organizational values, and 2) make decisions and act accordingly while taking these values (and possible conflicts between them) into account. In this sense, military professionalism shows great similarity with the concept of moral professionalism. However, the first can be considered to be a general state of mind, specifically associated with leadership, whereas the latter has much more to do with the explicit, preconditioned qualities for moral judgement and behaviour.

Tradition vs. Business

As mentioned, military professionalism can be addressed by means of two perspectives. The first perspective, the more traditional, is called chivalry. Chivalry occurred in the 12th century[14] as a legitimate, socially respected code for warriors to perfect their craft. This perspective is still recognizable today, mainly within manoeuvre-units (e.g., the Infantry), through their *esprit de corps* and by honouring traditional values like courage, honour, brotherhood, hardiness and heroism. In this perspective, these traditional military values are the determinants of the degree of military professionalism.

NETHERLANDS

The second perspective is a more modern and managerial view in which organizational values such as efficiency, cost-consciousness, control and integrity are indicators. The organization implements this perspective through the education and training of its employees, but also by implementing a certain working-strategy. What the leaders often hear (and sigh about), is that there is too little time to actually "lead" and invest in the relationship with their team-members as a result of the increasing amount of management tasks.

Another example is related to financial cut-backs. In times of economic (and political) crisis, organizations need to operate with fewer financial resources. This is also the case for the Dutch defence organization. Interestingly, however, cut-backs seem to focus on short-term financial issues whereas the long-term military ambitions are not adjusted downwards. As a consequence, the army is forced to do more with less. On the one hand, the troops are expected to operate in the "champions league," meaning they can be deployed anywhere in the world in any type of conflict, whereas on the other hand the number of operational units and servicemen is economized. Another issue related to financial cut-backs deals with the availability of resources. Since the organization needs to economize, less spare-parts are purchased. Troops, however, are still deployed and/or are training for deployment.

An interesting parallel seems to run between the dichotomy mentioned above with the distinction between military deployment abroad and non-operational functioning in barracks and offices. Chivalry values seem to be especially important on the battlefield, whereas managerial values (and qualities) seem more applicable in a peace context where managing daily administrative processes is the core business of the mother-organization. Another important (and in some ways ambiguous) concept within this perspective is the sense of responsibility and ownership. First, from a chivalric perspective, when deployed, servicemen often carry great responsibility, for deployed equipment, the mission itself, and ultimately the lives of team-members. "Mission Command" is carried out in full extent by decentralization of power and decision-making-authority. This is often felt as liberating since, in this case, great responsibility comes with relatively great influence. During a mission, servicemen are given significantly more room to make their own decisions and are usually given authority over a much larger command area. In addition, the effects of decisions made during a mission are usually felt to have a more profound effect and meaning in comparison with the less substantial effects of non-operational functioning. Secondly, from a managerial perspective, responsibility has much to do with being held accountable. Several systems and processes (such as Rules of Engagement), originally meant as guidelines in order to give the individual margin of manoeuvre and appeal to an individual's sense of responsibility, are actually often used and organized in a directly opposite manner, namely as control mechanisms that appeal to feelings of accountability in order to avoid being held responsible and face possible punishment.

One could say that organizations using control mechanisms this strictly, are incapable of learning, since "intelligent failure" and taking risks are necessary ingredients for a learning organization.[15] We consider this to be a negative consequence of the professionalization-strategy the Dutch defence organization uses. This exact kind of administrative avoidance of responsibility can ultimately lead to what is known as administrative evil.

Administrative evil is "regrettably a recurring aspect of public policy and administration in the modern era".[16] It refers to a bureaucratic mechanism that results in people engaging in acts of evil without being aware that they are in fact doing anything wrong. After all, ordinary people may act in accordance with what is considered normal and appropriate from their organizational and role perspective, whereas an outside observer would call their activities wrong and morally irresponsible. In worst cases, under conditions of what is referred to as "moral inversion" – in which something evil has convincingly been redefined as good – all individuals may easily engage in acts of administrative evil when at the same time believing that what they are doing is not only correct, but even the right thing to do.[17] The term "administrative evil" arose in 20th century as an attempt to explain what role bureaucracy played in the Holocaust. Of course, this article isn't about genocide as a result of bureaucratic accountability. A more common example of administrative evil within the Dutch Armed Forces concerns the manner of dealing with issuing (new) military identification cards needed to access barracks and offices. These cards are necessary for identification purposes both in the Netherlands as well as during deployment. The procedure that needs to be followed in order to achieve such a card (which expires, meaning every employee must repeat the procedure every few years) is so non-transparent, complex and fragmented that it literally takes months to successfully complete. This results in frustration among employees who take part in this procedure: for those trying to obtain such an identification card and for those who are releasing the cards since they are often considered to be non-supportive as they stick to the rules and procedures without taking into account the circumstances which in many cases do not comply with the oversimplistic model situations the rules and procedures were based upon. By introducing the concept of administrative evil we show that accountability is not synonymous with military professionalism. The way accountability is pursued in the Dutch defence organization, however, counteracts even the military professionalism that is aimed for, since accountability, as such, is opposite of the vital elements of professionalism mentioned before: self-leadership, ownership and moral professionalism.

DEALING WITH MILITARY PROFESSIONALISM – THE ORGANIZATIONAL CHALLENGE

Being a professional military organization means that the Dutch Forces need to overcome the organizational challenge professionalism causes. In this section we go into the dimensions that are, in our opinion, prerequisites to overcoming this organizational challenge. First, we describe what is needed for an organization to be considered a learning organization. Next, we discuss the bureaucratic management strategy. Finally, we discuss the organization in relation to the individual employee.

Organizational Learning

The military organization needs to continually adapt to changing situations due to the fact that the world changes continuously and the operational context is different for each mission. Our contention is that the organization is currently not a learning organization and therefore, it is not capable of adequately adapting to changing circumstances. The following illustrates this point:

> Since 1648 (Peace of Münster, after 80 years of war with Spain) the Dutch forces were deployed in situations in which the territorial integrity or the political sovereignty of the state were under attack. After the fall of the Berlin wall, the end of the Cold War, the military realized a broad scale of tasks of which most (due to the absence of a direct enemy) are of a humanitarian and peacekeeping nature. Since the last two decades, warfare has changed greatly. Nowadays there is talk of asymmetric warfare, meaning there is no definite enemy but insurgents using guerrilla tactics. So, warfare is no longer large-scale. This implies a fundamental change in the nature of the military profession, however the military ethos does not seem to follow these changes.[18]

It is strongly suggested that the Dutch organization invest in stimulating a learning culture. Several elements have been described that, to a large extent, determine whether the learning ability of an organization is used to its fullest potential to establish areas where matters could be improved.[19] Max Visser, an organizational scientist, categorized these elements in the following four dimensions:

1. the extent to which responsibilities are decentralized; the more responsibilities that are placed with lower levels in the organization, the greater the risk of mistakes being made at this level;

2. the extent to which, within an organizational culture, failures are tolerated; the more open and tolerant an organizational culture is, the more failures are laid out on the table, discussed and fixed;

3. the extent to which lessons learned are anchored within the organization; the more an organization internally records and shares these lessons learned, the greater the organizational learning potential; and

4. the way an organization generally treats its members; the better members are selected, trained/educated and deployed, the more responsibility they can bear.[20]

When these four dimensions are applied to the Royal Netherland Armed Forces, it becomes clear that the organization can improve. The first dimension (a decentralization of responsibility) is present in the organization, but could be further enhanced. Of course, this is the foundation of the strategy of Mission Command. In order to be effective, however, a culture of trust needs to exist between the hierarchical levels. The second dimension centres around the openness of the organizational culture regarding the reporting of mistakes and problems. The organizational culture of the Dutch military can be improved on through effective feedback, trust, and initiative. Feedback and trust are necessary in order to ensure that all leaders can and will take the initiative. The third dimension is about the transfer of training-on-the-job, otherwise known as lessons learned. This encompasses supplementing the formal training program with up-to-date insights from the field on the organizational, unit and personal levels, and in this way, allow these insights to be put into practice. The defence organization has established an institution (Defence Institute for Lessons Learned) that aims at analyzing deployment experiences. Collecting these lessons, however, does not guarantee they are actually learned. The process followed in this matter can be questioned in its effectiveness. Further, only deployment experiences are addressed. Clearly, the organization also needs to learn from non-operational situations. Finally, according to Visser's fourth dimension, better training, higher education and selection for more specific tasks can enhance the ability of individuals to deal with the complex situations they encounter in the military context. Currently, military personnel are not selected for specific functions or tasks, and as such, they do not necessarily work in their field of expertise. It is therefore suggested that by selecting servicemen for specific functions it could help the organization professionalize.

A Bureaucratic Challenge

The second dimension to confront the threat to military professionalism is bureaucracy. First, we should ask ourselves, "Is bureaucracy a threat to professionalism?" In the managerial perspective, military professionalism broadly refers to the degree to which accountability is achieved by using bureaucratic principles. Bureaucracy is a way to control systems, activities, and structures within an organization. As such, it is not necessarily a bad thing. However, the organizational context of military organizations becomes more and more complex, therefore flexibility and adaptability are needed.[21] At the same time, the one thing that bureaucratic organizations have a hard time dealing with is being flexible.[22]

On the one hand, the military organization uses bureaucracy to create a predictable and manageable working environment. However, this bureaucracy leads to the illusion of working in a predictable and controlled environment instead of making it actually controllable. To deal with this, the organization increases the level of control. This creates a bureaucratic monster with a lack of understanding that over-bureaucratization is not a translation of professionalization and will not necessarily make the organization more effective. Noticing that bureaucratization is not a complete answer, the organization reaches for the organizational culture and the traditional military values (such as tradition, trust and chivalry) in order to inspire and motivate its personnel to complete their missions. Subsequently, a vexing problem arises in this dual nature of military professions. Professions are by nature reflective institutions, as they continually need to adapt by using new knowledge and experiences in order to meet the needs of the situation.[23] It is argued that in this light, the challenge for any military organization is to make sure that the bureaucratic nature does not outweigh and compromise its professional nature.[24] This is a point of view which, not surprisingly, is strongly held by the authors of this chapter. As we see it, the pitfall for the Dutch military lies in the fact that in general one believes there is a need to choose between bureaucracy and traditional military values. We believe a choice does not necessarily have to be made. In some situations, military values are relevant, say for example, when a sacrifice is asked for or when honour and pride are needed in battle. Yet, in other non-operational situations, a commercial perspective is needed in order to improve quality and efficiency. We believe, following Snider, former Professor of Political Science at West Point, that it is not a matter of choosing only one perspective when professionalizing the organization. Instead, it is through differentiating and finding the balance between these two perspectives that enable professionalism.

An Organizational Challenge

The final dimension concerns opportunities for the organization to manage military professionalism. In our opinion, the biggest challenge with which the organization needs to cope lies within the fact that professionalization is not only relevant at the individual level, the organization as a system needs to be subject to the process of professionalization. Where the organization falls short is in its ability to communicate transparently about the goal and subject of professionalization. Clear definitions in this matter are simply lacking. We believe that a first step towards professionalism is to recognize what the organization truly considers to be important values, or in other words, it needs to define, transparently, what it stands for and identify the shared values. This means that the organization must not only formulate values which stem naturally from its core business identified in close consultation with the members of the organization, but also put effort into pursuing a culture in which these values are actually put into practice. If, for example, tradition, uniformity and loyalty turn out to be truly important values (which seems to be the case in certain units within the Dutch Armed Forces), the organization should accept this fact and behave and communicate those values accordingly, instead of enforcing behaviour that contradicts these values, for example by promoting on the surface values like progression, uniqueness and critical thinking. In our opinion, an organization should actively strive for congruence between values, culture and daily practice. One can easily see the parallel with the earlier mentioned concept of individual self-leadership, resulting in congruence between motives, beliefs and behaviour. At an organizational level this congruence is, in our perception, exactly what makes an organization a professional organization.

CONCLUSION

In this chapter we described military professionalism within the Royal Netherlands Armed Forces. The aim of the chapter was to argue that it is professionalism itself, as it is currently put into practice, that poses a threat for true professionalism within the Dutch Forces. As stated in this chapter, professionalism is an ambiguous and ill-defined concept. This is also the case within the Royal Netherlands Armed Forces; there is no clear-cut concept of what professionalism comes down to and what the subject of the process of professionalization should be. Professionalism is thus an organizational challenge in itself. In order to overcome this challenge we believe the organization needs to put effort into three dimensions: 1) creating an organizational

NETHERLANDS

culture in which learning is the key characteristic, 2) using bureaucracy in an effective manner in order to control systems and activities without losing the competence of flexibility and adaptability, and 3) finding the balance between focusing upon individual professionalism and organizational professionalism.

We want to conclude this chapter by arguing that military professionalism indeed poses an organizational challenge for the Royal Netherlands Armed Forces. However, we believe that this challenge can be managed by devoting effort to integrating values, culture and behaviour, into a congruent system. In other words: by dedicating oneself to organizational and individual self-leadership, the Royal Netherlands Armed Forces can further improve and sustain professionalism.

ENDNOTES

1. David J.B. Trim, "Introduction" in David J.B. Trim, ed., *The Chivalric Ethos and the Development of Military Professionalism* (Leiden: Koninklijke Brill, 2003), 1-40.

2. Ibid.

3. Desiree E.M. Verweij, "Morele professionaliteit in de militaire praktijk" in Jos Kole and Doret de Ruyter, eds., *Werkzame Idealen. Ethische Reflecties Op Professionaliteit* (Assen: Koninklijke Van Gorcum, 2007), 126-138.

4. Ibid.

5. Don Snider, "Once Again, the Challenge to the U.S. Army During a Defense Reduction: to Remain a Military Profession", *Professional Military Ethics Monograph Series - Vol. 4*, (Center for the Army Profession and Ethic (CAPE), Carlisle, Pennsylvania, 2012).

6. Ibid.

7. Ibid.

8. Trim, 2003, 6-7.

9. Peter Olstoorn, Marten Meijer and Desiree Verweij, "Managing Moral Professionalism in Military Organizations" in Joseph Soeters, Paul Fenema and Robert Beeres, eds., *Managing Military Organizations* (New York, NY: Routledge, 2010), 138-149.

10. Nick Van Dam and Jos Marcus, *Een Praktijkgerichte Benadering Van Organisatie en Management* (Groningen: Wolters Noordhoff, 2005).

11. Verweij, 2007.

12. Miriam De Graaff and Coen Van den Berg, "Moral Professionalism Within the Royal Netherlands Armed Forces" in Jeff Stouffer and Stefan Seiler, eds., *Military Ethics* (Kingston, ON: Canadian Defence Academy Press, 2010).

13. Marc Van Gils, "Leiderschapsontwikkeling. De Basis: Zelfleiderschap en Eigenaarschap", *Militaire Spectator*, Vol. 180, No. 2 (2011), 87-98.

14. Matthew Bennet, "Why Chivalric? Military 'Professionalism in the Twelfth Century: The Origins and Expressions of a Socio-Military Ethos", in David J.B. Trim, ed., *The Chivalric*

Ethos and the Development of Military Professionalism (Leiden: Koninklijke Brill, 2003), 1-40.

15. Miriam De Graaff and Eric-Hans Kramer, *Leadership and the Principle of the Hiding Hand,* paper presented at the International Leadership Association, Boston, Massachusetts, October 2010.

16. Guy Adams and Danny Balfour, "*Leadership, Administrative Evil and the Ethics of Incompetence: Lessons from Katrina and Iraq*", Leading the Future of the Public Sector (2003), and/or The Third Transatlantic Dialogue University of Delaware, Newark, Delaware, USA (May 31–June 2, 2007), 3.

17. Ibid.

18. Jos M. H. Groen and Desiree E.M. Verweij, "De Onlosmakelijke Band Tussen Professionaliteit en Ethiek", *Militaire Spectator,* Vol. 177, No. 6 (2008), 349-360.

19. Max Visser, "Designed by geniuses to be run by idiots: (on)mogelijkheden van een lerend leger", in Nicolette van Gestel, Jos Benders and Willem de Nijs, eds., *Arbeidsbestel en werknemersparticipatie: liber amicorum voor Fred Huijgen* (Den Haag: Lemma, 2008), 183-187.; Max Visser, "Learning under conditions of hierarchy and discipline: the case of the German Army, 1939-1940", *Learning Inquiry,* Vol. 2 (2008), 127-137.

20. Ibid.

21. Rudy Richardson, Desiree Verweij and Donna Winslow, "Moral Fitness for Peace Operations", *Journal of Political and Military Sociology,* Vol. 32, No. 1 (2004), 99-113.

22. Herman Kuipers, Pierre Van Amelsfoort and Eric-Hans Kramer, *Het Nieuwe Organiseren – Alternatieven Voor de Bureaucratie* (Leuven: Acco, 2010).

23. Snider, 2012.

24. Ibid.

CHAPTER 5

The Challenge of Maintaining Military Professionalism in the Face of Transformation: The Indonesian Army Experience

Lieutenant-Colonel Eri Radityawara Hidayat*

> We should create a TNI soldier who is aware of his/her Core Identity,
> A soldier who does not know his/her identity does not have the moral
> strength to defend the interest of the nation.
>
> *General Endriartono Sutarto, Commander-in-Chief of TNI,*
> *Briefing to the Joint Staff and Command School students on 4 August 2005.[1]*

INTRODUCTION

Considering that the Indonesian government has a limited budget, traditionally, it has had to prioritize funding to those sectors which can promote economic growth.[2] Therefore, in 2010, the Ministry of Defence of the Republic of Indonesia officially adopted a defence strategy which is known as the Minimum Essential Force (MEF).[3] In MEF, the Indonesian Defence establishment outlined the country's strategic defence requirements and the development of its capabilities, based on projected and actual threats, and its projected budget for the next twenty years.[4] Basically, the concept of MEF is a combination of a capability-based and military task-oriented model.[5] While the capability-based model lays out the foundation for future development of Indonesia's force posture and weapon systems, the military task-oriented model reoriented the strategy of military deployment for launching war operations as well as military operations other than war.[6]

In the context of the Indonesian Army or *Tentara Nasional Indonesia Angkatan Darat* (TNI AD), as an organization that relies on "men who are armed," MEF requires the availability of competent soldiers who are capable of performing their military tasks.[7] As stated by the current Army Chief of Staff, General Pramono Edhie Wibowo, in order to achieve the government's

---

*   The views expressed in this chapter are those of the author and do not necessarily reflect
    those of the Indonesian National Defence Forces or the Indonesian Army.

objective, apart from modernizing its weaponry, the focus of the TNI AD is to develop its human resources, so that its soldiers can possess the Army's traditional core values of mental toughness and militancy, coupled with high moral standards and ethics.[8]

In the past decade, following advances in the behavioural sciences, especially related to its application in the human resources field, many civilian and military organizations have adopted the Competency-Based Human Resource Management System (CBHRM).[9] As this development also influenced Indonesian organizations, including the private sector and the government, inevitably, there were pressures on the Defence establishment to also adopt this method. Consequently, the Ministry of Defence of the Republic of Indonesia, as part of the government's bureaucracy reform agendas, declared that it will also implement this method.[10] In light of this, the Indonesian Army decided to implement various changes in its personnel management system so that it could better reflect these agendas.

Considering that CBHRM is a concept that was born out of a need to stay competitive in the business world, the author argues that in the Indonesian context, care must be given in its implementation in the military establishment, especially in relation to its competency-based pay system. Efforts must be made to ensure that the Army's professional ethos will not be compromised.

This chapter will first discuss the concept of MEF, especially its relation to the Indonesian Government's Bureaucratic Reform agenda. It will then examine the subject of CBHRM from an academic point of view, showing examples of how CBHRM is being implemented in militaries, and arguing why its implementation can be a threat to a traditional values-based military organization. Finally, this chapter will discuss efforts to implement CBHRM in the Indonesian Army as well as what should be done in the future.

MINIMUM ESSENTIAL FORCE AND THE GOVERNMENT REFORM AGENDA

Minimum Essential Force

It is common knowledge that the Indonesian Defence Force (*Tentara National Indonesia* or TNI), must work with a less than optimum budget that cannot cover both operational requirements and logistical support.[11] In fact, the Indonesian Defence budget is quite small, not only in comparison to the other departments in the Indonesian government, but also in comparison to other countries in the region.[12] As a reflection of the improving condition of the Indonesian economy, only recently was the government able to allocate more money to the Ministry of Defence. Although the current 2012 defence budget (US $8 billion) has increased by almost three times as compared to six years ago, it is still very modest in comparison to its nearest neighbour.[13] Realizing that the defence budget will not increase to an amount that is deemed neccesary to design an ideal long-term defence architecture for the country, defence planners started to propose the concept of the MEF, which was mentioned for the first time during the President's brief for the TNI Commander's Call in 2008.[14]

In the MEF, the focus is on how to build defence forces that are capable of facing the predicted threat and yet at the same time, can meet budgetary requirements.[15] Essentially, this means that the TNI must adopt a capabilites-based defence strategy so that in the long term, it can face any threat that will emerge in the strategic environment.[16] For the TNI AD, the MEF is then translated into two actions, namely, the development of the Army's Force Posture 2005-2024 and the development of weapon systems and organizational structures related to the stated posture.[17] In addition, as mentioned in the beginning of this chapter, this military transformation will require the Army to develop its human resource capability so that it can perform any military tasks assigned by the government.

Bureaucratic Reform and Competency-Based Human Resource Management

As stipulated by the *Government's Grand Design for Bureaucratic Reform 2010-2025*, all Government Ministries are required, by law, to implement various reform agendas.[18] Actually, the Indonesian government's reformation effort was started by President Abdurahman Wahid in the 1990s, after the fall of the Suharto's New Order government, by partially borrowing concepts from Osborne and Gaebler's *Reinventing the Government*.[19] Based on this concept, the state is encouraged to become a competitive government, that can inject competition among its units so that it can deliver the best service to the public.[20] Consequently, the government is required to become an "enterpreneurial government", which is more or less market driven.[21] To achieve this objective, the government must create a system of good governance based on accountability, transparancy, and efficiency in its resource management systems.[22]

In terms of human resource management systems, ultimately, this will lead to a "zero growth policy" for personnel recruitment, because delivery of goods and services to the public does not neccesitate the heavy involvement of the state apparatus in the market.[23] To achieve this objective, government bureaucracy must place and promote its staff through a "fit and proper" mechanism, in which competent staff are promoted based on merit, and rewarded accordingly.[24] In short, this means the adoption of CBHRM to create a professional government apparatus, and the use of the Assessment Center method to assess the top echelon.[25]

As part of the government, the Ministry of Defence is required to implement these reform agendas. For example, in terms of human resource management, the Ministry of Defence adopted a zero growth policy, which means that new recruitment for Defence personnel for the next twenty years can only be done to fill empty billets that result from retirement or change of military status, such as promotion from NCOs to officers.[26] In addition, to achieve the reform agenda, the Ministry of Defence anounced that it will implement CBHRM and that it will utilize the Assessment Centre method to assess officials in the Defence establishment.[27]

Considering that CBHRM is a relatively new concept in Human Resource Management, it should be appropriate to examine it from a theoretical point of view. The following discussion will elaborate on the concept of CBHRM as it relates to superior performance by organizational members, and the challenges of implementing it in the defence establishment.

COMPETENCY-BASED HUMAN RESOURCE MANAGEMENT

Factors Influencing Superior Performance

Research in the field of human resource management has demonstrated that individual performance will depend on four factors, namely experience, technical competencies or hard skills, behavioural competencies or soft skills, and personality.[28] Experience is related to what has been done by an individual and can be measured through track records or biographical analysis, while technical competencies refer to what is known by an individual and can be ascertained through professional qualifications such as certification programs or ability tests.[29] However, there is no guarantee that an individual who has the right experience and possesses the required technical qualifications will be able to demonstrate outstanding performance.[30]

Richard Boyatzis, one of the founders of the competency movement, considered behavioural competencies and personality as the two factors neccessary to produce superior performance.[31] More related to psychological aspects, behavioural competencies have a big role in determining what a person will do in his/her job given his/her experience and qualifications. While behavioural competencies can be measured through a performance appraisal system or Assessment Centres, personality traits are usually measured through classical psychological tests.[32]

In addition, unlike business entities which are more or less driven by market forces, institutional competency represents another factor that can influence the performance of its members.[33] Comprising unique organizational values that reflect the organizational culture, these values are important for members of military organizations, who often join the military for some abstract reason such as patriotism.[34] In fact, modern militaries such as the United States Army still consider values-based competencies, which were derived from long held Army values and attributes, as unchangeable and form the basis for other Army competencies.[35] However, although values are important, the mismatch of values might undoubtedly demotivate members of a military organization, and measuring values is very hard indeed.[36]

Moving on to the next step in CBHRM involves finding ways to develop the competencies. While experience can be improved by providing the opportunity to serve on various "tour of duties" and technical competencies can be gained through specific training to improve the required skills and knowledge, values-based competencies can only be inculcated through indoctrination and other organization-based efforts.[37] Behavioural competencies on the other hand, can be developed through individual and group development programs such as experiential training, coaching and the use of individual development plans.[38]

CBHRM in the Military

Although there is no known record available, implementation of the CB-HRM in the military may have started with the publication of the US Army Field Manual 22-100 "Be-Know-Do".[39] The competency framework probably inspired other military organizations, such as the Canadian Forces and the Australian Army, to follow suit.[40] One example of its implementation was presented by a New Zealand Defence Force officer during the 49th International Military Testing Association (IMTA) meeting in 2007, in Gold Coast, Australia.[41] With a total of 36 competencies spread over 13 competency groups, it was indicated that there would be measurement and development programs for each competency, and that the whole system would be integrated through an information technology system.[42]

Surely, implementing CBHRM in the military is appealing, because with its performance appraisal system and the related developmental and mentoring guidelines, CBHRM can create a highly-prescriptive template of desired behaviour that in the end, will produce members who can think and act in similar fashion.[43] Yet, the challenge of implementing such a system in a military organization is, of course, the business orientation of the CBHRM system. A unique aspect of a military organization is that it can demand the ultimate sacrifice of its members, that is laying down their life if neccessary for the security of their country. While uniformity might be desirable for organizations such as the military, one might question the ability of CBHRM to address these kind of issues.

As an example, a full implementation of CBHRM will ultimately be linked to some sort of competency-based or performance-based pay.[44] Related to remuneration, certain Western governments that have implemented competency-based pay, showed that these can be achieved either by linking it to the ability of public servants to get certifications for their competencies, or to the way they perform based on their competencies.[45] While this reward system might be appropriate for profit-oriented companies, or for organizations operating in an individualistic culture setting, previous studies have shown that in a culture that values equality more than equity, such a system might not work optimally.[46] In fact, in collectivist Japan, value congruence is considered as being more important than reward-for-performance in motivating individuals to perform.[47]

While the author has not been able to find research on the effect of implementing a competency-based pay in military organizations, research has shown that even in individualistic Western countries, soldiers are much more collectivist than their average countrymen and women.[48] Therefore, it can be argued that if care is not given to recognize the unique nature of the military organization, the implementation of CBRHM, especially its competency or performance-based pay system, might reduce the intrinsic motivation of the soldiers to perform; since they have shared goals and values.

In fact, the main difference between military competency frameworks and its business counterpart is the existence of institutional competencies related to military values.[49] For example, the Canadian Forces competency framework includes a competency cluster called Profesional Ideology that they believe differentiates them from other industrial/business related institutions.[50] Similarly, US Army military authors suggested that the values-based competency cluster of the "Be" domain from the "Be-Know-Do" model were derived from unique Army values and attributes.[51] Therefore, adopting a values-based institutional competency in CBHRM will become essential to ensure that military members remain true to their calling, which is living a value system that can guide them in their day-to-day job of defending their country.

CBHRM IN THE INDONESIAN ARMY

Field Commander's Competency Profile

The TNI AD must implement the CBHRM as mandated by the Ministry of Defence. In reality, the TNI AD has partially implemented this system, albeit, not in an integrated manner. Starting in 2004, the Psychological Service of the Indonesian Army, or *Dinas Psikologi Angkatan Darat* (DISPSIAD), designed competency-based profiles for certain job targets in the Army. One such profile is for field commanders (Figure 5.1).

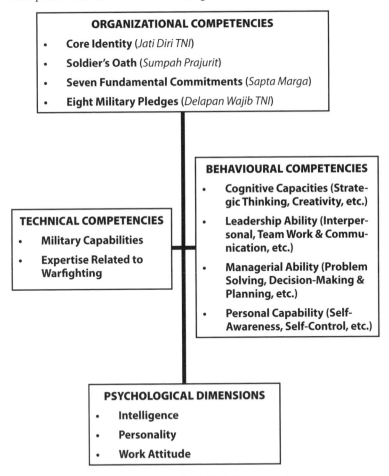

ORGANIZATIONAL COMPETENCIES

- **Core Identity** (*Jati Diri TNI*)
- **Soldier's Oath** (*Sumpah Prajurit*)
- **Seven Fundamental Commitments** (*Sapta Marga*)
- **Eight Military Pledges** (*Delapan Wajib TNI*)

BEHAVIOURAL COMPETENCIES

- **Cognitive Capacities** (Strategic Thinking, Creativity, etc.)
- **Leadership Ability** (Interpersonal, Team Work & Communication, etc.)
- **Managerial Ability** (Problem Solving, Decision-Making & Planning, etc.)
- **Personal Capability** (Self-Awareness, Self-Control, etc.)

TECHNICAL COMPETENCIES

- **Military Capabilities**
- **Expertise Related to Warfighting**

PSYCHOLOGICAL DIMENSIONS

- **Intelligence**
- **Personality**
- **Work Attitude**

Figure 5.1: Competency Framework of TNI AD Field Commanders

Based on this framework, a competency-based development matrix can be created; Army units will have the responsibility to implement the different development programs. As an example, each corps and branch is responsible for the development of the technical competencies, while DISPSIAD is responsible for the development of the behavioural competencies and the psychological dimensions. On the other hand, the Mental Guidance Service of the Army of *Dinas Pembinaan Mental Angkatan Darat* (DISBINTALAD) is responsible for creating programs to inculcate soldiers with the Indonesian Army's traditional values, which were derived from the struggle that was experienced during Indonesia's War of Independence with the Dutch between the 1940s and 1950s.

Position Competencies Assessment Program

The TNI AD has implemented competency assessments related to certain job positions. For example, candidates for the field commander position, such as Batallion Commanders or Territorial Commanders, must undergo a competency test prior to being placed in these jobs. This is called the Position Competencies Assessment Program (PCAP), or Program Penilaian Kompetensi Jabatan (PPKJ). The PPKJ was officially introduced in 2004, by the Chief of Staff of the Army, after officers from DISPSIAD conducted benchmark studies on the competency framework of civilian and military organizations, both in Indonesia and in other countries.

In the PPKJ, the behavioural competencies of the candidates were assessed using the Assessment Centre method, while the psychological dimensions were assessed through paper-and-pencil tests. As can be seen from Figure 5.1, the behavioural competencies consisted of four main competencies; cognitive capacities, leadership abilities, managerial abilities, and personal capabilities. In turn, each of these core competencies consist of several sub-competencies. The psychological potentials observed are intelligence, personality, and work attitude. In fact, since its establishment in June 1950, DISPSIAD has used field simulations that were handed over from the Psychological Service of the Dutch Colonial Army or *Leger Psychologiesche Dienst, Koninklijk Netherlands-Indische Leger* (KNIL). These simulations were very similar to the original Assessment Centre method that were developed by the German Armed Forces during the First and Second World Wars to select intelligence officers.[52]

In terms of technical competencies, such as military capabilities and expertise related to warfighting, the responsibility for assessment lies with each corps and functional unit. For example, the Infantry Training Centre or *Pusat*

Pendidikan Infantri (PUSDIKIF) is responsible for the selection of battalion commanders, while the Territorial Training Centre or *Pusat Pendidikan Teritorial* (PUSDIKTER) is responsible for the selection of territorial commanders. Among the assessment methods is academic or knowledge testing on the various topics related to the target job. On the other hand, since values-based organizational competencies are harder to measure, the PPKJ does not include tests for them. However, superior officers and personnel officers from the Army Headquarters will only nominate candidates for the PPKJ if these candidates have been deemed to uphold these values in their daily life. While these evalutions can indeed be very subjective, unless a scientifically proven method to better assess them is developed, then it is very likely that the PPKJ system will remain unchanged.

Competencies Development Program

Competency development programs are still very much in the planning stage. Although the TNI AD has implemented various development programs, they have not done so in an integrated manner. Candidates who pass the PPKJ test will attend courses designed to prepare them for their target job at the respective training centers. While these courses cover topics mostly related to the technical competencies. Materials related to the behavioural and institutional competencies remain to be developed.

As an example, at the end of 2011, the organizational structure of DISPSIAD has been validated by the Army Headquarters and a new unit called the Psychological Development Institute was established to implement a behavioural competencies program. This institute is in the process of designing the software to implement these programs in the form of Standard Operating Procedures and Field Manuals. It is expected that by 2013, the TNI AD will have development programs for behavioural competencies as part of the post PPKJ system.

For values-based competencies, there has been no concrete effort to systematically address the development of these competencies. Actually, long-term courses such as the Army's Staff and Command School, or *Sekolah Staf dan Komando Angkatan Darat* (SESKOAD), delivered materials related to TNI AD values which are called *Kejuangan* or the Warrior Code. In these *Kejuangan* classes, prominent members of the TNI, including the Commander-in-Chief of the TNI, the Service Chiefs and former freedom fighters deliver lectures and war stories.[53] The students are then evaluated based on topic assignments, participation in the seminar and observation by the lecturer. Classes cover discussions on the four core values of the TNI.

The first being the TNI's Core Identity or *Jati Diri TNI*, as a people's army, a patriotic army, a national army and a professional army, that reflects the historical establishment of the TNI during the revolutionary war as an army of the people, who possess mental toughness and militancy.[54] Next, is the Soldier's Oath or *Sumpah Prajurit*, which basically asks the soldier to be loyal to the government and the state ideology, *Pancasila* or the Five Principles, which are considered as being the philosophical foundation that unites Indonesians, regardless of race, religion or ethnicity.[55] Then, there are the Seven Fundamental Commitments, or *Sapta Marga*, which explain the responsibility of a soldier as a member of the TNI, and as a citizen of the Unitary State of the Republic of Indonesia.[56] Lastly, there are the Eight Military Pledges, or *Delapan Wajib* TNI, which detail the moral standards and ethics that must be upheld by TNI soldiers when dealing with fellow Indonesian citizens.

In terms of the PPKJ, however, there is no systematic plan to implement a development program for the values-based competencies. This is likely because the available literature on CBHRM itself does not dwell much on the subject, and most of the result findings on the assessment and development of values-based competencies are not conclusive. This fact is also reflected in the CBHRM concept formulated by the government itself. However, as argued by the author in the beginning of this chapter, these values-based competencies are essential since they reflect the organizational character of the TNI AD that differentiates it from other organizations. Granted, if the government's bureaucratic reform is successful, the TNI AD might have more transparent and efficient ways of conducting its affairs. However, the implementation of a CBHRM program that is too business-oriented and lacking in concern and/or in developing the institutional competencies will, in the long term, make the TNI AD soldiers indistinguishable from any other profession in the civilian sector.

Without these values, the TNI AD soldiers will lack a moral compass, and might not be willing to have unyielding fighting spirit, put the nation's interest above anything else, and always be close to the people. These values demand this from them. While possession of the technical competencies can create capable soldiers who might meet the MEF requirement, it is from the TNI values that will make them willing to perform the military tasks without question. While it might be different from the definition of professionalism in the Western sense, in the Indonesian context, soldiers can only be regarded as professionals, if they are not only capable of performing their military duties, but can also uphold the TNI's institutional values.[57] Considering that some experts argue that values-based competencies can also be developed, provided they are "behaviourized," the author believes that this is the main challenge for the behavioural scientists who work in the TNI AD. It is imperative that these scientists, in the future, be able to design assessment and development programs for the values-based competencies that are scientifically valid and reliable.[58]

Competency-Based Pay

The Indonesian government's current policy of Bureaucratic Reform also includes remuneration policy that is attempting to improve the compensation package for civil servants, the police and military members, without linking it directly to competency or performance.[59] For example the remuneration package for TNI members is divided into 21 pay classes, from the lowest ranking private to four-star general.[60] Therefore, one can say that this remuneration policy is essentially still based on seniority and is not yet linked to any individual performance or competencies.

Critics have argued, however, that similar to the business and public sector in other countries, the remuneration policy for Indonesian public sector employees, including the police and the military, should also be linked to performance.[61] Indeed, studies in other Asian countries with similar characteristics to Indonesia, have shown that it is possible to implement competency-based pay in certain public sectors that result in a marked improvement in performance as measured by customer satisfaction in the delivery of the services.[62] However, the organizations that were researched are very different in nature from military organizations, since these organizations conduct day-to-day transactions with external customers, such as the Immigration Department.[63] Since no research to date has shown the utility of competency or performance-based pay in the military, the jury is still out on the wisdom of implementing competency-based pay in the TNI.

CONCLUSION

The Indonesian Army is currently undergoing a transformation effort as part of the government's reform agenda, as well as it's own modernization strategy in the form of MEF. Following recent development in the civilian public sector, one strategy that will be implemented through the Ministry of Defence is CBHRM. While it is believed that this method can be utilized to improve the quality of the Indonesian Army's human capital, as a military organization that is steeped in tradition and values, it is essential that the TNI AD find ways to implement CBHRM in an approriate way that will not be detrimental to its nature as a military organization. Special consideration must be given in finding methods to measure and develop the values-based competencies. In addition, the TNI AD must also be very careful in implementing competency or performance-based pay. Otherwise, the current transformation effort might erode the professionalism of the soldiers as seen from the Indonesian context.

ENDNOTES

1. Endriarto Sutarto, *Kewajiban Prajurit Mengabdi Kepada Bangsa* [The Duty of the Soldier is to Dedicate His/Herself to the Nation] (Jakarta: Pusat Penerangan TNI, 2005), 19.

2. Yuddy Chrisnandi and Leonard C. Sebastian, "Defence Budgeting in Indonesia: Some Policy Options", *RSIS Contemporary*, Vol. 126 (2007).

3. Evan Laksmana, "Indonesia's National Defence Forces: Recent Strategic Changes and Implications", *RSIS Contemporary*, Vol. 101 (2010), 1.

4. Ibid.

5. Andi Widjajanto, "Transforming Indonesia's Armed Forces", *UNISCI Discussion Papers*, Vol. 15 (2007), 28.

6. Ibid., 28-29.

7. Saktia Andri Susilo, "Pramono Fokus Tingkatkan SDM dan Alutsista" [Pramono Focus on Personnel and Weapon System], *Suara Merdeka*, 7 July, 2011.

8. Ibid.

9. Eri R. Hidayat, *A Case Study of the Use of a Competency Framework in the Australian Army for Performance Management and Development* (Unpublished Master of Human Resources Management and Coaching Research Thesis, University of Sydney, Australia, 2005).

10. Kementerian Pertahanan Republik Indonesia, *Reformasi Birokrasi: Peningkatan Manajemen SDM* [Ministry of Defense of the Republic of Indonesia, Reforming the Bureaucracy: Improving Human Resource Management], retrieved on 22 April 2012 from <http://ropeg. kemhan.go.id/rebiro.php pada tanggal>.

11. Patriot, "Strategi Membangun Kekuatan TNI di Tengah Keterbatasan Anggaran: Minimum Essential Force Sebuah Solusi" [Developing Strategy to Build TNI Forces in the Midst of Limited Budget: Minimum Essential Force as a Solution], *Patriot*, Vol. I, No. 65-66 (2010), 11.

12. Chrisnandi and Sebastian, 2007, 1.

13. Anonymous, "Indonesia's Army: Seeking a Modern Role", *The Economist*, 30 March 2012.

14. Ibid., 14.

15. Ibid., 15.

16. Mabesad, *Revisi Pembangunan Kekuatan Pokok Minimum* [Minimum Essential Force] *TNI AD tahun 2010-2029* [Revision of the Development of Minimum Essential Force in the Army for 2010-2029] (Jakarta: Mabesad, 2011), 3.

17. Major-General Hotma Marbun, "Menata Postur TN AD Sesuai Dengan Kebijakan Minimum Essential Forces Guna Mewujudkan Daya Tangkal Aspek Darat Yang Tangguh" [Developing Army Posture in Accordance with the Minimum Essential Forces Policy to Create Strong Land Defence Detterence Power], *Yudhagama*, Vol. 83 (2009), 11.

18. Kementerian Pendayagunaan Aparatur Negara Dan Reformasi Birokrasi, *Peraturan Presiden Republik Indonesia nomor 81 tahun 2010: Grand Design Reformasi Birokrasi 2010-2025* [Presidential Regulation No. 81, 2010: Grand Design for Bureaucratic Reform 2010-2025] (Jakarta: Kementerian Pendayagunaan Aparatur Negara Dan Reformasi Birokrasi, 2010).

19. Syafuan Rozi Soebhan, "Model Reformasi Birokrasi Indonesia", *Widyariset*, Vol. 1 (2000), 219.

20. See also: David Osborne and Ted Gaebler, *Reinventing the Goverment* (New York, NY: Addison-Wesley, 1992), ix.

21. Soebhan, 2000, 222.

22. Eko Prasojo and Teguh Kurniawan, *Reformasi Birokrasi dan Good Governance: Kasus Best Practice Dari Sejumlah Daerah di Indonesia*, paper presented at the 5th International Symposium of Indonesian Journal of Antropology, 22-25 July 2008, Banjarmasin, Indonesia.

23. Soebhan, 2000, 223.

24. Soebhan, 2000, 224.

25. Kementerian Pendayagunaan Aparatur Negara Dan Reformasi Birokrasi, 2010, 1-8. See also: Badan Kepegawaian Negara, *Sistem Operasional Assessment Center bagi Pegawai Negeri Sipil* [Assessment Centre Operational System for Civil Servant] (Jakarta: Pusat Penelitian dan Pengembangan Badan Kepegawaian Negara, 2003).

26. Mabesad, 2011, 28.

27. Kementerian Pertahanan Republik Indonesia, 2010.

28. Vina Pendit, *Pemanfaatan Assessment Center Dalam Berbagai Sistem Pengelolaan SDM*, [The use of Assessment Centre in Human Resources Management System], paper presented at the 2nd National Congress on Assessment Centre, 24-26 July 2007, Hotel Borobudur, Jakarta, Indonesia.

29. Mark Brundrett, "The Question of Competence: The Origins, Strengths and Inadequacies of a Leadership Training Paradigm", *School Leadership & Management*, Vol. 20, No. 3 (2000), 353-369.

30. Mei-I Cheng, Andrew Dainty and David Moore, "The Differing Faces of Managerial Competency in Britain and America", *Journal of Management Development*, Vol. 22, No. 6 (2003), 527-537.

31. Richard Boyatzis, *The Competent Manager: A Model for Effective Performance* (New York, NY: John Wiley & Sons, 1982).

32. Jeffery Shippmann, Ronald Ash, Mariangela Batjtsta, Linda Carr, Lorraine Eyde, Beryl Hesketh, Jerry Kehoe, Kenneth Pearlman, Erich Prien and Juan I. Sanchez, "The Practice of Competency Modeling", *Personnel Psychology*, Vol. 53, No. 3 (2000), 703-740.

33. João Thomaz and Carlos Bana e Costa, *Decision Conferencing Within a Multimethodological Framework: Developing a Performance Appraisal Model for the Portuguese Army Officers*, paper presented at the 46th International Military Testing Association (IMTA) Conference, 26-28 October 2004, Brussels, Belgium.

34. See Pi Shen, "A Culture For Transformational Change: Strategies For The Singapore Armed Forces", *Pointer: Journal of the Singapore Armed Forces*, Vol. 28, No. 3 (2002).

35. William Steele and Robert Walters, Jr., "21st Century Leadership Competencies: Three Yards in a Cloud of Dust or the Forward Pass?", *Army Magazine*, Vol. 51, No. 8 (2001), 31.

36. Luann Barndt, *Developing Character and Aligning Personal Values with Organizational Values in the United States Coast Guard* (Master Of Military Art And Science, US Army Command and General Staff College, 2000).

37. Timothy R. Athey and Michael S. Orth, "Emerging Competency Methods for the Future", *Human Resource Management,* Vol. 38, No. 3 (1999), 215-225. See also: Lyle M. *Spencer and* Signe M. *Spencer, Competence at Work: Models for Superior Performance* (New York, NY: John Wiley & Sons, 1993).

38. Louis Wustemann, "New Dimensions to Competencies: An Interview with Bill Byham", *Competency & Emotional Intelligence Quarterly,* Vol. 8, No. 1 (2000), 15-19.

39. Brian Cronin, Ray Morath and Jason Smith, "Army Leadership Competencies: Old Wine in New Bottles?", paper presented at the 45th International Military Testing Association (IMTA) Conference, Pensacola, USA, 3-6 November 2003.

40. See: Robert Walker, *The Professional Development Framework: Generating Effectiveness in Canadian Forces Leadership* (Kingston, ON: Canadian Forces Leadership Institute, 2006), 29-30.; and, Doctrine Wing, *Australian Army Land Warfare Doctrine, LWD 0-0 : Command, Leadership and Management* (Tobruck Barracks: Doctrine and Simulation Group, Land Warfare Development Centre, 2003), 3.8-3.9.

41. Emma Davis, "New Zealand Defence Force Competency Framework On-Line Reporting Tool", paper presented at the 49th International Military Testing Association (IMTA) Conference, 8-12 October 2007, Gold Coast, Australia.

42. Ibid.

43. Barbara Townley, "Nietzsche, Competencies and Übermensch: Reflections on Human and Inhuman Resource Management", *Organization,* Vol. 6, No. 2 (1999), 285-305. See also, Wusteman, 2000, 17.

44. Richard I. Henderson, *Compensation Management in a Knowledge-Based World* (New Jersey: Prentice-Hall, 2009).

45. Sophie O. de Beeck and Annie Hondeghem, "Managing Competencies in Government: State of the Art Practices and Issues at Stake for the Future", draft report, *Annual Meeting of the Public Employment and Management Working Party,* 15-16 December 2009, OECD Conference Centre, Paris.

46. Richard Bruce Money and John L. Graham, "Salesperson Performance, Pay, and Job Satisfaction: Tests of a Model Using Data Collected in the United States and Japan", *Journal of International Business Studies,* Vol. 30, No. 1 (1999), 149-172.

47. Ibid.

48. Joseph Soeters, "Values in Military Academies: A Thirteen Country Study", *Armed Forces and Society,* Vol. 24 (1997), 7–32.

49. Hidayat, 2005, 17.

50. Walker, 2006, 26.

51. Steele and Walters, 2001.

52. OSS Assessment Staff, *Assessment of Men: Selection of Personnel for the Office Of Strategic Services* (NY: Rinehart & Co., 1948).

53. Head of the Kejuangan Departmen, *Jam Kadep Juang Seskoad kepada Pasis Dikreg XLIV Seskoad TA 2006,* Lecture for the 2006 Seskoad students.

54. Lieutenant-Colonel Eri R. Hidayat and Lieutenant-Colonel Gunawan, "People's Army, Patriotic Army, National Army and Professional Army: History, Challenges and the Development of Core Identity in the Indonesian National Army", in Jeff Stouffer and Justin C. Wright, eds., *Professional Ideology and Development: International Perspectives* (Kingston, ON: Canadian Defence Academy Press, 2008).

55. Imam E. Mulyono and Eri R. Hidayat, "*Sapta Marga*: The Indonesian Armed Forces' Code of Conduct and its Implementation in the Post New Order Era", in Stefan Seiler and Jeff Stouffer, eds., *Military Ethics: International Perspectives* (Kingston, ON: Canadian Defence Academy Press, 2010).

56. Ibid.

57. Ibid.

58. Wusteman, 2000, 17.

59. Wahyudi Kumorotomo, *In Search of Pay-for-performance System in Civil Services: A Challenge of Administrative Reform in Indonesia*, paper presented at the International Conference on Borderless Public Administration, 7 July 2011, Department of Public Administration, Gadjah Mada University, Hotel Sheraton Mustika, Yogyakarta, Indonesia.

60. Hadi Suprapto, "Dapat Remunerasi: Berapa Gaji Jenderal TNI?" [Getting Remuneration: How much is the compensation of a TNI General?], *Viva News*, 16 December 2010.

61. Kumorotomo, 2011, 4 and 12.

62. Ilhaamie Abdul Ghani Azmi, Zainal Ariffin Ahmad and Yuserrie Zainuddin, "Competency-based Pay and Service Quality: An Empirical Study of Malaysian Public Organisations", *Asian Academy of Management Journal*, Vol. 14, No. 1 (2009), 21-36.

63. Ibid., 27-29.

CHAPTER 6

Threats and Opportunities for Military Professionalism from Social Media

*Lieutenant-Colonel Psalm B. C. Lew**

NATURE OF THE MILITARY PROFESSION IN SINGAPORE

Singapore's lack of natural resources, small size and population as well as its multi-ethnic and multi-racial society, necessitates a unique approach to its defence via the implementation of National Service (NS), making the Singapore Armed Forces (SAF) the guardian of the country's sovereignty as well as a national building institution.[1] The practice of conscription over the past forty-five years has created the "NS citizen soldier" – where the National Servicemen (NSmen) form the main bulk of the fighting force alongside their active counterparts.[2] This integration was deliberate. Singapore Infantry Brigades command a mix of both active and NSmen units and Brigade Headquarters are staffed by both active personnel and NSmen.[3]

After completing two years of full time National Service, the NSmen maintain their operational readiness with annual In-Camp Training (ICT) sessions over a ten-year NS Training Cycle.[4] In fact, NSmen in the 7th year of their training cycle[5] are considered just as proficient as the full-time National Servicemen in terms of applying professional expertise to perform multi-faceted military tasks. They are expected to apply the same professional expertise within the same jurisdiction to uphold the SAF's legitimacy as a profession.[6] In a country of 3.2 million citizens[7] where 700,000 men have served or are currently serving in the SAF,[8] National Service in Singapore is considered a rite of passage and an issue close to the hearts of the people. In fact, citizens who default on NS, for example, by staying abroad, experience severe criticism for evading their duties.[9] National Service is a sense of duty shared by both regulars and citizens alike.

---

* The views expressed in this chapter are those of the author and do not necessarily reflect those of the Singapore Armed Forces.

SINGAPORE

THREATS TO MILITARY PROFESSIONALISM FROM SOCIAL MEDIA

In the SAF, professionalism demands the highest standards of excellence and competence from each soldier, sailor and airman.[10] Citizens of Singapore, who invest a deep personal stake in the armed forces, demand that these standards of excellence and competence also extend to their conduct in public life. Three elements define a profession – expertise, jurisdiction and legitimacy.[11] It is this legitimacy, or how it could be jeopardized, that is the focus of this chapter. Legitimacy is based on the perceptions of the people, which can change very quickly with events. Social media becomes a multiplier because it allows perceptions to be exaggerated and re-transmitted rapidly. This is an issue for Singapore because internet penetration is high at 72.4 percent (ranked 25th in the world)[12] and Facebook penetration is 56.52 percent. (ranked 11th in the world).[13] As shown by the recent 2011 uprising in the Arab states, the military's task became increasingly complex as the result of the use of social media as it could be used to link many stakeholders in a complicated web or system to fan dissent.[14] As such, the effect of social media on military professionalism in Singapore cannot be ignored.

In Singapore, the first threat that social media poses to the SAF's professionalism is that it permits the public to put the SAF under immediate scrutiny that can be re-transmitted very quickly. For example, Singapore's main English newspaper online media, the *Straits Times Online Mobile Print* (STOMP), encourages citizen journalism or mass self communication.[15] A story on STOMP featured the actions of two young NSmen who were photographed helping a cyclist hurt in a traffic accident. In short order, it was viewed by more than 60,000 citizens and a STOMP opinion poll reported an approval rating of 86 percent as well as over 600 Facebook likes.[16] While this story portrays a positive image of the SAF, it also highlights how the actions of every SAF serviceman can be examined, made public, and how the military's professionalism can be scrutinized at an unprecedented micro level.

The second threat that social media poses to the SAF's professionalism is the "Strategic Corporal"[17] phenomenon by which even the actions of an enlistee, like those of the two young SAF personnel in the above story, can have an enormous impact at the organizational or even national level of outcomes as it spreads through social networking sites.

In the traditional discussions on professions, Huntington and Janowitz limit professional membership to the Officer Corps; this excludes the non-commissioned ranks as well as members of the reserves.[18] This suggests a submissive and also non-participative role for any combatant other than a regular officer. This notion may not have been out of place in the 1960s where decision-making structures were centralized and revolved around the Officer Corps. It is not consistent, however, with today's reality. In today's world of social media, to suggest that only SAF officers are duty bound to the profession is incorrect as a lack of professionalism by warrant officers, specialists and enlistees, as potentially reported by social media, could contribute to the erosion of the SAF's legitimacy as a profession. The "Strategic Corporal" effect created by social media requires the SAF to review how it must inspire the full spectrum of ranks to the highest standard of professionalism.

The third threat that social media poses to the SAF's professionalism comes from its ability to blur the lines between a military members personal and professional lives. This is a problem faced by several other professions such as doctors[19] and psychotherapists[20] as well as many other professional groups. For example, in a study of the Facebook accounts of medical graduates from the University of Otago in New Zealand, it was found that of 37 percent publicly accessible accounts, 10 percent showed images of doctors being intoxicated, 6 percent showed doctors nude or cross-dressing and 3.6 percent showed images that breached patient confidentiality.[21] This study raised concerns about the state of the medical professionalism in New Zealand.[22]

Recently in Singapore, a physical education (PE) teacher's Facebook page showed photos of him hugging various women at night clubs. This drew considerable concern from parents, especially the parents of his female students; they questioned his credibility as a role model.[23] As the world becomes increasingly connected, the flow of information enables the rapid inception of meaning in the public's consciousness.[24] Hence, personal information about professionals in the social media can be detrimental because the meaning attributed by public perception could erode or destroy the public's trust and in turn, undermine a profession's legitimacy.

A military profession can lose its legitimacy when either a combination of the following situation occurs; when it loses its ethical anchor, when the leadership is somehow corrupted or when it is no longer able to fulfil the responsibilities of its jurisdiction.[25] The military professional, like other professionals, is subject to the moral proposition "to whom much is entrusted, much is expected."[26] This sentiment is rooted in the SAF Act that provides the military professional with the legal jurisdiction, including a wide range of powers, most significantly to *"take measures (including the use of force) reasonable and necessary."*[27] Therefore, like all other professions, the SAF is expected to regulate the behaviour of its members.[28] An increase in the incidents of SAF servicemen who are compromised on social media (i.e., that are not demonstrating military professionalism), will lead to a decrease in the SAF's social jurisdiction.

In most democracies, a military profession's legal jurisdictions and powers are not sacrosanct. As legitimacy and social jurisdiction are lost, the political leadership and elected government could be pressured by the public to remove these powers and/or apply more restrictions as they question the military professional's ability to fulfil its purpose. If not properly managed, social media could land a professional in a situation that could eventually spell a "death in its character."[29]

MITIGATING THREATS FROM SOCIAL MEDIA

The first response to mitigate the effects of the increased scrutiny caused by social media, as well as the Strategic Corporal phenomenon, is to raise the standards of military professionalism across all ranks through values inculcation; the end state being that all servicemen would demonstrate positive behaviours, both in operations as well as during their private life or out of camp. The challenge of being a National Service armed force is that service in the military is not optional. The newer generations of servicemen in Generation "Y" have a greater desire for a work-life balance. They also feel the need to not think and feel restricted by their work for some aspects of their lives, especially out of camp and during their personal time.[30]

In this respect, a dissonance will arise in the mind of a serviceman whenever there is a mismatch between their actions and the espoused beliefs and standards they are supposed to live up to. In studies of individual behaviours in groups, some coping strategies include leaving the group or engaging in intra-group or intergroup competition to reinforce their sense of self-worth when dissonance has occurred.[31] Clearly the law does not allow conscripts who don't identify with the SAF Core Values to leave. As low identifiers, however, they are not likely to align their self-concept with the SAF character and will more likely act in a way where their personal identities are affirmed at the expense of others.[32] This may result in self-centred or sometimes, anti-social behaviour in public, even while in uniform. This of course can be a problem given the pervasiveness of social media.

As such, raising the standards of military professionalism will require SAF leaders and commanders across all ranks to continuously inculcate values in all their servicemen. This will help to ensure that each serviceman forms an identity anchored on the SAF Core Values of Loyalty to Country, Leadership, Discipline, Professionalism, Ethics, Fighting Spirit and Care for Soldiers.

Ultimately, the personal identity of every member of the SAF is a collection of the in-group or out-group categorizations of himself across a span of groups including the SAF.[33] Researchers have argued that this is done through in-group and out-group distinctions by cognitively categorizing the self and others based on cognitive prototypes that describe the ideal attributes of in-group membership in a particular social context.[34] The in-group and out-group categorization and the development of each serviceman's social identity based on the SAF Core Values is important because the more they feel part of the SAF, the more it exerts a powerful influence to regulate their behaviour, at all times, to a standard of military professionalism.

Here, the experience of socializing new conscripts to the SAF Core Values is meant to shape their perceptions by imbuing in each of them a mental model which they hold of themselves as members of the SAF. This mental model of being a SAF member will eventually shape the behavioural traits that they display both in and out of camp, the attitudes they adopt in public, as well as the norms that guide their behaviour. The SAF attempts to achieve this through values inculcation where the desired outcome is for the SAF Core Values to shape the attitudes and traits of all leaders and servicemen in the SAF. Figure 6.1 illustrates the three-level model of the SAF theory of values inculcation,[35] which provides a framework for the socialization of values as the ethic of the military profession.

Level 1: Values Clarification and Alignment. The most important stage is Level 1 where the clarification of a SAF serviceman's personal values and his identification to the SAF Core Values assists his development of a sense of duty.[36]

Level 2: Values Based Actions. At this Level, self-awareness helps the SAF serviceman identify the dissonance between his choices and the SAF Core Values. Thereafter, he needs to engage in self-management to reduce this dissonance and translate his values into desirable attitudes, traits and norms.

Level 3: Application of Values in Reasoning. This Level is about reasoning through the application of values. In today's environment of a pervasive social media, the SAF serviceman will also need to be self-aware. When he is in uniform, he needs to reflect upon how his actions and behaviours are based on the SAF Core Values and how they contribute to a sense of moral goodness to the society, thereby maintaining military professionalism.

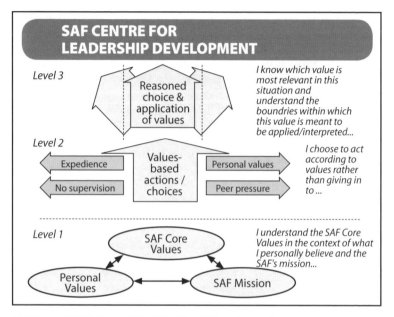

Figure 6.1: SAF Three-Level Model of Core Values Inculcation

The second response to mitigate the effects of the blurring of private and professional lives in social networking sites like Facebook, is to develop a framework for the military's use of social media that could comprise both policies and leadership. In terms of policies, the SAF has certain guidelines on the release of information based on the Official Secrets Act,[37] but it does not provide actionable guidelines on how SAF servicemen should behave on social networking sites. In this respect, there are guidelines proposed by other Armed Forces that could be adapted by the SAF to regulate the use of social media.[38]

First, SAF servicemen should not upload anything that isn't theirs or is prohibited.[39] With the tagging of photos and the sharing of content on Facebook, it is very easy to forget that legal restrictions exist, and examples include copyrighted songs, videos and other trademarked materials. Ultimately, in taking the Oath of Allegiance,[40] all SAF personnel promised they will "Obey the laws of the Republic of Singapore." Hence even the personal use of Facebook should be law abiding. Posting a colleague's naked photograph on Facebook after a prank may seem like good fun, but the serviceman should not forget that this violates the sections of the SAF Act concerning the conduct to the prejudice of good order[41] or in some cases, it constitutes an offence against decency under the Singapore Penal Code.[42] The following guidelines, adapted from the US Army Social Media Handbook, serves as an excellent resource:[43]

- Set security options to allow visibility to "friends only."

- Do not reveal sensitive information about yourself such as schedules and event locations.

- Ask, "What could the wrong person do with this information or photograph?"

- Closely review photos. Make sure they don't give away sensitive information.

- Make sure to talk to family about operations security and what can and cannot be posted.

- Videos can go viral quickly. Make sure they don't give away sensitive information.

- Avoid mentioning rank, locations, dates, or equipment specifications and capabilities.

Second, SAF leaders and commanders need to lead by example in the way they use social media as role modelling is a critical method in the development of professionalism.[44] For a start, those leaders not on social media need to be. In doing so, they can set the norms and demonstrate the importance of projecting an online persona that is characteristic and appropriate for professionals.[45] This includes the way we express ourselves in the social media space. In this regard, the US Army Social Media Handbook[46] has some very useful tips based on the principle that "Leaders online are the same as Leaders in person":

- Manage online relationships in the same way as professional relationships (e.g., Commanders and subordinates could befriend each other online but the way they relate to each other should be the same).

- Manage conduct professionally (e.g., things that a leader wouldn't say in person should not be posted on social media because a post is a semi-permanent representation, and similarly, leaders should correct their servicemen online just as they would in person).

- Manage online comments respectfully (e.g., comments a leader makes on a post must be done respectfully and intelligently so that they don't inadvertently raise issues that reflect poorly on the chain of command or on the SAF).

SINGAPORE

OPPORTUNITIES FOR MILITARY PROFESSIONALISM FROM SOCIAL MEDIA

While social media presents some threats to military professionalism, these same threats can also serve as opportunities for the profession. That is, social media tools (i.e., STOMP, Facebook, YouTube, Twitter, etc.), if understood, can be used effectively by leaders and commanders. Ultimately, their usefulness depends on how they are used. For example, during Operation CAST LEAD, the Israeli Defence Force used new media tools extensively and crossed swords with the Hamas in cyberspace as the ground-air campaign unfolded.[47] Here, one of the key lessons learned about social media was "if you don't engage [in social media], someone else will fill the void."[48]

In this respect, the SAF could use social media as a platform to build a culture of engagement. There are four elements to pay attention to while using social media to engage both internal and external stakeholders: being proactive, innovative, adaptive, and leader driven and sustainable.[49] Being proactive has already been dealt with earlier in this chapter. Responsiveness is where the SAF need to pre-empt issues and challenges and present their message first.[50] Innovation refers to how we find new ways of employing new media to serve the development of engagement, recognizing that social media platforms are constantly evolving.[51] On the point of being adaptive, it requires the engagement to support adaptive decision-making to the information and content being posted. This in turn requires the process to be decentralized in order to respond to changes in the perception of the social media.[52] As mentioned earlier, engagements on social media need to be leader driven and sustained, otherwise, someone else will very quickly fill the void with messages that may not help the SAF's image.[53]

The first opportunity for the engagement of social media centres around how it could be used to broadcast messages to improve the SAF's image. Here, SAF leaders need to learn how to be gatekeepers and agenda-setters.[54] There is a real war going on today in cyberspace for the hearts and minds of all soldiers, sailors and airmen as well as the larger public. In this war, the SAF needs to be the agenda setter for the stories that will strengthen Singaporean's commitment to defence. In this respect, the SAF has made some very positive in roads. For example, the 18 six to seven minute episodes of "Every Singaporean Son" posted on the SAF cyberpioneerTV on YouTube allowed the SAF to fill the void with its messages.[55] In terms of engagement, social media allows the SAF to engage its people "professionally."

The second opportunity for engagement presented by social media is how it can be used to strengthen the SAF personnel's identity as members of a military profession. For example, Facebook has created the opportunity for all National Servicemen to engage with the SAF *brands*, communicating their support by becoming "fans" of SAF-related groups, or through "likes" of a new group or post within the group.[56] Specifically, research has found that a Facebook users' desire to connect with brands on Facebook has been linked to social identity, trust, satisfaction as well as attachment.[57] Research has also found that larger networks and larger estimated audiences or "friends" for status updates predicted life satisfaction.[58] A large and vibrant Facebook group for SAF units or related events could strengthen a serviceman's alignment to the military because as the number of "likes" on an SAF-related group increases, the satisfaction of people with that group should also increase as this positively reinforces their sense of membership. In this case, social media allows the SAF to engage its people "intellectually" by identifying themselves with the profession publicly in cyberspace.

The third opportunity for engagement presented by social media is how it could be used to support efforts in values inculcation. The ultimate aim for values inculcation is to engender an emotional attachment to the SAF's beliefs. Here, research has shown that the status-update tool is predominantly used to express one's current emotional state to all the friends and groups one is connected to. This is important psychologically as it shows that intimacy development for emerging adults is now going public.[59] In addition, larger networks and friend groups for status updates also predicted perceived social support.[60] In this context, when Facebook groups are moderated professionally by leaders, SAF servicemen could discuss threats and challenges to how they demonstrate values and solicit feedback and support from other members of the SAF. This could serve to strengthen their conviction and commitment. Thus, social media allows the SAF to engage its people "emotionally" through the values.

CONCLUSION

While social media does present threats to military professionalism, the SAF, just like other militaries, could choose how it responds to this emerging information terrain. In this respect, social media becomes a threat especially when there is no effort to continuously raise the standards of military professionalism through values inculcation and when the use of social networking sites is not properly regulated by social media policies or properly led by the example of SAF leaders. On the other hand, when a National Service Armed Force like the SAF chooses to respond to social media by thinking of

SINGAPORE

it as a tool for engagement, the outcomes for the members can change very quickly. Military professionalism demands the highest standards of excellence and competence from every serviceman and this can be achieved when social media is exploited to improve the SAF's image, strengthen identity as members of the SAF and support efforts in values inculcation so that all SAF serviceman are engaged professionally, intellectually and emotionally. A renewed sense of military professionalism will further mitigate the negative effects brought about by social media and ultimately further strengthen the SAF as a profession.

ENDNOTES

1. See Singapore Government Press Statement Speech by the Minister of Defence, Dr. Goh Keng Swee, in moving the second reading of the National Service (Amendment) Bill in the Singapore Parliament on Monday, 13 March 1967, Document Number: PressR19670313b, retrieved on 20 May 2010 from <http://www.a2o.com.sg/a2o/public/search/index.html>.

2. All Singaporean males who reach the age of 18 are conscripted to render NS to the country. NS comprises two years of full time service and 10 years of NS liability during which they render service up to a maximum of 40 days per year. Upon completing 10 years of NS liability, they will enter MR. In essence, everyone is a National Serviceman. Those serving full-time are known as National Servicemen or NSFs as opposed to NSmen who are serving their annual liability.

3. Tim Huxley, *Defending the Lion City: The Armed Forces of Singapore* (Singapore: Talisman Publishing, 2004), 123-125.

4. NS Admin Department, *NSmen Handbook 21st Edition* (Singapore: National Serviceman Publication, 2010), 14.

5. Ibid.

6. See, James Burk, "Expertise, Jurisdiction and Legitimacy of the Military Profession", in Don M. Snider and Lloyd J. Matthews, eds., *The Future of the Army Profession* (New York, NY: McGraw Hill Custom Publishing, 2005), 47.

7. See, Department of Statistics, *Yearbook of Statistics Singapore 2010* (Singapore: Ministry of Trade and Industry, 2010).

8. The figures were drawn from the government's plan to grant an NS Anniversary tax bonus to NSmen on the 40th Anniversary of NS in 2007. See, Ministry of Information Communications and the Arts, *Singapore Yearbook 2007* (Singapore: MICA Press, 2007), 72.

9. See, MINDEF Singapore Media Room, *MINDEF News Release 16 Jan 2006, Ministerial Statement on NS Defaulters by Minister for Defence Teo Chee Hean*, retrieved on 20 May 2010 from <http://www.mindef.gov.sg/imindef/news_and_events/nr/2006/jan/16jan06_nr.html>.

10. *The SAF Core Values: Our Common Identity 2007 Edition* (Singapore: SAFTI MI, 2007), 41-44.

11. Eliot Friedson, *Professionalism Reborn: Theory, Prophecy and Policy* (Chicago, Illinois: University of Chicago Press, 1994), 16.

12. Miniwatts Marketing Group, "Top 50 Countries with the Highest Internet Penetration Rate", *Internet World Stats-Usage and Population Statistics*, retrieved on 19 March 2012 from <http://www.internetworldstats.com>.

13. Socialbakers, "Facebook Statistics by Country", *Socialbakers – The Recipe for Social Marketing Success*, retrieved on 19 March 2012 from <http://www.socialbakers.com/Facebook-statistics/>.

14. James Dorsey, "Arab Protesters and Social Media: Need for Engagement", *RSIS Commentaries*, No. 138 (3 October 2011).

15. Stuart Allan, "Citizen Journalism and the Rise of 'Mass Self-Communication': Reporting the London Bombings", *Global Media Journal Australian Edition*, Vol. 1, No. 1 (2007), 2.

16. STOMPER Luke "Army Guys in News Again – This Time They're Helping Cyclist Hurt in Accident," *STOMP*, 28 Jun 2011, Singapore Press Holdings Ltd. Co., retrieved on 19 Mar 2012 from <http://singaporeseen.stomp.com.sg>.

17. See Charles C. Krulak, "The Strategic Corporal: Leadership in the Three Block War", in *Marines Magazine* (Arlington VA: Marines Corps News, January 1999).

18. See Samuel Huntington, *"The Soldier and the State": The Theory and Politics of Civil-Military Relations* (Cambridge, MA: Harvard University Press, 1957), 9.

19. Lindsay Thompson, Kara Dawson, Richard Ferdig, Erik Black, Jeff Boyer, Jade Coutts and Nicole Paradise Black, "The Intersection of Online Social Networking with Medical Professionalism", *Journal of General Internal Medicine*, Vol. 23, No. 7 (2008), 954–957.

20. Ibid.

21. Joanna MacDonald, Sangsu Sohn and Pete Ellis, "Privacy, Professionalism and Facebook: A Dilemma for Young Doctors", *Medical Education*, Vol. 44 (2010), 810.

22. Ibid., 811.

23. STOMPER Anon, "OK For Teacher to go Clubbing but Why Post Pics of Women Hugging Him?", *STOMP*, 1 Apr 2012, Singapore Press Holdings Ltd. Co., retrieved on 1 April 2012 from <http://singaporeseen.stomp.com.sg>.

24. See Manuel Castells, "Communication, Power and Counter-Power in the Network Society", *International Journal of Communication*, Vol. 1, No. 1 (2007), 238-266, cited in Stuart Allan "Citizen Journalism and the Rise of "Mass Self-Communication": Reporting the London Bombings", *Global Media Journal Australian Edition*, Vol. 1, No. 1 (2007), 3.

25. See Douglas Bland, "The Government of Canada and the Armed Forces: A Troubled Relationship", in David Charters and Brent Wilson, eds., *The Soldier and the Canadian State: A crisis in civil-military relations* (Fredericton, NB: Centre for Conflict Studies, 1996), 27.

26. See Jeffrey Pinsler, *Ethics and Professional Responsibility – A Code for the Advocate and Solicitor* (Singapore: Academy of Law Publishing, 2007), 4.

27. See Republic of Singapore, *Chapter 295, the Singapore Armed Forces Act, Part XIIA, Section 201B, Sub-Section (3), Paragraph (F)*, (1970).

28. Huntington, 1957, 16-18.

29. See Don Snider, "The US Army as Profession", in Don Snider and Lloyd Matthews, eds., *The Future of the Army Profession* (New York, NY: McGraw Hill Custom Publishing, 2005), 16-19.

30. See Shuo Hao, Andrew Wan and David Tang, "Gen WhY – So What?", *Pointer*, Vol. 35 (2009), 15-16.

31. See Amelie Mummendey, Thomas Kessler, Andreas Klink and Rosemarie Mielke, "Strategies to Cope With Negative Social Identity: Predictions by Social Identity Theory and Relative Deprivation Theory", *Journal of Personality and Social Psychology*, Vol. 76, No. 2 (1999), 229-245.

SINGAPORE

32. See Belle Derks, Colette van Laar and Naomi Ellemers, "Working for the Self or Working for the Group: How Self- Versus Group Affirmation Affects Collective Behavior in Low-Status Groups", *Journal of Personality and Social Psychology*, Vol. 96, No. 1 (2009), 183–202.

33. See Henri Tajfel and John Turner, "The Social Identity Theory of Inter-Group Behavior", in William G. Austin and Stephen Worchel, eds., *The Social Psychology of Intergroup Relations* (Chicago: Nelson-Hall, 1979).

34. See Kelly Fielding and Michael Hogg, "Social Identity, Self-Categorization, and Leadership: A Field Study of Small Interactive Groups", *Group Dynamics: Theory, Research, and Practice*, Vol. l, No. 1 (1997), 39-51.

35. See *The SAF Core Values: Our Common Identity 2007 Edition*, (2007), 41-44.

36. In clarifying Personal Values and how it is connected to the SAF Core Values, the SAF has largely adapted Kirschenbaum's concepts of Values Clarification. See, Howard Kirschenbaum, "Clarifying Values Clarification: Some Theoretical Issues and a Review of Research", *Group & Organization Management*, Vol. 1 (1976), 99-116.

37. See Republic of Singapore, *Chapter 213, Official Secrets Act, Section 4-5*, (1935).

38. Chondra Perry, "Social Media and the Army", *Military Review*, March-April (2010), 63-67.

39. Ibid., 65.

40. See Republic of Singapore, *Chapter 93, the Enlistment Act, The Schedule*, (1970).

41. See Republic of Singapore, *Chapter 295, the Singapore Armed Forces Act,Part III, Section 26*, (1970).

42. See Republic of Singapore, *The Penal Code, Chapter XIV, Section 292*, (1970).

43. Office of the Chief of Public Affairs, *U.S. Army Social Media Handbook – January 2011* (Washington, D.C.: Online and Social Media Division, 2011), 7.

44. See Katherine C. Chretien, Ryan Greysen, Jean-Paul Chretien and T. Kind, "Online Posting of Unprofessional Conduct by Medical Students", *JAMA*, Vol. 301, No. 12 (2009), 1309-1315, in Joanna MacDonald, Sangsu Sohn and Pete Ellis, "Privacy, Professionalism and Facebook: A Dilemma for Young Doctors", *Medical Education*, Vol. 44 (2010), 805-813.

45. Ibid.

46. Office of the Chief of Public Affairs, 2011, 8.

47. William Caldwell IV, Dennis Murphy and Anton Menning, "Learning to Leverage New Media: The Israeli Defence Forces in Recent Conflicts", *Military Review*, May-June (2009), 6-7.

48. Ibid., 9.

49. William Caldwell IV, Shawn Stroud and Anton Menning, "Fostering a Culture of Engagement", Military Review, September-October (2009), 13.

50. Caldwell IV, Murphy and Menning, 2009, 5.

51. Ibid., 15.

52. Ibid., 16.

53. Ibid., 16-17.

54. Ibid., 4.

55. Beth Anderson, Patrick Fagan, Tom Woodnutt and Tomas Chamorro-Premuzic, "Facebook Psychology: Popular Questions Answered by Research", *Psychology of Popular Media Culture*, Vol. 1, No. 1 (2012), 26.

56. Ibid.

57. Ibid., 27.

58. Adriana Manago, Tamara Taylor and Patricia Greenfield, "Me and My 400 Friends: The Anatomy of College Students' Facebook Networks, Their Communication Patterns, and Well-Being", *Developmental Psychology*, Vol. 48, No. 2 (2012), 369-380.

59. Ibid., 378.

60. Ibid., 379.

CHAPTER 7

The Profession of Arms and the Promotion of Ethics: The Profession of Arms and the Challenge of Ethics

Hugh Smith, PhD*

War – the business of killing – is an activity in which the very existence of ethics is often disputed. Military ethics, cynics claim, is an oxymoron akin to military intelligence. There can be no ethics in war because the stakes are too high – the life and death of individuals and nations. English philosopher Thomas Hobbes, for example, argued that ethics are simply not relevant to the relations of states since they exist in a condition of anarchy where moral judgements are merely opinions. Others have argued that seeking to inject ethics into armed conflict is counter-productive. The mistakes which come from kindness in war, as military theorist Carl von Clausewitz suggested, are often the worst. Good intentions may be morally bad.

Defenders of military ethics argue that as a matter of observation some, perhaps most, soldiers do seek to behave ethically most of the time. Prisoners of war, for example, are mostly not killed out of hand, though mistreatment is not uncommon; in most cases civilians are killed as a secondary effect of military action rather than as deliberate targets. Historically, too, many societies have sought to identify what constitutes a just cause for going to war. Ethical considerations in war may be weak and merely one factor among many, but they are not absent altogether. A sense of humanity, a respect for laws, and professional pride among military personnel all underpin ethical behaviour in war.

This study outlines the characteristics of ethics in the military environment. It examines the challenging and complex circumstances in which military ethics exists and why ethical dilemmas faced by military personnel are difficult and often unique. These dilemmas are often at their most acute in war but they are not absent in peacetime. The study concludes with reflections on how to develop ethical behaviour in a military force.

---

*   The views expressed in this chapter are those of the author and do not necessarily reflect those of the Australian Defence Force.

AUSTRALIA

There is no need to elaborate on a definition of ethics here. It will suffice to mention several characteristics of relevance.[1]

Ethics is about what is right and wrong, in particular what is right and wrong to do (or not to do). Whether behaviour is ethical or not is taken to depend not on subjective preferences but on various principles that are widely, if not universally, shared. Ethical debate in practice tends to arise less from disagreement about the existence of moral principles than about how such principles apply in specific situations or about how to reconcile principles that point in different directions.

1. Ethics involves choices that are difficult. If there is only one, undisputed choice of action, we are not talking about ethics – or at least not about interesting or important ethical questions. Ethical choices usually involve competing principles or obligations such that the actor is pulled in at least two different directions, each of which has legitimate claims. Often, whatever choice is made, some harm will result – hence the phenomenon of "dirty hands" which signify a degree of guilt whatever decision is made. A decision can also be difficult for different types of reasons which are discussed later.

2. The choice is made by a free agent. Automatic, unthinking behaviour means no ethical question is being consciously confronted and no ethical choice is being made. This point is illustrated by the problem of obedience to illegal or immoral orders. Do we regard the soldier ordered to shoot an unarmed prisoner as a conditioned automaton or as a human being with some degree of genuine choice, even if disobedience would be punished by death?

3. Ethics is not about "correct" choices but ones that follow from sincere and competent analysis of a dilemma. Ethical individuals will face dilemmas honestly and without casuistry. Their attempt to assess competing principles or obligations and to think through the consequences of various choices should be as good as they are capable of. While all are expected to be sincere, different levels of competence can be expected. Thus higher standards are traditionally demanded of officers than of their subordinates.

THE SOCIAL CONTEXT OF PROFESSIONS

All societies need some shared ethical values and certain basic rules for human interaction that have developed over millennia. Any community needs some respect for the lives and property of others; any community relies on its members keeping promises that have been made. Whether such ethical rules are seen as god-given or simply as essential for common survival, "natural law" matters little for present purposes.

Human law is also important. Though covering many non-ethical matters, legal systems incorporate moral rules and principles. As United States (US) Chief Justice Earl Warren put it: "In civilized life, law floats in a sea of ethics".[2] Where law exists, however, individuals are not relieved of moral choice. First, laws are often general and need interpretation. The law of armed conflict, for example, does not provide detailed guidance on the choice of targets. Second, commanders may have to choose whether or not to apply a given law – should a military offence, for example, be dealt with by legal process, by command authority or by informal means. Finally, the law itself may be morally abhorrent such that ethical behaviour demands disobedience. Law alone is never enough.

Complex societies also depend on professions to promote ethical behaviour. Those with expertise in areas such as medicine, law, the church, academic learning, engineering and so on are granted a substantial measure of autonomy by society – for example, to determine the qualifications necessary to practice as a professional, to set the standards of performance to be maintained, and to discipline members who fall short. In return for such privileges, a profession is expected to act not simply in the interests of its members, but also for the benefit of their clients and for society as a whole. While laws may set broad parameters, detailed control of professional activities can only be effective through formal and informal codes of behaviour set by the profession and internalized by its members.

From society's perspective, professional military ethics has distinctive characteristics. The military, first of all, is the only profession that works directly for a particular state (Diplomacy is arguably the only other, while police officers work for the justice system rather than the executive government). Armed forces exist exclusively to serve the state unlike other professions which for the most part serve individual clients or private organizations. Those in uniform normally work for only one master unless they become mercenaries or change nationality. The loyalty of the military professional to a single state limits his/her freedom of action though, as will be argued later, other loyalties may also make demands.

Second, the expertise of the military profession lies in deploying violence that can be directed toward any objective selected by the state. Other professions, by contrast, possess expertise that is directed toward relatively specific ends such as the health of human beings or the settlement of legal disputes. The open-endedness of military objectives, allied to the critical role of the state in providing security against a wide variety of threats, means that the military professional is likely to be employed in highly diverse activities.

Finally, civilian professions are essential to community life in that their expertise is continuously exercised and – mostly – contributes positively toward the benefit of society. Military professionals, by contrast, generally serve a negative purpose (i.e., preventing adverse changes in society or warding off harmful threats to society). It is, moreover, an activity that is contingent rather than continuing. Military professionals exercise their skills relatively infrequently and lack the continuous feedback on their performance enjoyed by their civilian counterparts.

Ethical standards in the military profession are essential to society for two main reasons. On the one hand, they influence how soldiers deal with enemies and non-combatants. Here, failures in judgement may produce illegal actions, adverse publicity and damaging consequences for the state. On the other hand, ethics is important in how the military organization manages its own members and maintains its professional cohesion and pride.

Failure on this front – such as episodes of sexual abuse or the bastardization (hazing) of officer cadets – undermines the loyalty and dedication of members of the force and loses the esteem in which a nation's citizens hold the military profession. Problems also arise in areas such as allocating responsibility in the event of accidents, assessing appropriate levels of risk in training and exercises, balancing demands on individuals against military requirements, ensuring equitable treatment of groups such as homosexuals, women and ethnic minorities, and maintaining a fair and effective system of justice within the armed forces. Nor should the question of the proper treatment of veterans and the families of those killed or wounded on duty be overlooked. An armed force must constantly examine its personnel policies and its culture to ensure that it treats its members in a fair and ethical fashion.

ETHICS AND THE PROFESSION OF ARMS

Military activities contain a far greater ethical element than is widely realized outside (or perhaps even within) the armed forces. Despite extensive legal frameworks and detailed regulations, individuals still need to make difficult ethical judgements, often with lives or careers at stake. What is it about the military profession that makes ethics not only important but extraordinarily difficult? A number of general reasons can be identified.

Life and Death

War is a matter of life and death, of killing and dying. The liability of the soldier is, in British Army General Sir John Hackett's formulation, "unlimited".[3] He – or she – must inflict death and injury on others and risk life and limb if ordered to do so. Perhaps only police forces are required to put themselves in harm's way in such a fashion though the level and frequency of violence they face is far smaller. At the same time, it is the unique *raison d'être* of the military profession to inflict harm on those who attack the nation, or to threaten harm in order to deter attack. Where other professions generally work to improve lives directly, the military serves society by killing its enemies. It thus falls to the military professional to make decisions about who lives and who dies among enemies, non-combatants and their own number.

Ethical judgements are especially needed where great disparities in power and position exist between people. A surgeon may daily perform operations in which a patient's life is at risk. Engineers may design faulty buildings that could collapse with loss of life. But an armed force enjoys – if that is the word – the greatest disparity in power (i.e., the power of life and death over individuals). Military forces are equipped with weapons designed to kill and are routinely placed in a situation where they deal with others who are less well-armed or not armed at all. At the same time, superior officers are often compelled to decide which among their subordinates must face the risk of death.

Military professionals may also deal with death and destruction on a large scale. Most professions deal with individuals on a one-to-one basis. A minister preaches to a congregation but is primarily concerned with each parishioner's soul. A doctor may work in public health and combat epidemics, but most treat individuals. The profession of arms, by contrast, is routinely involved in conflicts where deaths number hundreds, thousands or even more. A war with weapons of mass destruction could potentially eliminate human life in its entirety. When nuclear weapons first threatened to proliferate the Second World War, US General Omar Bradley (also first Chairman, Joint Chiefs of Staff) was prompted to observe, "Ours is a world of nuclear giants and ethical infants."[4]

Military personnel also draw a distinction between the lives of people in a way quite different from other professions. Doctors have their triage between patients who are going to die, those who will recover without treatment and those who will recover if treated. The triage for military personnel, by contrast, is based on the legitimacy of individuals as targets for attack as defined by legal rules and as determined by political factors:

- enemy troops are justified targets for killing since they pose a clear threat to the lives of one's own soldiers; once wounded or captured, however, they normally cease to be a threat and must be accorded protection.

- non-combatants belong to a special category, protected by the international humanitarian law of armed conflict. This protection is not absolute, but the burden of proof lies on those who conduct military actions likely to cause non-combatant deaths to show that such actions are necessary, proportionate to the military objective and discriminating as far as is reasonably possible. Whether there is a moral distinction to be drawn between one's own civilians, enemy civilians and third party civilians is a source of ethical debate.

- one's own troops are held to be a special responsibility of those put in charge of them. Minimizing casualties is usually a military and political priority, but dilemmas arise in deciding what risks one's own forces should be exposed to in order to reduce the possible loss of life among non-combatants.

Means and Ends

War is above all a practical activity that uses violent means in order to get results. This immediately raises the dilemma about what means are justified to achieve a given end. Once objectives are set, a presumption easily arises that any means are justified to secure those ends. This is so for several reasons. To begin with, the aim of a war itself is set by the state concerned. It is declared to be in the national interest and is liable to rouse patriotic support and a readiness to do whatever is necessary to secure victory. War in the name of the state can readily be interpreted as an unlimited license to kill and destroy.

Over the centuries, however, statesmen, scholars, lawyers, clerics and others have developed what can be called the Just War tradition or *jus ad bellum* – a set of principles intended to guide those contemplating war as to its justness or otherwise. Today the key justification for war is self-defence, a concept formally enshrined in the Charter of the United Nations.[5] Importantly, the Just War tradition does not permit a free choice of means even in the most justified of causes. One of its key principles is that any war, just or otherwise, should be conducted according to the prevailing law of armed conflict – *jus in bello* – even if an opponent breaks the law and gains an advantage.

The reasons for this are both principled and pragmatic. Principle argues that to respond in kind to illegal behaviour produces a common descent into barbarism. The whole point of the Just War tradition is to keep war more manageable and less destructive overall. Practice suggests that law-breaking behaviour in war often gives no great military advantage but may lead to criticism from the international community, a nation's own citizens and its own armed forces. It can also provoke an enemy into greater willingness to fight and a greater determination to prevail.

A classic ethical dilemma arises when it appears to one side that continued adherence to the rules could jeopardize its whole cause, even its survival as a nation. Thus in the early stages of the Second World War, as the American political philosopher Michael Walzer argues, Britain faced a "supreme emergency" and was justified in bombing German cities because: this was the only way it could divert some of Germany's military effort from conquest; and the need to defend democracy and freedom against Nazism was overwhelming.[6] The dangers of admitting exceptions of this kind, however, are evident.

The same applies at the tactical level. Important constraints are imposed by the international humanitarian law of armed conflict in an attempt to moderate the horror of war. In brief, these are the duty to ensure that only violence is carried out which is necessary to achieve given ends, the duty to keep death and destruction in proportion to the objectives sought, and the duty to discriminate between legitimate and non-legitimate targets (in broad terms military and non-military targets). These rules are based on the moral principle of minimizing harm, especially to those not directly engaged in war.

Yet the battlefield has its own imperatives: survival and winning. By instinct, individuals normally do whatever is necessary to save their own lives; by training, soldiers generally seek to achieve whatever objective has been set. Inevitable and constant tension arises between these behaviours on the one hand and the observance of rules or the instinct of humanity on the other. Perhaps there are circumstances in which legal and moral rules can be bent or broken? Classic dilemmas include the patrol behind enemy lines that is spotted by a civilian who must be killed before he/she raises the alarm if a critical mission is to succeed (the use of torture raises comparable dilemmas). At the very heart of military activity, therefore, is the tension between results-oriented and rule-oriented behaviour.

Military organizations, moreover, depend on rules, laws and regulations for their own efficient and effective operation. To ignore rules in order to achieve results is to risk disintegration of the moral and functional basis of the organization itself. In the same way, the military organization depends on command and obedience. Superiors must be confident that orders will be carried out. If subordinates are ordered to perform wrongful actions, this raises the prospect that they will disobey – not least because they may be trained to reject unlawful commands despite also being accustomed to follow commands. Other professions may face comparable dilemmas. What should a doctor do in response to a patient's demand for euthanasia when it is legally prohibited? But for the military profession, far more is usually at stake than a single life.

Fog and Friction

Military decisions are often made in the most difficult circumstances, especially in the course of operations. Several factors can be identified that make ethical choices difficult in this context, if not impossible. The discussion focuses on decisions within war, but the factors mentioned are also relevant to decisions about the resort to war itself.

First, reliable information is usually inadequate or lacking altogether. Commanders rarely have enough intelligence about the enemy, about non-combatants or even about their own forces. Nor will the intelligence they do have be totally accurate or up-to-date. Military forces, moreover, often seek to keep each other deliberately in the dark, using legal means such as deception, feints and *ruses de guerre*, and sometimes illegal means such as exploiting Red Cross emblems or places of worship for military advantage. Decisions amid such uncertainty are hard-pressed to meet the requirements of necessity, proportionality and discrimination.

Second, the range of consequences flowing from different courses of action in war are often unpredictable. Friction intrudes into every plan. Civilians turn up where they were not expected. The enemy fights more fiercely than anticipated. Bombs and shells fall in the wrong place. Countless twists and turns in battle cause death and destruction to be higher than expected. Decisions must be made in advance with only sketchy knowledge of how each possible course of action might turn out.

Third, the time available in which to make a decision is often extremely short. At the tactical level, the choice between killing a person and holding fire may have to be made in a split second. Even at higher levels, hours or days or weeks may not be long enough to gather as much information as a commander would wish to have in order to make accurate estimates of the likely course of battle.

Fourth, there are psychological and physical pressures that distort decision-making. Danger is inherent on the battlefield and it is natural for soldiers to see their own survival and that of their unit as having the highest priority. For example, commanders may unwittingly overestimate the strength of the enemy such that non-combatant losses appear more justifiable. And, of course, physical exhaustion, stress and deprivation are often very great in time of war. None of these circumstances are conducive to clear, reasoned and careful ethical decisions.

Publicity and Secrecy

Military decision-making is also liable to occur in two extreme situations, neither of which is likely to favour calm and principled decision-making. On the one hand, modern communications and media coverage make it possible for events to be reported nearly instantaneously around the world. This can cause the actions of a single individual, even at the lowest level, to hit the headlines and prompt instant government reactions – the phenomenon of the "strategic corporal".[7] Breaches of good conduct can provoke hostile responses among audiences both within the soldier's own country and in foreign states. Reports of mutilation of corpses by Australian soldiers in East Timor, for example, led to much bad publicity and public concern both in that country and in Australia – whatever their veracity. Fear of publicity can also stimulate attempts by military personnel to conceal questionable activities both from military superiors and from the wider world.

The positive side of this phenomenon is that knowing the world may be watching may cause soldiers to be more ethical and more careful in their actions. The "goldfish bowl" may work to encourage moral behaviour. Yet, much action in war takes place when there are no witnesses, when no close supervision can be exercised and where no records are kept. A soldier may be able to kill illegally, knowing that no one else need find out the circumstances or perhaps even discover that a killing has taken place. If such actions come to light, reasons for killing can easily be given that are plausible and difficult to challenge. The "fog of war" can thus serve to conceal actions from the rest of the world. In such situations, ethical behaviour depends more than ever on the moral qualities of the individual.

Detachment and Disconnection

War itself can cause participants to lose moral sensibility as human life becomes devalued either through familiarity with death or through remoteness from victims. Psychological detachment on the part of the soldier from the enemy and from the consequences of his/her actions can occur in several ways. In the face of death and destruction on a large scale or on a routine basis, some emotional numbing is a natural consequence. The horrors of war, however necessary and justified they may be, tend to reduce the ethical sensitivity of even the most compassionate soldier. Common psychological defences in war include demonizing the enemy so that he/she appears less than human, discounting the suffering of non-combatants who are perceived as covertly supporting the enemy or simply as obstacles to efficient military action, and repressing emotions at the time (often with a price to be paid later in the form of post-traumatic stress disorder). Such factors reduce the humane element in war and make ethical decisions more uncertain.

Detachment can also be found in the fact that individuals are members of a much larger organization that sets military objectives, determines the means of pursuing them and applies powerful pressure on members to achieve them. By their nature, military organizations develop a "can-do" and "must-do" ethos which is valuable in terms of achieving objectives, but which can reduce the accountability of individuals. Members of a hierarchical structure can find it easy to dissociate themselves psychologically from the actions which they take or contribute to in the name of the organization. Their deeds are not "owned" by them but by someone else.

The problems of identifying the moral responsibility of individuals when organizations are involved are well-known. Individuals can seek to avoid blame or shift it to others in many ways: "I did not make the policy or issue the order"; "It was not in my area of responsibility"; "What I did was minor and insignificant"; "If I had not done it, then someone else would have"; or "I did what I could to ameliorate a bad policy." In a disciplined and hierarchical organization such arguments are not altogether specious.

Technological advances in warfare have also played their part in psychological detachment by increasing the physical distance between soldiers and their human targets. The javelin and the longbow meant that an enemy need not be killed in face-to-face fighting (the introduction of the longbow in medieval warfare, indeed, was denounced as unfair and unchivalrous). Though sieges had always caused civilians to suffer in war, the cannon made direct attacks on cities and their inhabitants more feasible. But it was the development of explosives and of long-range means of delivery that placed the greatest distance between soldier and target. In less than 150 years, a rapid technological progression occurred from explosive shells fired by artillery to the Intercontinental Ballistic Missile (or ICBM) with a nuclear warhead.

Electronic communications have further added to the phenomenon of detachment. It is not simply that targets can be out of sight over the horizon, but that they can now be made to appear on a radar screen. A controller hundreds or thousands of kilometers distant can decide what is to be attacked, press a button and launch precision-guided munitions toward their targets. The screen will then display the results of the action. War becomes like a video game, one that can be played by civilians, as well as soldiers. More intelligent weapons platforms can seek out programmed types of target and fire their munitions automatically. Ethical choices are no longer made on the battlefield or in the war-room but entered into computer programs.

Multiplying Roles

Most professions encompass a range of activities, but none wider than the military profession, which focuses a particular means – violence. The ethical problems of war are complex enough, but other, increasingly common activities of military organizations, notably peacekeeping, law enforcement and counter-terrorism, raise additional ethical dilemmas.

Peacekeeping

Peacekeeping (or peace operations) takes place in a wide range of circumstances – from relatively stable situations to chaotic and dangerous internal conflicts. It is an area that is engaging armed forces of many countries to an increasing extent, yet is one in which ethical problems for the military have been little examined. Several distinctive factors making for ethical dilemmas can be identified.

As its name implies, peacekeeping is designed to promote peace or at least stability between states or, more commonly, between factions in an internal conflict. It may need to employ some level of force to achieve this aim but, unlike war proper, it does not seek to secure peace through the medium of victory (i.e., the military defeat of an armed enemy). Whereas victory is a fairly straightforward goal, peace or stability is an amorphous and complex objective involving the cooperation of several contending parties. In consequence, ethical judgements also become complex and difficult.

While war is a military contest between organized forces who know the rules (even if they are not always obedient to them), peacekeeping may involve the use of armed force in situations where some of the parties are ignorant of the law of armed conflict or deliberately flout it. Yet armed peacekeepers are required to observe the principles of necessity, discrimination and proportionality and may have restrictive rules of engagement and orders for opening fire. One reason for this is that many innocent and unarmed people tend to be caught up in a civil war. Another reason is that scrupulous observance of these principles is likely to promote the peace process or at least avoid undermining it. Such restraint, however, may clash with a perceived obligation on the part of the forces concerned to minimize the risk of casualties among their own personnel.

In peacekeeping, there are usually more players in the game than simply two identified combatant parties. Each different group is liable to have different ethical values and responsibilities. Is it proper, for example, for peacekeepers to do deals with local warlords who abuse human rights? Should they remain neutral *vis-à-vis* warring factions regardless of their behaviour? Should a peacekeeping force give medical assistance to the civilian community if it directly or indirectly assists one of the warring factions?

Peacekeeping is usually carried out by a combination of different organizations. It is thus necessary to work with other nations' military forces which may have different values from one's own (e.g., lack of professionalism, willingness to accept bribes, brutal treatment of captives, discrimination against women, whether locals or members of the peacekeeping force). Peacekeepers must also work with non-government organizations which can give rise to difficult dilemmas. To what extent can intelligence be shared with them if it will help save lives? Should scarce military resources be used to provide security for transport of food and medical supplies?

Any intervention in another country, moreover, must draw a fine line between respect for local customs, traditions and values on the one hand and the principles for which the peacekeeping force stands such as equality, democracy and freedom. Too much interference in the host country creates resentment and undermines the purpose of the mission. Too little betrays fundamental principles and, in extreme circumstances, costs lives. The reluctance of the UN and its members to take active steps against impending and actual atrocities in Rwanda and of the North Atlantic Treaty Organization (NATO) in Srebrenica exemplifies the dilemma.

International law provides little guidance in these areas though the rules of belligerent occupation have some relevance to peace operations. But there is a wide scope for greater study and training in the ethics of peace operations which seem set to expand rather than contract in the medium to long term.[8]

Law Enforcement and Counter-Terrorism

In some missions, the military's role is closer to policing or law enforcement than traditional soldiering. Yet the philosophies of each activity are very different. The law enforcement approach does not distinguish between friend and enemy but between criminals and law-abiding citizens. Its preferred means is to use no force or minimum force. Where soldiers are controlled by their government, police are responsible to the judicial system (at least in Western democracies). The ethical dilemmas of policing are themselves complex. The point to note is that soldiers engaged in law enforcement are likely to be less familiar with such problems and to have less training than law enforcement professionals when dealing with individual citizens.

Another key difference for military organizations is that whereas they normally direct their efforts against an external enemy – or in relation to foreign citizens in the case of international peacekeeping – law enforcement and counter-terrorism is generally directed against one's own nationals. Historically, armed forces developed as much as a bulwark against internal rebellion as against external attack, but in democratic societies, the former role has steadily retreated over time. Growing involvement in law enforcement and counter-terrorism on the part of armed forces make the use of force against fellow citizens increasingly likely, which will create its own dilemmas.

In the extreme case, soldiers may be required to shoot fellow citizens engaged in riots or reckless behaviour and are liable to question whether such actions are ethically right, however legal and necessary they appear. Since 11 September 2001, for example, air forces in the US and Australia have at times been placed on alert to be ready to shoot down passenger aircraft that have been hijacked and might be flown into a target. Governments are naturally reluctant to promote debate on such issues. Recruiting campaigns never mention them and training for such roles is not given prominence. Yet it seems only proper that more public, professional and scholarly debate should take place so that these dilemmas are examined in advance, rather than at the last minute or not at all.

Multiple Loyalties

The answer to the question – to whom does the soldier owe loyalty? – appears so obvious as to be hardly worth asking. On the face of it, those in uniform have a simple duty of obedience to their commanders and to their service, even though the demands placed on them are often peremptory, dangerous and destructive. Yet, closer examination shows the ethical obligations on the soldier to be far more complex and problematic than in other professions.[9]

Figure 7.1 sets out these loyalties under three headings: the soldier in his/her own armed forces; the soldier who wears a second hat (i.e., is responsible to another organization or profession); and the soldier as a social being.

AUSTRALIA

Soldier	Two-Hats	Individual
Nation	UN	Family
Parliament	Allies	Friends
Government		Community
	Dual Professional	Humanity
Australian Defence Force (ADF)	Reservist	
Service	Secondment	
Commander		
Peers		
Subordinates		

Figure 7.1: Soldier Loyalties

These obligations are not necessarily in conflict, but the potential for clashing loyalties within each set and between sets is always present.

The Soldier's Duty

The soldier as such, naturally owes loyalty to his/her immediate commander though obedience is conditional upon orders being legal and duly authorized. Potentially problematic, too, is conflict between loyalty to groups within one's service – such as particular military units, reservists or corps – which may be set against loyalty to the service as a whole. Equally, loyalty to one's service may clash with duty toward the defence force or the defence organization as a whole. Some of these tensions (often dubbed "tribalism") can be a matter of bureaucratic politics and manoeuvring for advantage. But genuine ethical dilemmas can arise over where an individual's priorities should lie.

The upward loyalty of a soldier to superiors is accompanied by loyalties to his/her peers and often, also to subordinates. The phenomenon of "mateship" (termed "buddy system" in the US) can mean that soldiers feel it is right to support their peers against the hierarchy. Covering for others, hiding inefficiencies and beating the "system" are often seen as virtues in an army, albeit problematic ones. Similarly, loyalty to subordinates is highly valued by those receiving it and adds greatly to cohesion and effectiveness. Yet, downward loyalty can be at the expense of loyalty to superiors (e.g., not reporting offences such as an unauthorized discharge of a weapon by a subordinate in order to "give him another chance").[10] The challenge is to manage these kinds of loyalties while preserving the integrity of the organization.

Finally, those in uniform owe a loyalty to the government which normally exercises ultimate control over the military. As long as political direction comes down the line, duty is clear, but a government that seeks to influence military activities outside the chain of command – for example, by direct ministerial intervention – will create problems. A minister for defence who seeks to control junior officers, for example, instantly creates a dilemma for those officers. At the same time, democratic legislatures have some claim to military loyalty since they not only fund the armed forces but often take an active interest in military affairs. By way of example, military personnel appearing before parliamentary committees are, like other witnesses, on oath to answer questions put to them even if this creates difficulties for their service.

Ultimately, of course, soldiers see themselves as serving their country, in some cases taking an oath of loyalty to the head of state or the nation in the abstract. In Australia, this bond is symbolized by the fact that the Governor-General is also the formal Commander-in-Chief of the Defence Force while the government of the day exercises actual control. But loyalties can become complicated if soldiers believe that government policies are not serving the national interest or are simply promoting party or factional interests. US Marine Corps Colonel Oliver North, for example, convinced himself that his country was best served by pursing policies not authorized by the President and by concealing the truth over the Iran-Contra arms deal from Congress. In retrospect, few would support North in his stance, yet many would applaud the handful of German officers who sought to assassinate Adolf Hitler, to whom they had sworn a personal oath of allegiance, once they were convinced he was leading their country to disaster. Such can be the unique ethical burden of the military profession which in extreme cases, may have to act to protect the state.

Wearing Two Hats

The problem of two hats is not new. For good reasons soldiers may take on a duty to serve not only their own organization but another (e.g., the "dual-professional" such as the soldier who is also a doctor, a cleric or an engineer). These professions exist largely outside the military and have codes or ethics that may conflict with military demands. Does an army doctor, for example, treat a severely wounded civilian or prisoner of war before his/her own less critically injured personnel? Can a chaplain publicly disagree if he/she considers government policy unjust? There is extensive research into the dilemmas faced by dual professionals.[11] A similar conflict can arise for the reservist who is, say, a police officer in civilian life. The duty to report illegal activities observed while on an exercise may clash with the obligation to get the military job done.

AUSTRALIA

Where a soldier is seconded to another organization, acute problems can arise. Working as part of an alliance or of a UN operation, for example, the soldier may be under national orders to provide only limited intelligence or limited support to the other contributors such that he/she is unable to assist them in significant ways, even to the point of saving lives. Other examples of divided organizational loyalties arise where a soldier is seconded to a private company, a government agency or a national institution such as the Parliament. In the course of duties in such a context, he/she may come across confidential information that would be of value to their military superiors but should be kept confidential to the other organization.

The Human Soldier

Ultimately, the soldier is also a human being who may be faced with a personal clash of loyalties. Few soldiers do not have family members or friends, a sense of belonging to some wider group or a basic sense of common humanity. In some societies, too, there are strong tribal or communal loyalties that directly cut across loyalty to military organizations. All of these demands can present ethical challenges to the individual soldier who must choose between loyalties to known individuals and military duty. English novelist, E.M. Forster, approached the dilemma in the following terms: "If I had to choose between betraying my country and betraying my friend, I hope I should have the guts to betray my country."[12] This might not be the conclusion of all.

Fortunately, there is often no dilemma. The laws of armed conflict are labeled "humanitarian" for good reason. They win general acceptance precisely because they coincide with most people's sense of humanity and reinforce their notions of chivalry. There are also occasions when soldiers will form a genuine conscientious objection to fighting during a war, an occurrence that is not always harshly dealt with by military and political authorities. By and large, armed forces are learning how better to deal with matters of personal convictions among personnel.

It might be further argued that there is a professional duty to refuse to fight in a conflict that an individual believes to be unjust.[13] Traditionally, determination of what constitutes a just war was left to governments rather than soldiers who were not expected to make judgements on such matters and are often not in a position to do so. Yet, in more recent times, it seems that soldiers are coming to expect more explicit justification. Prior to the Iraqi war of 2003, for example, the British Chief of Defence Staff sought a statement from the government affirming the justice of the approaching hostilities precisely on the grounds that soldiers and their families ought to be reassured about the legal and moral rightness of risking their lives and taking others' lives. The official response did not satisfy all British soldiers.

THE CHALLENGE OF ETHICS

Military organizations pay much attention to moulding the ethical values of their members through formal and informal education, training and leadership. But members are never totally isolated from the society from which new recruits are drawn and with which they constantly interact. It is relevant to note the changes in Western society in recent decades that have made the development of professional military ethics more difficult.

Individualism has grown apace in many societies. The so-called "me generation" has good points – for example, the idea of realizing one's own potential as a human being to the fullest – but it can also devalue ideas of selflessness, loyalty and sacrifice which are central to the military ethos. It is perhaps a natural consequence of the shift, as noted by American writer and futurist Alvin Toffler, from the industrial era to the information age in which knowledge rather than possessions is the dominant source of wealth.[14] It is in the individual, above all, that knowledge resides. As more people attain higher levels of education and skills, the result is greater empowerment of individuals and perhaps greater reluctance to subordinate one's life and career to the control of others. *Ethical questioning has reduced confidence and certainty in values.* Western societies in particular, have seen greater readiness to challenge and reject traditional values. Individualism has no doubt contributed to the view that people are free to choose their own values, even to argue that there is no basis for shared values at all (postmodernism). Multi-cultural and multi-ethnic societies are perhaps less willing to be dogmatic on ethical questions for the sake of communal harmony. Such tolerance has much to commend it, but can promote ethical uncertainty. A military force, by contrast, is usually more comfortable with clear and certain values.

Distrust of traditional institutions in Western societies has increased. This is due in part because many have failed to maintain the high standards they proclaim. Much-publicized abuses and scandals have occurred in the church, medicine and the law, as well as in business, politics and banking. Nor has the military itself been unscathed. A profession that relies more than most on trust in leaders and on the acceptance of authority has not always responded effectively and convincingly to ethical challenges. A military force that seeks to represent the best values in society must be particularly vigilant in maintaining its ethos.

AUSTRALIA

Military practices are increasingly converging with those of civilian organizations. To attract volunteers, many armed forces offer conditions of service that resemble those of civilian society (e.g., living out rather than on base, greater choice in career paths, fewer demands on families, and the promotion of individual rights such as privacy and legal representation). At the same time, many military positions have been civilianized, functions contracted out to civilians and managerial approaches adopted. All this undermines the traditional notion that the military world is separate and distinct, with the right and duty to run its affairs according to its particular values.

These social and organizational trends present an enormous challenge to the military profession. They make recruitment and retention of individuals more difficult and make the setting of rewards and career development more complex. The rights and interests of individuals need to be respected while the demands of the military mission must also be met. The armed forces have long been familiar with personal responsibility for ethical behaviour but need to pay even more attention in modern times. High ethical standards are essential to military effectiveness, to military self-respect and to the military's standing in society.

The traditional military approach to ensuring and maintaining ethical behaviour has relied largely on two approaches: character development of trainees and the leadership of senior personnel. The former usually focuses on moral traits or "virtues" expected of leaders and followers – such as honesty, integrity and loyalty. While such qualities are admirable, inculcating them is not a simple matter. Rote learning and recitation are clearly insufficient. Formal codes of behaviour tend to be remote from the sort of real-life ethical dilemmas that trainees will encounter in which emotions and personalities are often involved. It is all too easy for such codes to be:

- no more than motherhood statements – that can be safely ignored;
- didactic, delivered from on high, provoking scepticism and resistance by those targeted;
- unable to impress the backsliders and the unprofessional – precisely those who need them;
- a source of resentment on the part of those who are responsible and who do not need them; and
- unrealistic – demanding a standard of behaviour that is little short of perfection.

The result is often that efforts are made to remain within the letter of the code rather than embrace its spirit. Irish writer and poet Oscar Wilde once referred to the "seven deadly virtues," implying that they are static and lifeless, deadening rather than inspiring. Codes of behaviour can play a positive role in some circumstances, but their limits need to be recognized.

Leadership is clearly influential in any organization, and in the military more than most. Do military leaders at all levels display the virtues of integrity, acceptance of responsibility, trustworthiness and respect for others that are considered essential to ethical behaviour?[15] Setting an example demonstrates ethical behaviour in real life and shows that positive values are no bar to leadership positions. The key problem, however, is that bad leadership also sets a powerful example. It demotivates subordinates, encourages cynicism about leadership and directly undermines whatever positive values do exist in the organization. Bad leadership drives out good.

It is thus unwise for an organization to rely on good leaders alone – they are necessary but not sufficient and are never guaranteed. Pressure for ethical behaviour needs to come from below as well as from the top. There is no foolproof system to ensure this is the case. What can be attempted is to create a sense among military personnel that:

- ethical behaviour can and should permeate all military activities; and
- ethical behaviour results more from debate than *diktat*.

This debate can take three forms. It must be personal (i.e., within the conscience and thinking of each individual). It must be between members of the military profession in its broadest definition. And it must be between the military profession and the wider society.

The aim of ethics education should be to promote such debate, recognizing that ethical behaviour is a struggle for everyone, even (or especially) senior leaders. It is not a matter of observing "unbreakable rules," but of wrestling with complex and in some cases insoluble problems. Debate also serves the purpose of informing those in uniform about the values shared with others – or sometimes not shared. What is needed are people in uniform who understand the nature of ethical thinking, who acquire and develop appropriate analytical skills, and who recognize the ethical dimension of a problem instinctively and immediately. Values and ethics are things primarily to work out for oneself … with some help from others. As the author John Mortimer once put it: "My father… never told me the difference between right and wrong … that's why I remain so deeply in his debt".[16]

AUSTRALIA

There is no single best method of education and training in ethics. Debate, character development and leadership must all play a part. Nor are there clear and immediate tests of the effectiveness of ethical development in the military – as in any organization. Spectacular lapses in behaviour may be evidence of failure of some kind, but in themselves do not prove that progress has not been made across the board or will not be made in the future. Ethical improvement is a long-term process and continuous effort is required. The challenge of ethics for the military profession is not only that its members should act ethically as occasion demands but that it establish strong cultural norms and enduring organizational practices that promote ethical behaviour in all foreseeable (and unforeseeable) situations.

ENDNOTES

1. This is based on the author's analysis and is not drawn from previous work.

2. Speech at Louis Marshal Award Dinner, New York City, 11 November 1962.

3. General Sir John Hackett, *The Profession of Arms* (London: Book Club Associates, 1983), 202.

4. "An Armistice Day Address", 10 November 1948, in Omar N. Bradley, ed., *Collected Writings - Vol. I* (US Government Printing Office, 1967), 584-589.

5. Article 51: "Nothing in the present Charter shall impair the inherent right of individual or collective self-defence if an armed attack occurs against a Member of the United Nations".

6. Michael Walzer, *Just and Unjust Wars* (New York, NY: Basic Books, 2006), 255-262. See also, Alex Bellamy, "The Ethics of Terror Bombing: Beyond Supreme Emergency", *Journal of Military Ethics*, Vol. 7, No. 1 (2008), 41-65.

7. General Charles C. Krulak, "The Strategic Corporal: Leadership in the Three Block War", *Marines Corps Gazette*, Vol. 83, No. 1 (1999), 18-22.

8. See James Burk, "Strategic Assumptions and Moral Implications of the Constabulary Force", *Journal of Military Ethics*, Vol. 4, No. 3 (2005), 155-167.

9. See for example, Stephen Coleman, "The Problem of Duty and Loyalty", *Journal of Military Ethics*, Vol. 8, No. 2 (2009), 105-115.

10. Robert Hall, "Accidental Discharges – The Soldier's Industrial Accident in Vietnam and East Timor", *Australian Defence Force Journal*, No. 149 (July/August 2001), 27-34.

11. See for example, Leslie London, Leonard Rubenstein, Laurel Baldwin-Ragauen and Adriaan Van Es, "Dual Loyalty among Military Health Professionals", *Cambridge Quarterly of Healthcare Ethics*, Vol. 15, No. 4 (2006), 381-391.

12. Edward Morgan Forster, *Two Cheers for Democracy* (New York, NY: Harcourt, Brace, 1951).

13. Jessica Wolfendale, "Professional Integrity and Disobedience in the Military", *Journal of Military Ethics*, Vol. 8, No. 2 (2009), 127-140.

14. Alvin Toffler, *The Third Wave* (New York, NY: Bantam Books, 1981).

15. For a critical discussion see: David Schmidtchen, "Developing Creativity and Innovation through the Practice of Mission Command", *Australian Defence Force Journal*, No. 146 (January/February 2001), 11-18.

16. Kevin J. Connolly and Margaret Martlew, *Psychologically Speaking: A Book of Quotations* (Hoboken, NJ: John Wiley & Sons, 1999).

CHAPTER 8

The New Economic Togetherness: Globalization of Economics and Some Implications for Security and the Military Profession

Mie Augier
Jerry Guo
*Robert M. McNab**

INTRODUCTION

"War is not only a military struggle, but also a comprehensive contest on fronts of politics, economy, diplomacy and law."[1]

"[M]y greatest fear is that in economic tough times that people will see the defense budget as the place to solve the nation's deficit problems.... [A]s I look around...and see a more unstable world, more failed and failing states, countries that are investing heavily in their militaries...I think that would be disastrous...."

Secretary of Defense Robert Gates, August 9, 2010[2]

The increasing pace and range of globalization and technological change have created new opportunities to improve national security. Globalization has lowered the costs of collaboration, widened the span of communication, and created new tools to influence perceptions and beliefs around the world. Global shifts in the division of labour have lowered the cost of manufactured goods; improved the breadth of goods available to consumers throughout the world; and have led to dramatic increases in income in some countries. Competition now occurs on a global scale.

There is, however, a darker side to globalization, the increasing interdependencies in the global economy and the "New Economic Togetherness", to use Nathan Leites' terminology.[3] Globalization creates and amplifies opportunities and fragilities as well as direct and indirect threats. It changes the global balance of power and it changes the perception of who is in power. The fragility

---

* The views expressed in this chapter are those of the authors and do not necessarily reflect the official policy of the United States Navy or the Department of Defense.

of the financial systems in the United States and Europe, for example, has increased fiscal imbalances, leading to substantial pressure to lower defence expenditures. China, on the other hand, has continued to increase defence expenditures, increasing concern about its ability to project power in Southeast Asia in the near-term (*The Economist*, April 7, 2012). The shifts in power are not limited to the military arena, as the financial crisis has brought into question Western models of economic growth.

In this chapter we examine aspects of how the new "economic togetherness" (or globalization of the economies) may influence the military profession. Reductions in defense expenditures, for example, may pose a direct threat to the military profession through reductions in force, declining capabilities, and reducing the ability to operate in partnership with other nations. Shifts in relative economic power, on the other hand, may more subtly influence the military profession. The ability to project influence may suffer due to shifts in perception, relative attractiveness, and negotiating powers. In the long run, these shifts may result in a reduction of expenditures on research and development (physical capital) and training and education (human capital). A decline in investments can lead to an undermining of the core values of "professionalism" in the sense of Abraham Flexner (1915). Although Flexner wrote mostly about medical schools and medicine as a profession, his thoughts apply to discussions of professions and professionalism in general. Like in medicine, *professionalism* is an essential feature of good *professional practice* in our militaries.[4] Thus, the links between economics and security and military professionalism are embodied in our societal and social cultures and practices, making the challenges to them more complex, but no less essential.

In the next section, we discuss some of the linkages between economics and security in terms of conceptualizing the economic competition in different ways, and especially suggesting a (broad) definition of "economic warfare" as one that might capture some of the elements that are crucial for understanding some future security issues. The section after that discusses some instruments of "economic warfare" that might be particularly relevant to the military profession in the future security environment. We hope to illustrate that economic warfare is an important topic for strategists and probably deserves a more explicit part in the discussions of "our national strategy."

DEFINITIONS & HISTORY

Economic warfare is a practice that is old and yet new again. Ancient Carthage, for example, dominated maritime trade in the Mediterranean, placing it not only in direct military conflict with Rome but also economic conflict.[5]

Sir Francis Drake's expedition against the Spanish not only created havoc for Spanish shipping but resulted in a dividend of 4,700 percent; a return which allowed Elizabeth I to eliminate the existing national debt of England.[6] The US-China Commission concluded in 2011 that the government of the Peoples' Republic of China manipulated the value of the Renminbi to reduce the price of its exports and artificially increase the price of imports.[7] More recently, the international community has imposed severe economic sanctions on Iran, to include the removal of the Iranian Central Bank from the global financial transactions system in an attempt to curtail development of a nuclear weapons' capacity.[8]

While economic warfare may take many forms, the predominant forms are those of sanctions and blockade, that is, the attempt to prevent the transportation of various goods and services into and out of a specific country. These overt forms of economic warfare are potentially complemented by covert methods that could include currency counterfeiting, sabotage, and the arming of rebels with the specific intent of sowing economic destruction.[9] Yet, there are emerging methods that could be viewed as economic warfare but are outside the current scope of international norms. China, for example, dominates the refining of rare earth elements employed in the production of a wide variety of defence systems in the United States.[10] China, given its market power, recently increased the price of rare earth elements and could do so again in the future, inhibiting the ability of the United States to build and maintain crucial defence capabilities. Currency manipulation may be another form of economic warfare that undermines the ability of a country to generate export earnings, creating economic imbalances that lower the long-term growth potential of an economy. In light of these emerging threats, we argue that the traditional view of economic warfare is increasingly outdated in the multi-polar, multi-actor environment that characterizes the modern security environment and the United States is particularly vulnerable to these new forms of economic warfare.

Historical Treatment

Whether or not the term "economic warfare" has a precise definition in international law or in the academic literature remains a matter of debate. While the practice of economic warfare is recognized by international law, there is a distinct lack of consensus on defining it. On one end of the spectrum, economic warfare employs international economic measures that seek to directly or indirectly reduce the economic strength of an adversary, thus increasing one's relative economic strength.[11] Economic warfare may also be considered the use of economic weapons (sanctions, embargoes, and cartels) for strategic purposes, although these classical approaches may be expanded to include industrial mobilization, arms races, and the stockpiling of strategic materials.[12] A country may engage in a "guerrilla-type" economic warfare through the provision of foreign aid, subsidies, and propaganda to sow distrust and to increase the relative dependence of developing nations.[13] The United Nations General Assembly, for example, has, on several occasions, expressed concern about the employment of "economic coercion" against developing countries.[14] Economic warfare may be an intense, coercive disturbance of the economy of an adversary state, aimed at diminishing its power.[15] Others have argued that economic warfare is increasing without explicitly defining it or its associated outcomes other than a focus on free markets and economic growth.[16] Non-state actors may be engaging in economic warfare through attacks on tourists, projects funded by foreign investment or foreign aid.[17] At the end of the spectrum, economic warfare involves the employment of military power to interrupt the flow and use of resources among countries to diminish the power of an adversary.[18]

The lack of consensus in the literature suggests that there is not one form of economic warfare and that it evolves over time. Cultural and technological change may reduce the threat from one form of economic warfare and give rise of another type. A blockade in the 18th century may have effectively impeded the flow of information into and out of the blockaded nation; such a blockade would likely be ineffective today given the rise of the Internet and satellite phones. On the other hand, the power grids of the mid-20th century were relatively robust to external sabotage on a widespread scale as command and control was physical rather than virtual. Cyber attacks, however, are cheaper, unconstrained by distance, easier to replicate and duplicate.[19]

This leads to a definitional issue that is not explored in the literature. While for the purposes of this review "economic warfare" is taken to be purely economic activities, which could include subsidies, sanctions, research funding, tariffs, or direct government ownership of enterprises, in the literature there can be some bleeding between the realms of military and economics. The British, for example, considered different options to deny the Germans iron ore for production, including purchasing all Swedish iron ore, a modest increase in purchase, and finally military action to strike at German shipping (blockade) or factories.[20] Military action to prevent an adversary state from acquiring an economic capability or resource, like in the British case, is sometimes considered to be economic warfare. It does not necessarily impact the immediate material capability of the state to make war, and if attacks are not launched on military targets, this sort of action could be considered economic warfare. This, however, makes defining actions messy, as it is conceivable that any sort of military action that does not attack military targets will somehow negatively influence the target state's economy, thereby becoming economic warfare.

Most existing studies of economic warfare are historical case studies, with a disproportionate sample considering the Second World War and the relationships between Axis, Allied, and Neutral powers. Researchers have examined at how the United States attempted to prevent Germany from acquiring tungsten ore in Spain.[21] They note that in recent years the United States has attempted sanctions as a means of statecraft, focusing on the political component, "because the alternatives, military force and diplomatic persuasion, are often so unattractive".[22] With regard to the study of sanctions, the authors acknowledge the study of their effectiveness and underlying incentives is still at a formative stage. They argue that economic warfare during the Second World War took a variety of forms, including "oil embargoes, offers of loans, blacklisting of firms that dealt with the Axis, and even the buying of strategic materials to keep them out of enemy hands".[23] The authors focus on the latter and ask whether Allied attempts to keep Spanish tungsten out of German hands were effective.

In an attempt to deny the Germans this critical resource, the Allies, and particularly the United States, embarked on a major buying campaign to purchase as much Spanish tungsten as possible. This had the dual effect of denying the Germans this critical resource (with Spain and Portugal their only possible suppliers), while giving the Allies a larger supply. Once the United States was onboard with a pre-emptive buying program, both tungsten prices and supply skyrocketed between 1941-1944. The authors find that this buying program "reduced German purchases of Spanish wolfram by a bit more than a third, by about 1,500 tons".[24] In the authors' estimation, this justifies a claim of success. In the absence of Allied buying, German capabilities could have stayed at pre-war rates for an extended duration. The authors also cite evidence that the scarcity of tungsten damaged the German war effort.[25]

It has also been argued that economic warfare is different from how it was originally proposed.[26] The British government in 1939 defined its purpose as "so to disorganize the enemy's economy as to prevent him from carrying on the war." The Roosevelt Administration in the United States broadened the concept to include domestic supply and international finance. The Department of Defense defines economic warfare as "aggressive use of economic means to achieve national objectives." It further discusses the difference between basing definitions on *ends* or *means*, that is, whether it is economic means used or the end desired of eliminating an enemy economy.[27] Discussing the means is narrower in scope and closer in concept to modern economic warfare – more covert, purely economic means, to disrupt enemy production or growth.

While economic warfare could pertain to blockades to deny materials (like in the British case) or aggressive competition to achieve market dominance, the attempt by the US to deny the Soviet Union critical materials is an example of a "peacetime strategic embargo".[28] These controls sought to deny the export of materials that could improve an adversary's military capability. After the Second World War, Western European states along with the United States established a body called the Coordinating Committee (COCOM), which drew up a list of items from western states that would not be exported to the communist bloc. This was supplemented by a similar body for the People's Republic of China.[29] The idea of a strategic embargo shifted with the loss of China, the Korean War, and general expansion of communism overseas. The idea became a euphemism for policies "aimed not only at denying the Soviet bloc strategic materials, but also at retarding her economic growth: this was economic warfare".[30]

Under President Reagan, the intent of the peacetime embargo shifted from economic warfare to a pragmatic strategy that eventually led to moderation. British diplomat, historian and political scientist Alan Dobson claims "unlike his more ideological colleagues, Reagan never intended or expected to destroy the Soviet Union. Instead he strove to draw it into constructive negotiations".[31] Therefore, economic sanctions and COCOM were used not to destroy the Soviet Union, but to draw the Soviets to the negotiating table. Reagan thought that the Soviet Union would collapse anyway, and there is no real evidence to think that he personally believed that he could economically ruin the Soviets. The US had limited capacity to damage the Soviets economically, there was a lack of compliance among US allies, there were bureaucratic difficulties within the administration, and Reagan always intended to negotiate with the Soviets.[32]

Another important contribution is James Schlesinger's 1960 book, *The Political Economy of National Security*. Referring to the competition between the Soviet Union and the western powers, he notes "in international trade, the economic and strategic elements are inextricably intertwined. Traditionally, the main arguments for international trade were the economic ones; the strategic implications were largely ignored. In recent years, however, the strategic elements in trade have come to outweigh the economic…"[33] In this regard, he is an early proponent of economic warfare with respect to trade. In a chapter regarding international trade, Schlesinger discusses protectionism as a form of defensive economic warfare. While free-market principles are generally better for an economy than protectionist policies, he quotes Adam Smith: "Defense is more important than opulence."[34] In other words, there are certain industries that contribute to national security and which may be necessary to protect from foreign influence or competition.

Schlesinger identifies two types of power embodied in trade: the supply effect and the influence effect. The supply effect has two aspects – one connected with total supply and real income and another connected with the supply of vital commodities. For the former, trade is the means by which some states become rich and provide resources that are necessary for national power. As Schlesinger notes, "unless there exists a disposable margin, a nation is unable to allocate sufficient resources to provide itself with the instruments of security".[35] The second element relates to the supplies of essential elements of warfare, like in the tungsten case referenced above.

The influence effect is also important. It operates on the demand rather than supply side, giving nations the idea that important markets could be closed unless the appropriate foreign policy is followed. In effect, it is blackmail. Whereas the supply effect is concerned with building up a home state's capabilities, with the influence effect, "a major power may use trade as a weapon of economic penetration".[36]

In summary, the history of the study of economic warfare has centred on the study of how sanctions and export controls have been used to weaken adversary economies, incite specific political action, and weaken adversary war-making capabilities. So far, there has been relatively little discussion about other economic tactics that could be used to make economic war. The remainder of this review will survey some of the recent literature or cases of economic warfare and provide some thoughts on possible means by which adversary states could perpetrate action against the US, as well as ways in which the US could respond.

TOOLS OF ECONOMIC WARFARE

There are various tools of economic warfare that might become important to better understand some of the current threats to the military profession. These tools are representative of emerging trends in economic interaction between states that might be indicative of a new economic warfare. Military professionalism might be endangered by any of these tools; they influence all sectors of the economy, including the security sector.

USA

Sanctions

Sanctions could take a number of different forms, but they probably would be restrictions on domestic firms operating in foreign countries or totally blocking the export of certain goods. Firms could be prohibited from starting operations in adversary states, prohibited from investing in foreign-related assets (bonds, funds, or stocks), and could be barred from entering into joint ventures with adversary-based firms. Additionally, firms could be prohibited from working with the adversaries government and could not provide consulting or respond to requests for proposals. Associations with citizens of the adversary state would be limited or monitored, and there would be strong pressure in the international community for allied states to not do business with the adversary state. Economic sanctions are a common means of economic warfare and could substantially weaken an adversary state, leaving them without critical materials or investment to sustain growth. This example has been practiced in a number of states, including North Korea, Iran, Iraq, and Libya. In practice, sanctions meet with mixed results, as some findings in the literature suggest. Pape has argued strongly that sanctions do not result in desired outcomes, noting that in 115 cases where sanctions were used, in only 5 cases were they successful.[37] Other research has shown that sanctions can actually weaken respect for human rights in target countries.[38]

Subsidies

One means of warfare could be subsidies for domestic firms. To some extent, every country in the world practices this. The US and Western European countries regularly promote massive agricultural subsidies to support the growing of selected crops, and the US in particular has been noted for its financial support of the corn and sugar industries, not to mention its support for green energy initiatives like solar power. For subsidies to count as warfare, there must be an adversary state in mind that is building capability in one of its own domestic industries. For example, consider the United States' green energy industry. A competitor state might begin to invest heavily in its own domestic green energy industry, perhaps even by acquiring or luring away technology or personnel from the adversary state. At some point, if there has been enough investment, the competitor state's industry will outcompete that of the United States, leading to the aggressor state taking control of the market, denying the technology and profits to the US. This tactic requires a long-term view and significant financial commitment, meaning it is probably less common than other tactics.

Investment

There first should be a distinction between public and private investment, although this delineation could be muddied in states without a clear rule of law. There should then be a distinction between investments in adversary states for a takeover of certain firms or knowledge and investing in allied states for future economic or political support. Any combination of these things could occur, and examples of states doing this abound. China regularly invests in African and other Asian states to shore up economic and political support, and Chinese state-owned enterprises (SOEs) regularly invest in or acquire firms across the world.[39] This increases Chinese support in target countries while building up Chinese capabilities, a potentially dangerous combination.

Sovereign wealth funds are a prime vehicle for this sort of activity, and they have historically been opaque to the outside world. The funds of the various Arab emirates are non-transparent, as are Chinese and Russian foreign investments.[40] Where these funds are targeting and why is an excellent question that could open up new thinking about their intentions, if answered.

This is a major reason most countries have some sort of agency tasked with reviewing foreign investment. As an example, if a domestic economy only supports two or three shipbuilders for naval vessels, a foreign takeover of the entire industry could be feasible with enough resources. It is up to the domestic government to ensure that this does not happen by strict monitoring of nationally sensitive industries.

Predatory Lending

This tactic requires the tacit acceptance of the adversary state to work. If an adversary state regularly runs government deficits or engages in major spending, it will have to issue bonds if it wishes to avoid inflation. The aggressor state could then purchase large quantities of these bonds, thereby gaining a sort of leverage over the adversary state. This works when the aggressor state has large quantities of cash to spend, does not purchase too many bonds (e.g., the famous idea of the bank owning you with a small loan, but you owning the bank with a massive loan), and an expectation by the aggressor state that the adversary state will be too weak in the future to resist aggression to pay back loans. Examples of this tactic include Western Europe indebted to the US after the Second World War, and the US indebted to a variety of Asian countries to support government deficit spending.

USA

Trade Practices

There are several trade practices that could have a direct impact on adversary states. Various import or export tariffs could be levied on the adversary state, making it very difficult to conduct trade profitably. These will work best against smaller economies that cannot afford to purchase from or sell to other markets. Against a more powerful state, these could lead to a trade war that could be very damaging for both, hence the modern practice of general liberalization of trade in most sectors and a strong desire to avoid tariffs. Since modern governments now take in much less revenue in tariffs than they did in the past, they are less attractive to governments and are easy targets for removal when relations need to be improved.

Financial Controls

Financial controls can mean several things. First, it can mean the freezing of foreign assets. For security, members of regimes sometimes deposit funds in foreign banks.[41] States with control over those channels can freeze access to those funds and deny wire or funds transfers; this has been used with success in the cases of Libya and North Korea. It tends to work best with despotic regimes where the paramount leader is corrupt and tends to hide money overseas to enrich himself and his inner circle. It also tends to work well with states that have devalued currencies; access to foreign "hard" currency is valued and necessary for foreign exchange or trade.

The other way an aggressor state could influence financial controls is by denying access to financial markets. This works best when the aggressor state already sets the rules of the road; this holds for states like the US or the United Kingdom where large volumes of international financial transactions flow through domestic markets. If the US were to bar foreign firms from transactions in the New York Stock Exchange or the Chicago Commodities Exchange, there would be significant disruption to those firms and their host countries. The US also has the luxury of denying access to US bond and currency markets, and with the US dollar still serving as the world's preferred reserve currency, this could prove to be challenging.

Pre-emptive Purchasing

This is a tool used by many states around the world, principally for military affairs. The examples referenced above (the US and United Kingdom (UK) purchasing Spanish tungsten to keep it out of German hands), demonstrate its effectiveness and operation. An aggressor state will begin pre-emptively purchasing large quantities of commodities to prevent another state from acquiring them. Often, these commodities are used in the manufacture of weapons or weapons systems. To take this further, it is conceivable that this could be extended to actual technological knowledge or human resources. That is, an aggressor state could begin purchasing or acquiring firms or patents that hold the key to technological development, denying a targeted state access. It could also begin instituting policies that "poach" highly talented personnel from target states.

Currency Manipulation

Currency manipulation occurs when an aggressor state intervenes in international foreign exchange markets to ensure that its currency is undervalued relative to what its actual market value should be. By making currency undervalued, it makes its exports cheaper relative to those coming from the rest of the world, attracting much more business from foreign buyers. This requires the aggressor state to have large reserves of foreign currency with which to buy or sell its domestic currency and maintain a fixed price. The aggressor state therefore runs the risk of entering a currency crisis, wherein it runs out of foreign currency to maintain a fixed price and ends up having to deal with wild swings in the value of its domestic currency, requiring International Monetary Fund (IMF) or other intervention. China has been alleged to practice currency manipulation in how it treats the yuan.[42]

Immigration

A state's immigration policies could conceivably be considered economic warfare. Following the discussion above regarding "poaching" human capital, a state could offer favorable immigration policies to immigrants from particular target states to take them out of the workforce of those states. A state could also deny entry to immigrants from particular target states. For example, to prevent immigrants from being educated in high-quality universities only to return to their home countries and have the knowledge used to the detriment of the host state.

Alternatively, a state could send a large number of immigrants abroad for the purpose of learning, either in universities or in the workforce, with the intention of them returning later. This gives those students international experience (useful for international business expansion), a high-quality education, and foreign language training. It is no wonder that states like China regularly send tens of thousands of students a year outside of the country for study, despite the possible political dangers this may pose.[43] While students may come back with knowledge of "freedom" or alternate political systems, the economic advantage they bring to Chinese industry is immense and worth the possible sacrifice.

USA

Foreign Aid

Related to investment, this tactic sees an aggressor state making large foreign aid investments to secure favorable trade agreements or political support. An aggressor state could provide materials, knowledge, funding, and personnel for any number of aid projects in a target state, with the aim of securing that market for itself. In doing so, it would shut competitor states out of that market, effectively adding it to its sphere of influence. This is a dual-use strategy, allowing for both economic and political gains. Both China and the US have practiced this tactic in Africa. The competition between the two to attract African client states has created a sort of new "Race for Africa".

Dumping/Counterfeiting

While it is unlikely that a state would ever actively promote counterfeiting, it is possible that it would tacitly approve of it. For example, if State A exports several important products to the world that comprise a large portion of its foreign trade, it is probable that those products will be counterfeited in some way. Normally, the counterfeiting would be halted in whatever state it is happening. But if counterfeiting happens in State B, but B does nothing to stop it, would that not be considered a form of economic warfare? The tacit acceptance of a practice that erodes the economic value of State A while giving State B increased market share and revenue could reasonably be called an aggressive action.

Dumping is another trade tactic that is similar to counterfeiting. By supplying cheaper, possibly lower quality goods to the world marketplace to challenge established products from State A, State B could undercut the market, dump all of its products, and quickly establish a monopoly. While World Trade Organization (WTO) regulations strictly prohibit dumping, not all states are members of the WTO and even members do not necessarily abide by the regulations at all times. Counterfeiting is more common than dumping due to these regulations, and the fact that counterfeiting is far more difficult to detect and address. This has become truer with the rise of the Internet and electronic communication.

Espionage

Economic and industrial espionage are not new, but they are increasingly common tactics because of the relative ease of communication and transportation across countries. States could direct, through government agencies or state-controlled firms, personnel to go abroad in search of new technology or knowledge. These personnel would go abroad and work for foreign firms, while funneling information back to masters in their home country. Alternatively, the aggressor state could invite foreign firms to engage in joint-ventures or operations at home, supplying local staff (by limiting the number of allowed expatriates through immigration regulations), and take knowledge that way.

THE INFLUENCE OF ECONOMIC WARFARE ON PROFESSIONALISM

This section will explore some challenges the military profession might face as a result of some of the tools of economic warfare. Greater economic togetherness increases the susceptibility of an economy to economic warfare, and the effects on a national economy could quickly influence military professionalism. The methods described in the previous section could have three primary effects on a national economy: (1) higher costs for a domestic government; (2) relative technological decline; and (3) increased political pressure on the military as political leaders find their other options constrained. This section explores these three concerns and their influence on how the military operates.

Higher Costs

Economic warfare can increase the cost of providing security. First, key inputs into national security may increase in cost if another nation controls the production of these inputs. Second, a country that undervalues its currency at the expense of the currency of another nation gains an unfair advantage in the global marketplace. This may induce firms to move to the currency manipulator, undermining the ability of other states to produce their own security over time. Finally, soft power competition may increase the cost of projecting military power.

The United States and China are, for example, currently engaged in a competition in Sub-Saharan Africa using a variety of techniques. The Chinese government expends considerable resources in a "soft power" outreach, to include the provision of loans on favourable terms, material goods, humanitarian aid, and Chinese-run infrastructure projects.[44] The United States may be at competitive disadvantage with regards to soft power competition as its resources for foreign aid are diminishing in real terms over time. On the other hand, the attractiveness of the professionalism of the US military and its ability to project national power are countervailing influences. Yet, if the US wished to compete directly for influence using similar soft power methods as the Chinese, it would have to increase its commitment of resources.

Economic warfare techniques may also reduce government revenues. As industry moves out of a country, the revenue base of the country declines.

Currency manipulation may also increase import dependency, leading to significantly higher trade imbalances. When the target state's economy is damaged like that, government revenues could decrease as growth slows. This places pressure on government budgets, with the potential for governments to run deficits or cut budgets if effects are strong enough.

The net effect of inflicting higher costs on a target state is to restrict its ability to spend. The obvious danger for the military profession is in smaller defense budgets. Smaller training, procurement, and operations budgets restrict the ability of military leaders to carry out the missions political leaders assign and could lead a country to be vulnerable in times of crisis. It might also lead to military leaders participating in politics outside of approved channels to lobby for preserving budgets. Finally, it could provoke conflict within a military – leaders of different branches or departments might struggle with each other for a large enough slice of a shrinking pie.

Austerity programs tend to have a perverse impact on defence budgets. A decline in procurement, for example, may increase the unit-cost of the procured good, leading to a further decline in the planned purchase. As defence is typically one of the largest discretionary items in the central government budget, it may bear the brunt of reductions. These reductions, if not well planned, could lead to a force that is unable to train, educate, equip, or deploy. The recent campaign in Libya, for example, illustrated some of these problems as some NATO countries needed US logistical support to participate in the air campaign.

Finally, higher costs could lead to myopia. Similar to how political leaders may defer investment in education and healthcare, they might also defer investment in other critical areas that sustain long-term productivity and security. These range from cutting future weapons programs, to decreased investment in basic scientific research, to a lack of government attention on hotspots around the world that could be future security concerns. This might put military and political leaders in direct conflict if their views differ.

Relative Technological Decline

A number of economic warfare techniques could have a detrimental impact on technological or industrial competitiveness. For example, the United States government has supported the development of a domestic solar panel industry with loan guarantees and tax incentives. China, however, has supported their domestic industry with direct subsidies and has purchased bankrupt US firms to acquire construction capability and intellectual property.[45] Increasing Chinese dominance of the solar panel industry has led the United States to consider import tariffs on Chinese cells of up to 35%, accusing the Chinese government of "dumping" underpriced panels on the United States to drive US firms out of business.[46] Here, a combination of "dumping" tactics and strong domestic subsidies has inflicted costs on the United States while supporting the rise of a domestic industry. The US solar panel industry is not as capable as its Chinese counterpart, to the detriment of US consumers and security. The economy of a domestic state could also be vulnerable from industrial espionage, resource restriction, and currency manipulation.

This could lead to relative technological decline or disappearance of capabilities. Although economists typically agree that free trade and specialization are almost always positive for a state's economic health, in the defence sector this might not be the case. Foreign acquisition of defence industry intellectual property or disruption of firms in manufacturing or research and development could severely damage entire industries. The loss of manufacturing and research capability is not easily solved; it requires sustained investment over time. The denial of critical resources could also negatively impact a state's economy, as the wolfram and tungsten examples from the Second World War show. The modern analogue would be rare earth elements (REEs) and/or rare earth oxides (REOs). As REEs are used in many high-technology applications, the economic implications are severe.

What is the effect of relative technological decline as a result of economic warfare? First, military leaders involved in acquisitions could be pressured by industry for support. The potential for negative relationships could increase as firm performance declines. Second, the military's future capabilities might be degraded if technological development lags. This complicates the ability of the military to carry out complex missions against high-technology adversaries (who might be employing economic warfare techniques in the first place).

Increased Political Pressure on the Military

One of the biggest effects economic warfare techniques could have might be on the relationship between political and military leadership in a target country. As the target state's economy weakens, industries become less competitive, and spending decreases, political leaders will be under significant pressure to solve problems with fewer resources. This increases the amount of pressure they place on military leaders to carry out missions. This could also increase the likelihood of political leaders attempting to use the military

USA

to carry out political or economic ends; if leaders feel pressured by foreign encroachment on markets or resources, it is possible they could turn to the military to secure them. China's activities in the South China Sea show how countries might do this.

EXAMPLE OF SOME US VULNERABILITIES

The potential impact of economic warfare on the military profession rises with globalization. Increased integration is likely to influence economic vulnerability. The leadership challenge is to anticipate the challenges of globalization and to adapt over time. To illustrate some of the challenges that may face developed, integrated economies in the west, this section will explore some US vulnerabilities to each of the tools listed above and discuss possible amelioration if there is indeed a threat. It takes as an example one of the United States' largest trading partners, China.

US economic integration with China continues to grow. While in volume, Canada is still the US' largest trade partner. The US does not share a border with China, so its status as the second largest partner, even with geographic separation is worthy of note. This does not imply that China conducts an active economic warfare campaign against the United States, but that these are examples of typical challenges that face the US and similarly developed states.

Sanctions

Typically it is the US imposing sanctions rather than being the subject of sanctions, the 1974 oil embargo notwithstanding. At present, there is little danger of the world cutting the US off from importing or exporting materials, with the exceptions being critical commodities like rare-earth elements and fossil fuels. US Geological Survey reports indicate that the short-term supply of rare earth oxides is highly constrained and dependent on China, but prospects for longer-term resource development outside of China are good.[47] This could be a concern for US high-technology manufacturing if the Chinese government decides to constrict supplies in the short term, as REOs are used in the manufacture of high-technology military and civilian systems.

Investment

Due to greater economic togetherness, the US is vulnerable to foreign direct investment in at least two ways. First, it is unable to match competitor investments in foreign countries for the reasons explained above – a lack of fiscal sustainability precludes investment in the way that states like China can do it. Second, it is possible that the US is the state its competitors are investing in. Put another way, the aims of competitor investment in the US, such as by China, are unclear. Whether there is a profit motive, a desire to acquire technological knowledge, or a strategic motive, the US has no way of knowing why foreign countries are investing, or in what sectors they are investing. It is conceivable a government like China's, through state-owned or affiliated entities, is investing in critical national security sectors, like high-technology, communications, heavy manufacturing, or shipbuilding. It is equally unclear whether these investments are a danger to the US. The US therefore faces the dual dangers of being unable to take advantage of the value of investment abroad while also being unable to respond to its disadvantages at home. Possible policy prescriptions include better monitoring of foreign investment in the US, stronger regulatory controls over foreign interaction with critical industries, and renewed promotion of US investment abroad (tax benefits, subsidies, diplomatic support, etc).

Predatory Lending

Predatory lending by foreign governments is a national security concern. While the share of US government debt held overseas is low relative to Japan and the European Union, a significant amount of debt is still held overseas. A threat by China to curtail bond purchases could roil international financial markets, causing significant damage to the US economy. If the US could not sell its public debt at favourable terms, it might have to engage in significant austerity measures that could significantly dampen economic growth, if not result in an outright recession. It needs to be recognized, however, that due to the interdependencies between the Chinese and US economies, such a movement would also have significant negative impacts on the Chinese economy and is unlikely. Japan holds a larger share of US government debt and has never used it as a policy instrument. A more likely outcome is that the continued increase in US public debt will, at some point, result in rising yields on US debt, resulting in increased taxes and reduced public expenditures. Given that national defence constitutes the largest discretionary program in the US federal budget, it would be an obvious starting point for cutting US federal expenditures.

Trade Practices

US vulnerability to trade practices is lower than its vulnerability to several of these other tactics, but vulnerability still exists due to interconnected economic practices. The US remains the world's largest manufacturer (assessed by value of goods), and export of US goods is important for the domestic economic health. At the same time, the US is also one of the world's largest importers of goods (assessed by value) and leveling import tariffs or restrictions on certain states could seriously damage foreign economies. The biggest reason this is less of a threat than other tactics is that it is unlikely to be practiced in a serious way. Trade wars are damaging to all parties involved, and the US' largest competitor, China, cannot afford tariffs that would damage its export-oriented economy. This could be an emerging threat in the future as US economic power wanes, and potential steps that could be taken in the future include strengthening international trade institutions (WTO), strengthening ties with foreign trading partners, and building domestic industries to be relatively self-sufficient in the event of trade issues.

Pre-emptive Purchasing

The US is fairly vulnerable to this tactic as world resources become more and more constrained. Fossil fuels and rare earth elements are the biggest threats, as the US requires large quantities of both to fuel its high-technology economy. If its competitors were to purchase large quantities of oil from the Organization for the Petroleum Export Countries (OPEC) or REOs from other suppliers and restrict the supply available to the US, there would be significant disruption to the US economy. Prices of all goods would probably greatly increase, and in the event of a true cutoff in REOs, it is possible that some high-technology production (including advanced weapons systems) could halt entirely. An amelioration strategy here includes strengthening ties with providers of critical commodities to prevent backhanded deals in the future, exploration of new sources of commodities, and development of technology that could supplant the need for the rarest commodities in the future.

Currency Manipulation

The US is susceptible to foreign currency manipulation. Foreign governments could manipulate currencies to make their products look more attractive and thereby undercut US goods in the marketplace, though this also gives the US the benefit of being able to purchase cheaper products. It has some recourse for this in international institutions (World Bank, IMF, WTO), but these institutions would be able to do relatively little in the face of a determined adversary. The US might suffer from this tactic now in its trade relations with China, and the policy prescriptions that could lead to amelioration mostly have to do with building consensus among partners abroad that this behaviour is acceptable. The US and its allies can place diplomatic pressure on China to value its currency correctly, but since China is such a large economy, no state will be ready to take serious action unless manipulation becomes dire.

Dumping/Counterfeiting

The US experiences counterfeiting to an extreme in China.[48] US products are regularly counterfeited. There are some signs that the Chinese government is trying to deal with the problem, but efforts are slow. To date, counterfeiting has not truly negatively impacted the US, but there is the possibility that it could damage US product credibility abroad if it continues. To address this issue, the US could place pressure on the Chinese government – threatening tariffs or shutting off access to financial markets – unless they comply with international anti-counterfeiting efforts. A tandem effort to shore up support among international partners and allies could also do much to ensure this problem does not explode out of control.

CONCLUSION

It may be a reflection of the modern widening of the field of security studies that economic warfare has not been thought of in this way in the past. "Securitization," as it is termed, is a real phenomenon that attaches security implications (and the associated baggage) to issues that have not had it in the past. Security implications of natural resource deposits, climate change, and now economic factors have only recently been part of the security studies vocabulary even though all of these factors clearly play a role in the security environment.

All of these pose risks to military professionalism. In modern economies, the relationship between the security sector and the rest of the economy is complex. Members of the military might benefit from being aware of possible pressures facing the economy. A sophisticated understanding of economic pressures facing security and policy-making by military members could aid in the development and execution of policies in keeping with modern principles of civil-military relations.

Economic warfare is something that seems so obvious when described, but without the label, would be difficult to discuss in a way encompassing all of its factors. Prior research into economic warfare has focused on the use of sanctions or trade practices, typically during war, in an attempt to reduce an adversary's industrial and economic capabilities. During wartime, it often focuses on a discussion of how economic warfare is used to prevent enemies from acquiring critical materials for war-making. Economic warfare has posed both direct and indirect threats (and opportunities) for the military profession.

Emerging research has looked at how economic warfare could be practiced in peacetime, with the goal of not destroying an adversary state, but to weaken its economic base so that the home state can make relative economic gains.

USA

These gains may or may not be at its expense, but in the case of an aggressor state attacking an adversary that is stronger than itself, it would make the most sense for this to become a zero-sum game.

Economic warfare is a means of conflict that could be practiced by rising powers. Political science research has shown that conflict between states is most likely not when adversaries have disparate power, but when one adversary is rapidly overtaking another. The transition of one state losing a top position to a new adversary is when conflict is most likely. This could also hold true in the economic realm; when one economy begins to overtake another, there then could be the largest prevalence of economic warfare.

ENDNOTES

1. Peoples' Liberation Army Academy of Military Science Dictionary of Military Strategy.

2. Phil Stewart, "Pentagon to Shut Military Command and Cut Jobs", *Reuters*, 10 August 2010, retrieved on 17 May 2012 from <http://www.reuters.com/article/2010/08/10/us-usa-pentagon-budget-idUSTRE67855620100810>.

3. Nathan Leites, *The New Economic Togetherness: American and Soviet Reactions* (Santa Monica, CA: Rand Corporation, 1973). Nathan Leites was an expert on the Soviet Union and had been an associate at the Rand Corporation since 1947.

4. Professionalism and professional education is based on scientific and basic knowledge, and oriented toward a higher organizational purpose, of general social good and not narrow self-interest. Flexner found that all professions should inspire to be "objective, intellectual and altruistic" and devoted toward social goals; that is a noble aspiration and one that, in the context of our military profession, speaks to the importance of the underlying investment in long-term education and basic research. See: Abraham Flexner, *Is Social Work a Profession?* (New York, NY: The New York School of Philanthropy, 1915), 56.

5. Dexter Hoyos, "Carthage in Africa and Spain", in Dexter Hoyos, ed., *A Companion to the Punic Wars* (Oxford: Wiley-Blackwell, 2011), 218-241.

6. Thomas R. Naylor, *Economic Warfare: Sanctions, Embargo Busting, and Their Human Cost* (Toronto, ON: McClelland & Stewart, Inc., 1999).

7. US-China Economic and Security Review Commission. *2011 Report to Congress of the U.S.-China Economic and Security Review Commission*, (Washington: United States Congress, 2011).

8. Carol E. Lee and Jay Solomon, "Tehran is Warned Window is 'Shrinking'", *The Wall Street Journal,* 14 March 2012, retrieved on 17 May 2012 from <http://online.wsj.com/article/SB10001424052702304692804577281924174555332.html>.

9. Naylor, 1999.

10. Belva M. Martin, *Rare Earth Materials in the Defense Supply Chain*. GAO-10-617R (Washington, DC: United States Government Accountability Office, 2010).

11. Yuan-li Wu, *Economic Warfare* (New York, NY: Prentice-Hall, 1952).

12. Charles Johnston Hitch and Roland N. McKean, *The Economics of Defense in the Nuclear Age* (Cambridge: Harvard University Press, 1965).; Martin Shubik and J. Hoult Verkerke,

"Open Questions in Defense Economics and Economic Warfare", *Journal of Conflict Resolution*, Vol. 33, No. 3 (1989), 480-499.

13. Robert Loring Allen, "State Trading and Economic Warfare", *Law & Contemporary Problems*, Vol. 24, No. 2 (1959), 256.; Naylor, 1999.; James P. O'Leary, "Economic Warfare and Strategic Economics", *Comparative Strategy*, Vol. 5, No. 2 (1985), 179-206.

14. UN General Assembly, 79th Plenary Meeting, *Economic measures as a means of political and economic coercion against developing countries*. A/RES/46/210, New York, 20 December 1991.

15. Tor Egil Forland, "The History of Economic Warfare: International Law, Effectiveness, Strategies", *Journal of Peace Research,* Vol. 30, No. 2 (1993), 151-162.

16. Hazel Henderson, *Building a Win-Win World: Life Beyond Global Economic Warfare* (San Francisco, CA: Berrett-Koehler Publishers, 1996).

17. James M. Lutz and Brenda J. Lutz, "Terrorism as Economic Warfare", *Global Economy Journal,* Vol. 6, No. 2 (2006).

18. Michael P. Gerace, *Military Power, Conflict and Trade* (London: Routledge, 2004).

19. Sajal K. Das, Krishna Kant and Nan Zhang, *Handbook on Securing Cyber-Physical Critical Infrastructure* (Waltham: Morgan Kaufmann, 2012).

20. Patrick Salmon, "British Plans for Economic Warfare Against Germany 1937-1939: The Problem of Swedish Iron Ore", *Journal of Contemporary History,* Vol. 16, No. 1 (1981), 53-72.

21. Leonard Caruana and Hugh Rockoff, "A Wolfram in Sheep's Clothing: Economic Warfare in Spain, 1940-1944", *Journal of Economic History*, Vol. 63, No. 1 (2003), 65-99.

22. Ibid., 100.

23. Ibid., 101.

24. Ibid., 117.

25. Of course, this still does not exactly fit the definition above regarding economic warfare, a sign that the literature has not historically considered economic warfare in a way purely related to economics. Perhaps it is also a sign that economic warfare should also incorporate activities that lead to desired geo-political ends just as much as purely economic ends.

26. Tor Egil Forland, "'Economic Warfare' and 'Strategic Goods': A Conceptual Framework for Analyzing COCOM", *Journal of Peace Research,* Vol. 28, No. 2 (1991), 191-204.

27. Ibid., 192-194.

28. Alan P. Dobson, "The Kennedy Administration and Economic Warfare Against Communism", *International Affairs*, Vol. 64, No. 4 (1988), 599-616.

29. Ibid.

30. Ibid., 601.

31. Alan P. Dobson, "The Reagan Administration, Economic Warfare, and Starting to Close Down the Cold War", *Diplomatic History,* Vol. 29, No. 3 (2005), 555.

32. Ibid.

33. James Schlesinger, *The Political Economy of National Security: A Study of the Economic Aspects of the Contemporary Power Struggle* (New York, NY: Praeger, 1960), 129.

34. Adam Smith, *The Wealth of Nations* (New York, NY: Random House, 1937), 431.

35. Ibid., 135-136.

36. Despite this importance, however, Schlesinger actually disagrees with the concept of economic warfare. He notes that much of the power of economic warfare is based on the strategic implications of trade. However, he claims that "economic warfare is a much weaker weapon than is generally realized". See: James Schlesinger, *The Political Economy of National Security: A Study of the Economic Aspects of the Contemporary Power Struggle* (New York, NY: Praeger, 1960), 137. If certain goods are banned from export to the Soviet bloc, it encourages them to develop alternative sources of supply, typically domestic. In this way, there is no long-term pattern to economic warfare, as target states will find ways to arbitrage around restrictions. It is an ad hoc strategy that "cannot be used to achieve anything other than immediate purposes" (Ibid., 139). Moreover, he notes that many developing economies are essentially immune from economic warfare, particularly subsistence economies.

37. Robert A. Pape, "Why Economic Sanctions Do Not Work", *International Security*, Vol. 22, No. 2 (1997), 93. See also: Robert A. Pape, "Why Sanctions *Still* Do Not Work", *International Security*, Vol. 23, No . 1 (1998).

38. Dursen Peksen, "Better or Worse? The Effect of Economic Sanctions on Human Rights", *Journal of Peace Research*, Vol. 46, No. 1 (2009).

39. For example, see Julie Jiang and Jonathan Sinton, "Overseas Investments By Chinese National Oil Companies: Assessing the drivers and impacts", *International Energy Agency Information Paper* (Paris, 2011), retrieved on 15 May 2012 from <http://www.energidnews.com/newsletter/files/8cc4d5d6b70eea5e72502ef1c50ce5fe.pdf>.

40. The Sovereign Wealth Fund Institute has developed the Linaburg-Maduell Transparency Index to track the transparency of sovereign funds. It can be accessed from <http://www.swfinstitute.org/statistics-research/linaburg-maduell-transparency-index/>.

41. For example, see Anthea Lawson, "Don't make it easier for dictators to steal", *The Financial Times*, 23 February 2011, retrieved on 18 April 2012 from <http://www.ft.com/intl/cms/s/0/e23b6baa-3f91-11e0-a1ba-00144feabdc0.html#axzz1vFIdqikG>.

42. Anna Lowery, "China Curbs on Currency Still an Issue", *The New York Times*, 2 May 2012, retrieved on 18 April 2012 from <http://www.nytimes.com/2012/05/03/business/global/as-appreciation-of-china-currency-slows-manipulation-remains-an-issue.html>.

43. Li Mu, "China sends more students abroad, absorbs record high", *The People's Daily*, 3 March 2011, retrieved on 18 May 2012 from <http://english.peopledaily.com.cn/90001/90776/90882/7307378.html>.

44. Deborah Bräutigam, "Aid 'With Chinese Characteristics': Chinese Foreign Aid and Development Finance Meet the OECD-DAC Aid Regime", *Journal of International Development*, Vol. 23, No. 5 (2011), 752-764.

45. John Daly, "Seeking to Circumvent Possible U.S. Trade Sanctions, China Buys Hawaiian Solar Company", *Oil Price*, 24 December 2011, retrieved on 17 May 2012 from <http://oilprice.com/Alternative-Energy/Solar-Energy/Seeking-To-Circumvent-Possible-U.S.-Trade-Sanctions-China-Buys-Hawaiian-Solar-Company.html>.

46. Associated Press, "Commerce Department imposes stiff tariffs on Chinese solar panels; fees average 31 percent" *The Washington Post*, 17 May 2012, retrieved on 17 May 2012 from <http://www.washingtonpost.com/business/policy/commerce-department-imposes-stiff-tariffs-on-chinese-solar-panels-fees-average-31-percent/2012/05/17/gIQAuinaWU_story.html>.

47. Keith R. Long, Bradley S. Van Gosen, Nora K. Foley and Daniel Cordier, *The Principal Rare Earth Element Deposits of the United States – A Summary of Domestic Deposits and a Global Perspective, U.S. Geological Survey Scientific Investigations Report 2010-5220* (Reston, VI: U.S. Department of the Interior, U.S. Geological Survey, 2010); and Keith R. Long, "The Future of Rare Earth Elements; Will These High-Tech Industry Elements Continue in Short Supply?", *U.S. Geographic Survey Open-File Report 2011-1189* (Reston, VI: U.S. Department of the Interior, U.S. Geological Survey, 2011).

48. See for example: Paul Midler, *Poorly Made in China* (Hoboken: Wiley, 2009).

CHAPTER 9

Displaced Pride:
Attacking Cynicism at the United States
Air Force Academy

Brett A. Waring
*James J. Do**

The American flag is slowly lowered before the backdrop of the sun sinking behind the striking architecture of the Air Force Academy, descending for the final time before the Fourth Class cadets (first-year cadets) finish the Recognition activities that mark their ascension into the ranks of upperclass cadets. In the ranks of the assembled Cadet Wing, hearts beat with an unconstrained pride in the young men and women who have finally reached the end of their first year of military training, and perhaps the greatest ordeal of their young lives. For a moment, they are undefeatable; immortal in their triumphs and limitless in their potential. Three years later, as they complete their studies and join the ranks of fellow graduates, many will carry with them a debilitating emotion that taints every memory and image of the previous four years. How they carry out their active duty mission as officers, influence their peers and subordinates, and look back on the United States Air Force Academy (USAFA) and its purpose, mission, and experience will be affected by the amount of cynicism retained long after the white parade caps are hurled into the air beneath the roar of the passing Thunderbirds.

Cynicism is not unique to USAFA. As a natural response mechanism, it may affect every human endeavour. The United States' service academies represent a unique fixture in American culture, combining rigorous officer training with accredited undergraduate studies. Upon graduation, cadets from the service academies enter their respective military services as officers. While cynicism exists at all service academies and within any structured organization, this discussion will focus on the circumstances contributing to the development and promotion of cynicism at the Air Force Academy. Specifically, it will address cynicism through non-military models, discuss the perceptions and rationale concerning its origin and growth in cadets, and provide suggestions for attacking cynicism effectively. Although this discussion uses

---

* The views expressed in this academic research paper are those of the authors and do not reflect the official policy or position of the US Government or the Department of Defense.

USA

USAFA as the primary platform to discuss combatting and minimizing cynicism, the recommended suggestions may also apply across other institutions producing a military workforce. In a structured military organization with a hierarchy of personnel dependent on decision-making, communication, and adherence to rules and regulations, threats to professionalism negatively impact the mission and ultimately national security. Having an intimate knowledge of the Academy, as graduates and an assistant professor on the faculty, the authors use this unique environment as their example of tackling threats to professionalism due to familiarity with the system. The terms we use to describe our organization, including "cadet", [Air Officers Commanding] "AOC", and "squadron", may be interchangeable depending on the organization and situation. Ultimately, the Air Force Academy cadets, the subjects of our analysis of cynicism, enter the United States Air Force as second lieutenants. It is incumbent upon the faculty and staff at USAFA to ensure the cadet experience, including their time in the classroom and out in the field, results in an exceptionally trained professional ready to serve the nation they have sworn to defend with their life.

The Academy serves as an interesting microcosm in the analysis of cynicism simply due to the levels noted for such an institution. As a rigorous and scripted training environment purposefully created to forge officers of character in the pressure cooker of a four-year syllabus, one might expect to find comparable levels of this symptom as levied against other strenuous regimens. However, graduates of highly stressful and demanding training venues such as Special Forces indoctrinations or the USAF Weapons Instructor Course do not exhibit such attitudes as can be readily found amongst USAFA alumni. The extremely obvious pride in accomplishment that accompanies such other courses is expected, but noticeably overtly absent in a sizeable cross-section of USAFA cadets and graduates. With this foundational baseline, cynicism as it applies to both subordinates and leaders can be analyzed in the pursuit of increasing the pride that should naturally flow through military service and arduous training. We contend that cynicism does not exist as a solitary mindset in-and-of- itself, but rather on a sliding attitudinal scale also encompassing pessimism, sarcasm, and most importantly, *pride*.

Cynicism is an intangible emotional expression that exists in the chasm created by the difference between expectation and reality; "fostered by high expectations and subsequent disillusionment."[1] Cadets do not enter USAFA with inclinations towards cynicism but, somewhere along that arduous journey, *something* occurs that drives their outlook away from pride, through sarcasm and into cynicism. Several goals of the Air Force Academy provide a strategic focus on how it develops future officers: focus on character and leadership development, prepare and motivate the workforce, and strengthen our communications and reputation.[2] During the process of officer development at the Air Force Academy, how do all the personnel involved in this, including cadets and staff, lose sight of the Academy's strategic goals? Somewhere during their education and training at USAFA, cadets' development and passion become inhibited, which ultimately results in a cohort of freshly minted second lieutenants with sullied views about how the bigger Air Force and overarching military structure function. On a grander scale, cynicism, when left unchecked and allowed to deteriorate into resentment and indignation toward the very organization they have trained to serve, emerges as a threat to professionalism in our military forces.

Current research concerning cynicism, including its causes, effects, and suggested avenues for attack, deals primarily with business models and studies conducted in the private sector. Research within the corporate world, however, must be cautiously applied to military endeavours, as the purposes behind such disparate organizations do not necessarily support the indiscriminate application of common suggestions. In reference to the armed forces, close scrutiny must be applied to avoid recommending inappropriate solutions that undermine military order, discipline, and purpose. This inquiry is not intended to be a single source "cure-all" for institutional problems concerning cynicism, nor is it projected to be a series of checklist recommendations to follow in attacking cynicism. This discussion proposes simple suggestions in the hopes that the discourse on the subject will motivate cadets and officers to grapple with this difficult situation and work together in advancing a common mission. Finally, we do not presuppose that USAFA has not taken steps to combat cynicism, nor do we contend that such attitudes have not already been curtailed. In such instances, this work should serve to reinforce effective policies. Battling cynicism is a constant process and, as such, must continually be re-evaluated for effectiveness and improvement. It must also be fundamentally understood that cynicism cannot be viewed, approached, adjusted, or attacked singularly. The expression of cynicism cannot be seen as a fault of a subordinate or a leader in and of itself. Rather, the effective leader confronted with the expression of cynicism seeks to understand both the manifestation and the inspiration behind the attitude, specifically seeking to identify what actions the individual may have taken to inadvertently produce a cynical subordinate.

USA

CYNICISM AND THE CYNIC: DEFINITIONAL FOUNDATIONS

In ancient Greece, the Order of the Cynics, begun by Antisthenes, a follower of Socrates, held in their dogma "that even cherished institutions, such as religion and government, were unnatural and unnecessary—worthy only of scorn. Cynics were openly contemptuous of such institutions and were known for using dramatic and obscene displays to draw people into conversations."[3] In much the same manner that modern cadets attempt to express their frustrations and cynical tendencies, "humor was the favorite weapon of the Cynics, the privileged and the powerful their favorite target."[4] Regardless of the semantics surrounding the classification of cynicism, sources commonly surround the term with negative connotations that make it difficult to place cynicism on a common gradient with pride. However, turning to organizational descriptions of cynicism, the application and effects of external events enters the discussion. James W. Dean, Pamela Brandes, and Ravi Dharwadkar, professors of management who currently research organizational change, international management issues, employee attitudes, and performance improvement, describe cynicism as "an attitude consisting of the futility of change along with negative attributions of change facilitators."[5] Additionally, organizational cynicism is a "learned belief that fixable problems at work will not be resolved due to factors beyond the individual's control."[6] By this line of reasoning, a major contributing factor to the creation of cynical thoughts resides within *any* organizational change. Still, simply labeling cynicism as a negative attitude spawned by repeated or unsuccessful change initiatives remains shallow and incomplete. Cadets tend to focus their definitions on expectations, with several First Class cadets (in their fourth-year) identifying the source of cynicism as the difference between one's expectations of USAFA and reality.[7] As the cadets describe, the difference between expectations and perceived realities creates a significant amount of the negative emotion defining cynicism in the academic sense. Incorporating the influence of organizational change demonstrates the effect that a lack of consistency can play with fostering these same feelings. However, for all of the negative associations compiled into definitions of cynicism, one must return to the core theory that places cynicism on par with pride and understand that cynical tendencies do not spawn immaculately.

Arnon Reichers, John Wanuous, and James Austin, professors of management and psychology studying organizational commitment, employee motivation, and performance measurement, address both the realistic implications of cynicism as well as the causes in opining that "people do not deliberately decide to become cynical, pessimistic, and blaming. Rather, these attitudes result from experience, and are sustained because they serve useful purposes. Cynicism persists because it is selectively validated by the organization's mixed record of successful change, and by other people in the organization who hold and express similar views."[8] Thus, cynicism is understood to originate within significant organizational change and in the chasm between expectations and perceived reality. In addition, it is neither a preconceived nor sought-after emotional response, but one which grows in the absence of more desirable attitudes. With cynicism existing in a learned manner, its positional relevance to other attitudes can be examined.

With respect to attitudinal expressions amongst cadets, graduates, and faculty alike, pride remains the most desirable. Certainly, young men and women embark upon the Academy endeavour with just such an outcome in mind. From the outset, applicants are deluged with descriptions of the monumental tasks they'll confront as cadets: "It takes dedication, sacrifice, and stamina. Organization, time-management, and self-discipline amid mental, ethical and physical demands. The environment is one of structure, rules, and regulations. But the rewards are lifetime friends, honor, personal development, pride, and of course an exciting career."[9] Events such as completing Basic Cadet Training (BCT), Recognition, and the accomplishment of significantly challenging military courses throughout the curriculum support such a description and generate indescribable expressions of pride in such feats. Somewhere amongst these milestones, that same pride occasionally erodes, caustically forming negative emotions. A 2003 graduate of the U.S. Military Academy described this phenomenon, arguing that:

> When you apply to any of the service academies, they set you up with absurdly high expectations. As a high-school kid walking around the post, you can't help but paint a picture in your mind of a place that is a study in superlatives: the hardest, smartest, most honorable school in the whole country. Tapping into the vision cradled by that high-schooler about to head off to the academy is the first step to understanding the cynicism.[10]

Misapplied, misplaced, or even denied pride leaves an emotional gap that creates an opportunity to cultivate negative attitudes as an individual's viewpoint slides away from the positive. As reality fails to live up to expectations, the hopeful individual first begins to replace that pride with skepticism. Skepticism, in-and-of-itself, remains fairly non-intrusive attitudinally. "Skeptics doubt the likelihood of success, but are still reasonably hopeful that positive change will occur. It is also distinct from resistance to change, which results from self-interest, misunderstanding, and inherent limited tolerance for change. Cynicism about change involves a real loss of faith in the leaders of change and is a response to a history of change attempts that are not entirely or clearly successful."[11] At this stage, pride is relatively easily re-introduced through a reaffirmation or the reconciliation of expectations with reality. However, the further that an individual slides away from pride, the more confused the attitudes can become. Indeed, leaders looking to sharp-shoot emotions in subordinates often confuse or misdiagnose the expressed manifestations. "Cynicism has been frequently confused with skepticism. If all cynics were skeptics, the confusion might be innocent or trivial, and no real confusion would obtain. They are, however, quite opposite in many respects. Indeed, many cynical remarks are both skeptical and cynical."[12] Critical to this scale remains the fleeting nature of attitudes in falling from pride, through skepticism, and into cynicism. Just as skepticism can be quickly reinvigorated into pride, it can just as easily descend to the expressions of cynicism. Continuing to expand the chasm between expectation and reality drives cynicism into pessimism. Comparatively, drawing upon both the contemporary and classical definitions of cynicism, the particularly abrasive nature of pessimism comes into view. "Cynical remarks were barbs in the classic tradition to prod moral reform. Pessimistic remarks rhetorically tend to disincline one to action, not provoke it."[13] Thus, just as cynicism does not represent the worst attitude a cadet can express, it also contains an inclination toward affecting change and offers hope of progress when viewed in relation to the sliding scale of emotion. With a definitional foundation established, the discussion can analyze the unique situation of perceptions situated between expectation and reality at the Air Force Academy in discerning opportunities to attack cynicism.

EXPECTATIONS AND PERCEPTIONS: CYNICISM IN PRACTICE

The mere mention of cynicism draws an inherently negative connotation amongst officers, cadets, and even society itself. It is precisely this negative association with cynicism that causes grave concern amongst USAFA officials in their efforts to curtail and prevent such attitudes.

In expanding upon the causes of cynicism, researchers of management and business offer the assessment that "organizational change and quality improvement efforts particularly seem to engender cynicism."[14] With respect to their appraisal, the notion of organizational change presents a significant challenge for Academy officials. While the structure of the four-year class system and established curriculum would seem to support consistency, reality offers a starkly contrasting view. In their four years at USAFA, cadets will see their immediate supervisors and overall chain of command turnover multiple times. Though Air Officers Commanding, the active-duty officer commander of a cadet squadron, maintain a two-year controlled tour of duty, cadets can expect to see at least two or three different commanders during their Academy experience. The Commandant of Cadets (a one-star general), responsible for military training and curriculum, changes rapidly as well. Over the Academy's history, most Commandants have served roughly three years in the position, although the average has decreased to two years over the last fifteen years. Superintendents (three-star general) serve slightly longer, averaging three years in position, with the longest term being five years. Deans of the Faculty (one-star general) tend to average six-year terms. Examining the tenure of faculty highlights the fact that cadets face drastically different approaches and policies through what *should* be a consistent curriculum over the course of four years. Such changes represent a significant catalyst in the formulation of cynicism simply through constantly shifting administrative approaches to a common mission.

In numerous discussions with cadets, they highlight two problematic areas that coincide with corporate definitions concerning cynicism. First, they point to the significant differences between their expectations of the Academy experience with what they found in reality. One cadet put it bluntly: "Cynicism stems from the difference between cadet's expectations of USAFA to reality."[15] When asked to expand upon those expectations, this cadet stated that he "honestly expected that it would be much tougher militarily and was disappointed to see how scared the permanent party are to the press and members outside of the big black gates. It has gotten better since my [first] year but not by much." However subtle, such remarks also contain a glimpse into the promise held within cynical attitudes. This cadet also opines that "it is the cynics who still care because they want it to be an esteemed military institution—many try and change it for the better." Finally, he offers profound insight into the power and potential within such an attitude when he states, "I hold onto cynicism because I truly believe that USAFA is a great institution that exposes cadets to experiences that no other place in the world can. I have had some instances where my cynical 'episodes' inspire me to be a better role model for the underclassmen because I believe that if can instill the sense of pride in them that I have, then I have done my job."

Ultimately, the battle against cynicism must be fought not against the attitudes themselves, but against the *conditions* that allow perceptions to slide away from pride and into the negative expressions. Cynicism is a symptom, not necessarily a causal agent. "Researchers see cynicism as a result of violations of psychological contracts and describe this cynicism within the realm

USA

of attitudes."[16] With an institution that requires intense instruction, mentorship, and guidance in developing officers, the attitudinal divergence of the students away from those instructors must be carefully analyzed and scrutinized when the relationship becomes adversarial. Negative perceptions of leadership should be investigated as "organizational cynics believe that the practices of their organizations betray a lack of such principles as fairness, honesty, and sincerity."[17] Inadequately addressing such perceptions, or allowing the underlying conditions to thrive, drives cynicism dangerously closer to pessimism. Should the cadets reach this stage of a pessimistic outlook, significant efforts must be exerted to re-establish a sense of pride and purpose in that individual.

PRIDE IN OWNERSHIP: ATTACKING CYNICISM

Effectively targeting attitudinal manifestations such as cynicism represents a particularly difficult assignment for any organization. Cynicism, like any emotion or attitude, can be extremely elusive as it leaves few physical demonstrations of its presence. Unless expressed in the presence of commanders, cynical attitudes often appear as phantasms existing beneath the surface of everyday life. Foremost in discussing the existence of cynicism within an organization concerns the negative connotations associated with the term, as cynicism is not a particularly valued attribute in our culture.[18] However, cynicism exists and propagates within an organization with the perceived utility of the attitude within the holder:

> For the organization, cynics may provide a necessary check on the temptation to place expediency over principle or the temptation to assume that self-interested or underhanded behavior will go undetected. In their particular manner cynics may act as the voice of conscience for the organization, much as the Cynics did for their culture. Thus, we should see organizational cynicism as neither an unalloyed good nor an unalloyed evil for organizations.[19]

The first step in attacking cynicism relies upon the validation of the attitude as a human emotion. "Whatever their real or imagined basis, these attitudes are equally valid to the individuals who hold them. Moreover, it would be virtually impossible to distinguish between 'justified' and 'unjustified' organizational cynicism because so much of what happens in organizations is open to different interpretations. Determining whether cynicism is justified is ultimately a matter of opinion, which would be a very unstable basis for theory."[20]

Some commanders and leaders ineffectively target these attitudes through eradication campaigns that seek to eliminate any physical symptoms of cynicism. At USAFA, cadets once produced a monthly satire publication that often contained cynical cartoons and commentary. When administrative officers began heavily censoring the material, a group of graduates started an online website out of the reach of USAFA officials. Battle lines formed, pitting perceptions of good order and discipline against expressions of frustration and crude humour against one another. As defences solidified, few in either camp found it possible to compromise and view the situation from the other's viewpoint. Ultimately, beneath an external political pressure that pressed the Academy on unrelated topics, the Commandant of Cadets shut down the cadet publication, and online access to the "underground" website was blocked in accordance with standard Air Force web browsing protocols. Cadets found themselves unable to vent their frustrations through the medium originally employed by the Cynics of ancient Greece: *humour*. Corporate America faced a similar dilemma in the early 1990s when a frustrated engineer named Scott Adams began his incredibly successful assault on hapless managers and ludicrous policies in the comic strip, *Dilbert*. Employees across the nation immediately identified with his tales, and his cartoons quickly leapt from newspaper pages to the walls of cubicles and offices throughout the business community. While some managers attacked such expressions in fashions similar to that at the Academy, others found the expressions to be invaluable indicators of corporate morale. In an article describing this effect, Marc Greilsamer, a writer on business affairs and fan of *Dilbert*, contends that:

> This is a really clean way for employers to find out what people are worrying about—just walk down the hall and look at the cubicles." The best scenario, says Adams, is if there are some Dilbert cartoons on your walls: That means you have problems, but also that 'there's probably good communication and a receptive environment because they're not forcing you to take them down.' If the cartoons are so numerous that they resemble wallpaper, this obviously indicates very big problems. The worst-case scenario is if there are no cartoons posted at all: Not only do you have a slew of problems, but employees are afraid to talk about them.[21]

Still, simply permitting outward expressions of internal emotions only provides a forum for the venting of frustrations without assaulting the source of such feelings.[22] Were Academy administrators to re-open access to physical and online publications, there would be neither a guarantee nor even an assurance that such acts would markedly decrease the production of cynical attitudes. However, as a release mechanism, such a gesture could assist in preventing attitudes from slipping further from cynicism into outright pessimism through the allowance of a purge process. Perhaps this explains why the Cynics of old relied on such mediums, conflicting the apparently polar opposites of frustration with laughter in a positive expulsion of negativity. At the same time, cadets must accept the fact that such venting mechanisms may not remain completely unchecked, given the current political climate that exists at USAFA and society in general. For most of its existence, the physical publication produced by cadets had to pass through a series of officers who checked and censored inappropriate material. With such a process, there was always a struggle between cadets pushing the limits, and officers defining and maintaining boundaries constrained within the label of good order and discipline.

Little, if any, research has been conducted concerning efforts to curtail cynicism within military organizations. Because the demands of military service, coupled with the options afforded a commander, differ greatly from those of the corporate world, an appreciable demand for such studies generally has not existed. As mentioned earlier in this discussion, caution must be exercised when applying civilian solutions to military issues. However, the Academy offers a particularly inviting scenario for just such an application. While it exists first and foremost as a military organization, its primary purposes reside in officer training and the creation of a leadership laboratory from which cadets can practice the qualities that will be expected of them upon graduation and commissioning. Reichers, Wanuous, and Austin, who study cynicism and organizational change in the business world, formulate a strategy beneath the title, "Understanding and Managing Cynicism about Organizational Change." They offer ten tactics that directly confront the "issues of credibility and the relationship between employees and change agents. The suggestions build on some of what is now known about cynicism, credibility, and transformational leadership."[23] The authors make their premise upon the assumption that organizational change creates the greatest degree of cynicism within employees. They apply most of their suggestive efforts toward improving communication flow and enhancing the credibility of the information that flows between executives and employees. Where relevant, the authorial focus on information has been expanded to appropriately include aspects of military hierarchy and command instruction in areas not considered by the original article. While organizational change represents a substantial source for generating cynicism, it is certainly not the only cause. Still, given the constraints of these assumptions, the points offered by business and management scholars embody an effective yardstick by which policies can be referenced in their attempts to curtail or attack cynicism. Foremost in this discussion must remain the fact that these suggestions do not necessarily remedy cynicism itself, but rather seek to deny the attitudinal kindling that often pushes an emotional posture further from pride toward the dangers of pessimism. Leaders and subordinates alike can directly apply these steps (slightly modified in discussion here to bridge the original civilian applications to military service) to better understand the symptoms of cynicism and to reverse the manifestation back in the direction towards pride.

Keep People Involved in Making Decisions that Affect Them

In the corporate world, such a suggestion might appear particularly innovative in its delegation of responsibility and inclusive tendencies. The business model suggests that

> People more likely to be cynical about change were those who reported that they lacked meaningful opportunities to participate in decision making, felt uninformed in general about what was going on in the work place, and had supervisors and union representatives they felt were lax about communicating with them, and about getting back to them with answers to questions. These findings lend support to the idea that cynicism may be an attempt to make sense out of disappointing or puzzling events.[24]

At first glance, the proposition seems to conflict directly with the military culture as involvement is not necessarily a hallmark of a rigid chain of command. However, given the distinctive qualities of the USAFA mission, this proposition actually represents a touchstone submission for combating cynicism. In learning to become effective military officers, cadets must be given ample opportunities to practice leadership. They must be given the opportunity to create, enact, and learn from their own guidance and policies within the Cadet Wing. Such a practice must also allow for the possibility of recoverable failures. *Cadets must experience the consequences of their decisions firsthand.* To craft this discussion into an analogy, cadets must be allowed and encouraged to walk the tight rope without a safety harness on their person. The safety net of the leadership laboratory itself exists to catch them, should they fall. Without consequence and immediate feedback, and absent risk per se, the actual ability to learn leadership remains theoretical in an environment that should be stressing the practical. Colonel Lavanson Coffey, reflecting upon his tenure as a Group AOC, with more than a decade of his career spent at USAFA, admitted that the Academy can allow cadets a greater degree of autonomy in exercising leadership principles within their squadrons. The difficulty, he explained, lies within striking an effective balance between the forward progress of the Cadet Wing without allowing for a catastrophic failure when too much latitude is permitted. He also admitted that Academy officials maintained a posture that could be interpreted as micro-managing in the attempt to prevent a leadership practicum from running awry in the hands of relatively inexperienced cadets. Brigadier-General Susan Desjardins, Commandant of Cadets from 2006 to 2009 described the difficulty in balancing responsibility within environmental constrains as she suggested "I will never be able to give them enough responsibility. We give them a lot of rope. We give them just enough rope so they don't hurt themselves."[25] In direct contrast to this approach, a 2003 graduate of the U.S Military Academy contrasts the level of cynicism at Air Force with a comparable lower level in a sister service academy.

> I feel strongly that cadet leadership should be given real authority, even if that gift of authority leads to the possibility of failures. *Especially* if there is the possibility of failure. Everyone that is cynical is haunted by the vision of what they thought the academy was or had the potential to be. But this vision is not dead, and can still be called to life. We need torchbearers, who refuse to throw up their hands in the face of a disappointing reality.[26]

The effect of delegation to, and trust in subordinates creates an immediate possibility for the reduction in organizational cynicism.

A 2006 graduate of the Air Force Academy described just such a situation: "The best leadership example I experienced at the Academy was from my AOC during my Firstie [a fourth-year cadet] year. His style was hands off and he allowed us to run the show, and he acted as a mentor for the squadron leadership. I can't recall a time when he took away the power from the cadets. If someone screwed up and needed punishment, he'd offer his advice to the squadron commander and let him handle it from there."[27] This graduate continues to explain the lasting effects that such a leadership style had upon the squadron in contrast to the initial reception. "His ideas were pretty radical and a lot of AOCs initially laughed at him for how he commanded our squadron. It didn't help his cause that we were #36 [last] in the wing after the first 9 weeks of my Firstie year. However, things began to change. We started to improve rapidly and by the end of my Firstie year, AOCs from other squadrons were asking him for advice on how to run their squadrons." He concludes with a capstone comment: "By the start of the following fall semester (after I had graduated), my squadron was #1 in the Wing and a lot of the PTB [slang term for Academy officials: literally, the Powers That Be] were taking notes."

Positive and effective organizational change does not occur immediately, and leaders must have the will to weather initial setbacks and relapses before a new direction takes hold. With any change acting as a potential catalyst, leaders must expect an initial *increase* in cynicism, even with policies that will ultimately prove proper and effective in combating that response. Appropriately, the next suggestion deals directly with improving the leadership quality of organizations stricken with cynicism.

Enhance Credibility

An AOC has arguably one of the greatest impacts upon a cadet's professional development due to the command exposure from within their individual squadrons. To ensure high calibre officers fill these critical leadership positions, the Commandant of Cadets handpicks AOCs based upon the strength of their service records. This offers cadets a broad exposure to leaders of diverse Air Force Specialty Code (AFSC) backgrounds; however, the leadership abilities and philosophies of the AOCs remain inconsistent throughout the administration.[28] AOCs also receive one year of graduate education, resulting in a Masters Degree in counseling and leadership, prior to a 2-year role as an AOC. During their year of study, the officer has formal on-the-job training with a sitting AOC.

Enhancing credibility also maintains a significant footprint operationally within the execution of the Academy's mission. Credibility itself is bookended by standardization and enforcement. The enforcement of regulations and policies should be constant and expected throughout both the Academy and military service in general. However, in practice, the art and necessity of correcting peers, and occasionally leaders, remains an elusive and uncomfortable art. In the popular culture and slang of the Cadet Wing, individuals making corrective observations on fellow cadets are referred to as "strivers" and "tools." Essentially, the problem manifests through two avenues, example and expectation. With respect to example, it must be understood that *any* instance of non-adherence to or the ignoring of standards by a superior will be reflected then as acceptable by subordinates. The officer or cadet who walks past obvious infractions, or corrects discrepancies while displaying the same violation creates a culture of acceptable negligence and disregard for established protocols. Worse, the attitude is infectious and spreads rapidly. Peer leadership and exemplary corrective actions represent a necessary, albeit difficult, focus area for the Academy to redouble its efforts in officer training. At which level is it appropriate to initially address and exemplify this attitude? From an exposure perspective, the layman might identify AOCs as the primary point of attack with their increased exposure to cadets and daily life at the Academy. However, Coffey points out that while such exemplary representation is ultimately the requirement of *every* officer assigned to the Academy, such an institutional focus must come from the senior leadership. With the military mission, the Commandant of Cadets would represent the point from which such a focus could be enacted from a top-down push to permeate the ranks. From this perch, the Commandant must make the point that standardization enforcement is not a *goal,* but a *minimum*—an entry-level baseline that sets 100 percent compliance and enforcement as a standard of measurement. In a series of informal conversations with more than one hundred personnel who attended USAFA as cadets, the results are telling. When asked about the primary purpose of officers assigned to cadet development, about 44 percent of the cadets stated that they expected superiors to act as examples or mentors in their instruction. Interestingly, 12 percent of this group of cadets carried negative opinions of officers assigned to USAFA, labeling their primary duties as micromanaging, punishing, or disciplining cadets. At a basic level, cadets expect the officers above them to set and abide by the principles expected of their subordinates. Leadership by example remains an effective motivator throughout history, and cadets thirst for such exemplars in the men and women charged with instilling lasting values into these future officers.

Credibility must contain consequences. Current AOCs assigned to the Academy describe a particularly alarming phenomenon in the prevailing sense of "entitlement" amongst cadet attitudes. When allowed to confide anonymously, cadets admit that such a feeling springs from the lack of significant consequences. Specifically, cadets believe that rehabilitation reigns over disenrollment for most offences. The lack of a credible threat of reprisal or consequences emboldens those who would push the limits of regulatory guidance and policy while supporting the assumption that acceptance into the Academy somehow assures a cadet of the "right" to graduate. Rehabilitation versus expulsion remains a significant challenge for all military leaders confronted with subordinates who test the limits of authority. The Academy lies at a particularly precarious position as it must balance the natural tendencies of youth battling emotional, psychological, and physical passions alongside the demands of officership and a regimented lifestyle. The acceptance and realization of consequences directly affects the development of responsibility within cadets; officer and cadet alike must realize and accept the consequences associated with a failure to comply with established guidance, with a credible threat of disenrollment maintained for those who fail to adhere to established standards.

The issue of credibility within the crucible of the Academy's purported leadership laboratory ultimately comes down to the degree to which cadets should potentially be allowed to fail in their attempts at leadership. As commanders, AOCs often overlook their instructional positions in favour of managerial responsibilities. Cadets thirst for opportunities to affect their own destinies, and several AOCs suggest that the more time and power that can be given back to cadets within the competing demands of the Academy curriculum, the less cynicism will be bred amongst their ranks.[29] A current AOC explained the situation in relating cadet experiences during a major military training exercise. During planning events occurring months prior to the actual exercise, the AOC identified several critical deficiencies in the cadet plan that, if left uncorrected, would lead to failure in execution. Rather than correct their mistakes, the commander allowed the cadets to continue in their planning and leadership practice. As identified, the cadets did not recognize the oversight and failed at the tasks assigned during the inspection. During a "lessons learned" review session, the AOC traced the specific errors and demonstrated appropriate fixes that would have remedied the situation. At the conclusion of this session, the cadets had a common reaction to the manner in which their commander had served in his capacity as an example throughout the process: "Thank you for letting us fail."[30] With limited resources and time devoted to officer development, Academy administrators will always struggle with the appropriate and acceptable consequences available to cadets at all levels of their training. Still, the most effective means of teaching accountability comes through the realistic and practical application of responsibility itself.

Keep People Informed

People need to be fully informed and educated about any change within an organization since information minimizes opportunities to fill in the blanks of missing information.[31] With an imposing academic schedule and series of training events designed to overwhelm and monopolize an individual's time, cadets often fail to comprehend the objectives of every policy, regulation, and training event placed upon them. While such attitudes have always existed to some degree, these future officers have come of age in a world where information is readily available and limited only by the individual's ability or willingness to discern or search for it. Once again, the Academy must strike a particularly precocious balance between military discipline and efficiency with the instructional outcomes associated with training leaders who will issue such orders in the future. Major Michael Drowley, a recent AOC, and United States Air Force (USAF) Weapons School Risner Trophy recipient, contends that "no matter what the policy, or who implemented it, AOCs have to take the time to explain the logic and purpose behind it."[32, 33] He describes setting aside weekly meetings with his cadets for just such a purpose and has found that even when they disagree with a policy, they tend to support it when they understand the thought process associated with the directives. He emphasized, and warned, that such information sharing sessions required a significant and consistent commitment on the part of the supervisor to maintain effectiveness and relevancy. If cynicism exists in the disparity between perceptions and outcomes, then even apparently irrelevant events and outcomes can deny a cynical foothold through the proper application of information. In Major Drowley's example, he further cautioned that information sharing is not simply accomplished through meetings alone. He explained that effective communication requires distribution across multiple media, including mass meetings, email, and personal interaction. Finally, he instructs that the distributor must be prepared to offer that information through different techniques due to the variations in individual reception; effective communication for some is a message not received by others.

Enhance Timing and Minimize Surprises

In their proscribed plan of attack against organizational cynicism, experts in employee motivation and organizational commitment outlined two separate suggestions that have been combined here into one focus area to emphasize the need for consistency throughout the Academy experience. In their words, employers should enhance the effectiveness of timing and keep surprises to a minimum. In any informational gap, people begin to fill in their own answers, either independently or through interaction with co-workers, most of them equally uninformed.[34] With respect to minimizing surprises, they contend that routine notice about what is happening, and especially why it is happening, prevents anyone from being caught off guard.[35] Consistency should be the hallmark of any institutionalized curriculum and established course of study, thereby marginalizing the effects of surprises or rashly-timed policies. With a constant and recognized mission, the changing of leadership should have little effect on the overall progress and steadfastness of the institution itself. However, this is not the case. Each administration within the pillars of instruction at the Academy brings a unique perspective and approach to accomplishing the mission of producing officers. Consideration should be given to extending the tours of general officers assigned to the Academy in much the same way as faculty heads under the Dean are tenured "Permanent Professors." Such a dramatic change may offer a level of consistency in mission not currently afforded by the constant change of critical administrative personnel.

Publicize Successful Changes and Deal with the Past

A popular, albeit slightly sarcastic, saying permeates the Cadet Wing when describing the Academy's history: *half a century of progress unimpeded by tradition*. While cadets at the U.S. Military and Naval Academies use a photo-negative of this to describe the predominance of traditions and rites-of-passage over a sense of modern progressiveness, the USAFA sketch laments the *lack* of traditions in a comparatively young organization that appears to constantly reinvent itself. Tradition at the Air Force Academy generally resides in either heritage or the accomplishments of fellow graduates, visibly present in memorials and static displays in the cadet area. While such items link cadets to graduates through historical reference, they do not directly provide a forum for participation outside of reflection. Traditions that cadets can participate in seem fleeting, inconsistent, and reside in sordid tales that begin, "Back in my day…" Inconsistencies and dramatic alterations to major events in a cadet's career crack the very foundation of their perspective and the link between that class and other graduates. Certainly, curriculums evolve over time, but cadets come to expect certain experiences that their predecessors identified as unique and central to the shared experience. Repeated efforts to curtail or expand the cadet experience represent other examples of inconsistencies that make it difficult for current cadets to associate their experiences with those found in Academy folklore. This is not to say, however, that *all* tradition is good for tradition's own sake. However, the common ideals and experiences that define the unique experience of the Academy that draws youth to its curriculum over other commissioning sources must be identified, sanctified, and promoted exhaustively. Such successful experiences and policies represent the hallmark of this institution, and should be heralded accordingly.

The Academy must also take conscientious steps to specifically deal with negative incidents in a consistent and effective manner. In the past decade, a series of sexual assaults, cheating incidents, and drug abuses have triggered media attention, the consternation of a concerned citizenry, and scrutiny from the Cadet Wing. In these incidents, cadets immediately identified discrepancies in the manner by which some cases were handled differently from others. In other areas, cadets reported a lack of familiarity with the circumstances surrounding negative events and perceived an institutional cover-up to avoid having to display publicly the black-eyes associated with such an event.[36] The severity of such incidents can cause a dramatic shift from sarcasm to pessimism in very short order, particularly with individuals close to such an event. However, given an open forum based on effective communication, such gaps in knowledge may be preventable and ultimately inexcusable. Yet, even amongst such perspectives, communication remains a two-way street, and cadets must be afforded a voice within the construct of the leadership laboratory.

Perspective and Opportunities to Air Feelings

At the Academy, leaders have the unique perspective associated with instructing in a defined curriculum that affords them an ability to foresee mistakes and errors in subordinate actions. Actions taken to maintain a steady course often can be perceived as micromanaged instruction. The burden of experience sometimes prevents a superior from viewing a situation from the critical perspective of a student subordinate. The ability to discern this vital facet in cadet development cannot be overemphasized. Developing the ability to recognize and adjust leadership and instructional techniques to account for subordinate perspective must be institutionalized and constantly re-evaluated for effectiveness and improvement. Within that very perspective, cadets must be given a voice in their curriculum. Such a voice will run the gamut from simple complaints to viable feedback and should be both tolerated and encouraged. On the other side, officers should not feel threatened or uncomfortable by grumblings and complaints within the masses. Colonel (ret) Hector Negroni, USAFA class of 1961, explains this phenomenon effectively in instructing:

> I am one who has never been bothered by cynicism or complaints by the "troops." Bitching and moaning is a sign of spirit and a sign of a good military person. I favor "grumblers" over the silent types. That is why I always supported the old paper Dodo and I support its electronic version. As a commander, I learned that I needed to know what my 'troops' were complaining about and what they were cynical about.[37]

Specifically addressing cynicism, the Academy once had an established medium afforded to cadets in the form of their publication, *The Dodo*. Before it was banned in 2006, senior officers remarked that they used the magazine to gauge the effectiveness and manner by which policies were received by the Cadet Wing.[38] Cadets used the forum as a medium by which to purge negative feelings and emotions when confronted with scandalous situations.[39] Given the current political climate surrounding an institution still recovering from the shock of multiple scandals earlier in the decade, Academy leaders find little room to permit experimentation with sensitive subjects. At the same time, affording cadets specific, credible, and legitimate authority to police themselves and resurrect a tradition could serve to eliminate more cynicism than the magazine espouses.

Having a voice in Academy administration follows classic lines within the curriculum as well. When cadets see that their suggestions lead to implemented change, the resultant empowerment will produce instances of pride. Cadets must recognize that their constructive feedback (when appropriate) is taken seriously and provides tangible results. As maturing officers, they must also understand that all complaints and suggestions do not translate directly into change. The ramifications of any policy change will be cemented by highlighting specific cadet feedback that led to the improved policies and should foster increased and improved feedback. As direct participants invested in the system, cadets will both grow as future leaders and as the "owners" of a system which once may have been viewed more often than not as an adversarial entity. Most importantly, however, is the "pride" that naturally flows through the simple act of participation, and ultimately, ownership.

CONCLUSION

Cynicism should neither be feared nor lamented as a cancerous entity. Neither, though, can it be embraced or celebrated as a desired emotional expression. Existing on the same scale with pride, sarcasm, and pessimism, cynicism provides an attitudinal barometer that allows leaders to gauge how far from the desired expressions their subordinates have shifted. Such an assessment requires constant and faithful interaction, involvement, and study. As an entity, cynicism itself cannot be attacked directly. However, by understanding its causes and relative stature alongside other emotions, effective measures can be taken to undercut the effect and propagation of cynicism. The mere existence of cynicism should not cause immediate alarm among leaders. In describing the rhetoric of cynicism, George Yoos, professor emeritus of philosophy, offers a more optimistic prognosis in opining that "the cynic's sarcasm may be perceived as a form of moral shock therapy, and if the cynic is engaging in rhetorical therapeutics, then he cannot be in complete despair about his patient, especially if the therapy is free."[40]

In some respects, Academy administrators have more room for optimism than panic with established policies that may effectively assist in combating cynicism. The USAFA Strategic Vision offers guidance that aligns with the suggestions of this work. Of the seven strategic goals published by the Superintendent, the second goal looks to strengthen communications and reputation, only behind a focus on leadership and character development.[41] Such observations and directives represent methodologies that, if enacted effectively, could undercut cynicism's ability to cultivate within cadet perspectives. Strict adherence to these goals through a credible executive process will strengthen pride in the institution. However, it remains critical to recognize that such policies, even as perfectly crafted and expertly intentioned, can cause some degree of sarcasm and cynicism at the outset as they represent change to the organization. Adherence and consistency to the original intent should overcome such reactions, but the weathering of such responses must be anticipated and dealt with consistently.

Finally, whether cynicism comes about due to policy or organizational changes, it ultimately resides within the realm of a subordinate's perception. As both a defence mechanism and natural response, such perspectives must be recognized and validated in the spectrum of human emotion. Understanding this relationship creates the most succinct methodology and baseline knowledge required to effectively target cynicism. As perceptions open the door for attitudinal shifts toward cynicism, it is precisely these perceptions and expectations that must be aligned to focus upon the desired pride inherent in the original perspective. Consistency of message, effective dialogue, and a unified effort toward a common goal all work directly to both reinvigorate pride and deny cynicism an opportunity to gain an emotional foothold. In the end, despite the best efforts of experts in the field and diligent analysis of the issue, perhaps the best perspective on the situation again comes from the trenches as an admitted cynic as a recent graduate describes his outlook: "I'm cynical because, deep down, I think I actually have some pride in not just USAFA, but in who I am, what I stand for, and what USAFA should be. I'm proud to be cynical, because if I am not cynical about USAFA's failures, then I've either become blind to the problems, or I have lost my ability to care."

ENDNOTES

1. Lynne Andersson and Thomas S. Bateman, "Cynicism in the Workplace: Some Causes and Effects", *Journal of Organizational Behavior*, Vol. 18, No. 5 (1997), 451.

2. *United States Air Force Academy Strategic Plan, 2010-2014*, retrieved on 15 May 2012 from <http://www.usafa.af.mil/shared/media/document/AFD-100322-020.pdf>.

3. James W. Dean, Jr., Pamela Brandes and Ravi Dharwadkar, "Organizational Cynicism", *The Academy of Management Review*, Vol. 23, No. 2 (1998), 341.

4. Ibid., 341.

5. Ibid., 344.

6. Ibid., 344.

7. This was an anonymous interview conducted by the Author with a USAFA cadet, 15 December 2008.

8. Arnon E. Reichers, John P. Wanuous and James T. Austin, "Understanding and Managing Cynicism about Organizational Change", *The Academy of Management Executive*, Vol. 11, No. 1 (1997), 51.

9. United States Air Force Academy, Daily life, retrieved on 15 May 2012 from <http://www.academyadmissions.com/#Page/Daily_Life>. This is the official USAFA Admissions website, which provides prospective cadets and their family with information about the experiences and challenges they face. These comments are typical messages that welcome prospective cadets to USAFA.

10. This was an interview conducted by the Author with a USMA cadet known only as Wry, 11 December 2008.

11. Reichers, Wanuous and Austin, 1997, 48.

12. George E. Yoos, "The Rhetoric of Cynicism", *Rhetoric Review*, Vol. 4, No. 1 (1985), 57.

13. Ibid., 58.

14. Dean, Brandes and Dharwadkar, 1998, 341.

15. This was an anonymous interview conducted by the Author with a USAFA cadet, 11 December 2008.

16. Dean, Brandes and Dharwadkar, 1998, 344.

17. Ibid., 345.

18. Ibid., 347.

19. Ibid., 347.

20. Ibid., 347.

21. Marc Greilsamer, "The Dilbert Barometer", *Across the Board*, Vol. 32, No. 3 (1995), 2.

22. Interestingly, a significant fear of retribution currently exists among cadets.

23. Reichers, Wanuous and Austin, 1997, 52.

24. Ibid., 52.

25. Tom Roeder, "Great Leaders of the Academy", *Checkpoints*, Vol. 37, No. 3 (2008), 19.

26. Anonymous, *Attacking Cynicism at USAFA - 4 Oct 2008*, retrieved on 15 May 2012 from <www.edodo.org/rm>. The *eDodo* is an internet-based version of the cadet humor publication *The Dodo*. With no official connection to the USAFA Dodo, which was banned in 2006 by senior USAFA officials, the *eDodo* was established by former Dodo contributors and USAFA graduates in 1998 to act as an uncensored version of its mirror paper publication. A part of the *eDodo* website, called "The Rumor Mill", is an internet message forum which acts as a gathering place for graduates, current cadets, and friends (and enemies) of the Academy. Personnel who frequented the board signed their posts anonymously using unique monikers akin to call signs. This endnote, and remaining endnotes referencing *eDodo*, originated in the *eDodo* message forum. This comment is from a U.S. Military Academy graduate who participated in the message forum on a regular basis.

27. Ibid., 18 Dec 2008. This story came from a 2006 graduate who explained the transformational leadership style demonstrated by his AOC.

28. Interview conducted by the author with Colonel L.C. Coffey, 14 January, 2009. Colonel Coffey spent more than a decade of his career at USAFA working as a Group Air Officer Commanding, an instructor on the Dean of Faculty's Staff, and on the USAFA Headquarters staff as the Aide-de-Camp to the Superintendent.

29. Ibid.

30. Ibid.

31. Reichers, Wanuous and Austin, 1997, 53.

32. The Risner Trophy is an award for outstanding tactical fighter aircrew members. The annual award recipient is a graduate of the USAF Weapons Instructor Course (WIC) who is voted by a board of WIC squadron commanders as the top graduate for that year, based upon actions and accomplishments in the year following course graduation.

33. Interview conducted by the author with Major Michael Drowley, AOC, CS15, 4 February 2009.

34. Ibid, 53.

35. Ibid, 54.

36. Anonymous, *Attacking Cynicism at USAFA - 18 Dec 2008*, retrieved on 15 May 2012 from <www.edodo.org/rm>. Multiple users, on this topic of institutional cover-ups, provided commentary regarding the lack of communication from USAFA leadership and the perceived inability to deal with past issues in a timely manner.

37. Col (ret) Hector A. Negroni, *Attacking Cynicism at USAFA - 2 Oct 08*, retrieved on 15 May 2012 from<www.edodo.org/rm>. Col (ret) Negroni was the first Puerto Rican graduate of USAFA (Class of 1961) and was a founding member of the USAFA Association of Graduates.

38. Interview conducted by the author with Colonel L.C. Coffey, 14 January, 2009.

39. This represents the author's personal experience, Dodo Editor 1995-1996.

40. George E. Yoos, "The Rhetoric of Cynicism", *Rhetoric Review*, Vol. 4, No. 1 (1985), 59.

41. United States Air Force Academy, *Air Force Academy Strategic Vision, 2008-2013*, (US Air Force Academy: 2007).

CHAPTER 10

Military Professionalism of the Swedish Armed Forces in the 21st Century

Dr. Sofia Nilsson
Emma Jonsson, MA
Maria Fors Brandebo, MA
Dr. Gerry Larsson*

INCENTIVES FOR TRANSFORMATION AND PROFESSIONALIZATION

The West-European Armed Forces

At the beginning of the 21st century, the world order became increasingly challenged as global structures and transnational flows have brought forth new demands that pose threats to stability. The emergent and increasingly complex threat scenario has altered conditions for nation states and their relations with foreign powers, a development that has changed the overall societal/social, technological, economic and geopolitical contexts.[1] Globalization is one factor that is claimed to be a strong influential factor behind recent transformations of the West-European armed forces. In fact, Michael Moore, a former manager at the Department of Strategy at the Swedish Armed Forces (SAF), stated that the globalization effect on military organizations would be enormous:[2]

> The demand for change is claimed to be influenced by several factors: The technique, the threats, the surrounding world and our altered political view and ambition. It is difficult to point to one specific factor as most important but taken together, the effect is enormous. The change has resulted in the armed forces becoming a mission- and competence-oriented defense [authors' translation].

Military sociologists Haltiner and Klein discuss the development of the European states since the 1990s and the effect it had on the transformation of military organizations, in particular the end of conscription in favour of all-

---

* The views expressed in this chapter are those of the authors and do not necessarily reflect those of the Department of Security, Strategy and Leadership or the Swedish Armed Forces.

SWEDEN

volunteer forces (AVF).[3] The reform in the first half of the 1990s is referred to as the "downsizing wave." This period was characterized by the prompt downsizing in military personnel and material as well as shortened military service. In the second half of the 1990s, NATO "oriented phase of inter-nationalism and professionalization" occurred, which was characterized by international cooperation. During this period, multinational units became a common element of the western European armed forces. Arguments for joint military efforts included, for example, the difficulty experienced by single nation states in handling transnational challenges and threats on their own,[4] while at the same time managing reductions in public expenditures.[5] Accordingly, there were strategic advantages to be gained through coalition and alliance operations;[6] military presence in conflict areas was assumed to contribute to national security. For a long time, Sweden had been relatively sheltered from security alliances, however, it now became an actor within the supranational framework of the UN, a member of the European Union (EU), and a partner country of the NATO. The third reform, "the wave of modularization and flexibilization," can be seen as an aftermath of 11 September 2001,[7] which was characterized by an additional increase in both professionalization and international participation by the European armed forces.[8] During this time period, conscripts became more and more used as a reserve pool. Professionalism developed to be the standard in Europe while nation states that continue to cling to the conscript based system were exceptions to the rule.

Apart from the historical approach to the transformation of the European armed forces, crucial incentives have also been explained in terms of soci-etal/social, technological, economic and geopolitical changes,[9] which partly overlap with the three reform waves presented above. The societal/social driving forces are asserted to concern factors such as individualization and differentiation or changes in values. For example, it is claimed that young people are no longer interested in the armed forces. Due to modernization, specialization and professionalization, there was also greater demand for militaries to have personnel with special qualifications, and consequently the specialists increased in number at the expense of the conscripts. For example, technological driving forces replaced some competencies, which accounted for a reduced officer corps and undermined the need for a conscript-based system. Additionally, economic motives hastened the development toward an AVF as military organizations have continually been subject to cut-backs (i.e., reduced personnel requirements require less conscripts). Geopolitical driving forces are also claimed to be important in understanding the trans-formation of the European defence organizations. After the end of the Cold

War, the threat panorama diminished and consequently, military organizations adopted a new profile that emphasized peacekeeping operations abroad and increased international cooperation which, in turn, has brought additional prerequisites for the transformation to AVFs. For example, compared to a conscript-based system, the AVF obliges and consequently guarantees military personnel to serve in international operations.

In spite of the recent changes presented above, it should be noted that the transformation of defence organizations to AVFs was initiated long before the end of the Cold War. However, the conscript-based forces were particularly questioned and put to the test in the first half of the 1990s.[10] The United States of America (USA) abandoned the conscript system in 1973, which further affected the transformation of European defence organizations. With regard to the Swedish armed forces, professionalism is strongly associated with the notion of an AVF.[11]

This chapter draws upon the aforementioned changes by emphasizing the transformation of the SAF from a conscript-based system to an AVF and the resulting subsequent consequences from a military professionalism perspective. That many defence organizations that have been subject to organizational changes have experienced problems that, for example, concern the possibility to recruit sufficient numbers of individuals without a reduction in quality,[12] the aim of this chapter is to develop a deeper understanding of potential threats to the military professionalism of the SAF.

The Swedish Armed Forces

For over 100 years Sweden had a compulsory conscript system for men. The vast majority of them went through eleven months of military training. After the end of the Cold War, the SAF downsized and the number of conscripts and employees decreased significantly and rapidly. In July 2010, Sweden officially abolished the conscript system in favour of an AVF. This was the final step of a long process.

When the Swedish government presented "The New Defence" in 1999,[13] they argued that international developments required the SAF to re-organize to better adapt to the new demands, as well as the requirement to act at all levels of conflict, both nationally and internationally. The SAF transformed from an invasion-based defence (i.e., from defending national territory and preparing for an invasion), to a mission-oriented defence that emphasized international engagement. It was stated that the mission-oriented defence should be usable, accessible and flexible,[14] which also had implications for the personnel staffing system. Today, all categories of personnel apply voluntarily and enter the SAF in a standardized way, independent of position. After a selection process is completed, all recruits complete a common three-month basic training course. After this, the graduating recruits can apply for a military position in the SAF or for the officer education training (for example, a three-year academic education).

The conscript system was viewed as a guarantor for the Swedish defence as it had been firmly established among the public and viewed as a national affair[15] by guaranteeing social representativeness.[16] As such, one of the fears related to the transformation of the SAF was that it could create a greater distance between the Swedish people and the SAF.

Common problems for countries that have switched to AVFs are personnel supply and recruiting sufficient numbers of individuals without a reduction in quality.[17] The recruitment of specialists, retention of personnel and competition with the civil labour market have shown to be problematic.[18] These implications tend to be discovered a few years after the actual shift from a conscript system to an AVF.[19] The transformation of the SAF is still in its infancy, however, recruitment during the first year has shown positive results in terms of quantity concerning physiological and psychological qualities.[20]

THE CONSTRUCT OF PROFESSIONALISM

It was noted above that professionalism is strongly associated with the notion of an AVF.[21] The Swedish defence organization now states that:

> Joint trained units characterized by high cohesion and professionalism are some of the most important factors required of the SAF to complete their tasks. This needs to be continuously developed [authors' translation].[22]

The discourse of professionalism generally has a positive overtone as it is associated with exclusive ownership of an area of expertise, in addition to autonomy and discretion in work practices and occupational control of work.[23] In keeping with this, Sociologist Eliot Freidson suggests that professionalism comprises:

> Exclusive ownership of an area of expertise and knowledge, power to define the nature of problems in that area as well as the control of possible solutions, an image of collegial work relations of mutual assistance and support rather than organizational hierarchical, competitive or managerialist control, autonomy in decision-

making, discretion in work practices, and decision-making in the public interest unfettered only marginally by financial constraints, and in some cases, even self-regulation or the occupational control of the work.[24]

Sociologist Magali Sarfatti Larson is more concise when referring to professionalism as "the monopoly of competence legitimized by officially sanctioned "expertise," and a monopoly of credibility with the public."[25]

The positive overtone in military circles regarding the academization of the officer profession, could in one respect, be considered as a too late awakening. By this we do not imply a criticism of academization as such. On the contrary, we agree with all those who see this as a natural and necessary development. However, looking at the concept of professionalism more generally, the position of classical professions has been weakened. Through processes such as globalization, work standardization, financial control, the use of targets and performance indicators, etc., a process that has been labeled "proletarianization of the professions," appears to be universally ongoing.[26]

With regard to most European countries, there are specific conditions of relationships between the profession and the state which are assumed to make for a different course of professionalization and professional activity. Here, the state has both an active and influential role by being the professions' prime employer. For example, the state controls the instruments for legitimization and financial and institutional support.[27] These conditions are, in many ways, in a state of opposition to the aforementioned characteristics associated with professionalism. On such comprehensions, sociologist Julia Evetts challenges professionalism "as we know it" with regard to military organizations in European countries by stating that:

> It seems that the reality of the discourse of professionalism in the armed forces includes budgetary constraints and financial cutbacks; strict control of armaments and equipment costs; a decrease in numbers of personnel which at times is a more highly trained and disciplined work force; an increase in organizational features in the military which influence an increase in bureaucracy, managerialism, accountability and audit; an enlarged and expanded role, which includes global policeman alongside defensive and offensive combatant functions; and an international, as well as a national, identity to make more efficient organizational use of scarce defence resources.[28]

SWEDEN

Professor Harries-Jenkins similarly questions the ideal-type of professionalism as an analytical tool for understanding military professionalism. The author argues that since the military is both a highly bureaucratized and professionalized occupational group, thus a classical example of the ideal-type bureaucratic model, it needs to also be approached in terms of an ideal-type bureaucracy.[29] Both authors see a need to contemplate the fusion of profession and organization to assess military professionalism (i.e., institutional and practitioner professionalism).[30]

In keeping with the aforementioned approaches to professionalism, one key set of indicators refers to the state of the profession's relations with "the client," which in the case of the SAF, ought to be defined as the Swedish society. It is argued that "lay people must place their trust in professional workers" while "professionalism requires professionals to be worthy of that trust, to maintain confidentiality and conceal such [guilty] knowledge by not exploiting it for evil purposes. In return for professionalism in client relations, professionals are rewarded with authority, privileged rewards and higher status."[31] Likewise, for the military to enjoy military professionalism, the importance of "the relationship of the military and the individual to the society or culture at large"[32] must be understood. On the basis of such theoretical comprehensions, it is suggested that the phenomenon of military professionalism depends, among other things, on public support. Bearing in mind the officially sanctioned or legitimate right to use force, this should particularly hold true for the ideal-type bureaucratic model of the defence organization.

Another key set of indicators of professionalism, as presented above, comprises the notion of "monopoly of competence legitimized by officially sanctioned 'expertise.'"[33] It should be noted that the ideal-type model of a professional military holds that combat, or the management of violence, constitutes the core element of military competence and expertise. Some scholars direct criticism toward such a definition; they believe that it points to a conceptual problem, since combat or the management of violence is only part of the military task.[34] However, from a military professionalism perspective, we argue that one cannot disregard that the uniqueness of military competence and expertise comprises the practice of combat. If one undermines the uniqueness of military capability in the discussion of military professionalism, the military no longer fulfills the criteria of being a profession. Hence the discussions of this chapter would be needless.

In keeping with the above reasoning, this chapter will put emphasis on public support, as well as the monopoly of competence and expertise of the SAF to scrutinize potential threats toward the military professionalism of the SAF. It is assumed that lack of public support and decline in the monopoly of competences and expertise might eventually threaten military professionalism. Thus, we emphasize the professional characteristics of the officer corps while considering both profession and bureaucratization in the analysis of military professionalism.

PUBLIC SUPPORT

Recent Trends

Due to the aforementioned societal/social, technological, economic and geopolitical changes and the subsequent transformation of the SAF, it is argued that public support of defence-related issues can no longer be taken for granted. Researchers at the Swedish National Defence College (SNDC), Jonsson, Nilsson and Larsson, have made an attempt to understand attitudes among, or the opinion of, the Swedish population with regard to defence-related issues and the SAF (see Figure 10.1). It should be noted that public opinion refers to the local, regional and national anchoring of the SAF in Swedish society.

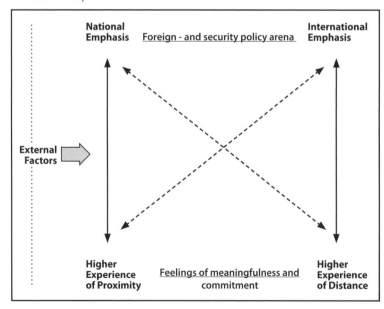

Figure 10.1: Theoretical model of central conditions behind public opinion of the armed forces.[35]

SWEDEN

These researchers suggested that there are three main areas of importance for understanding the public opinion of the SAF:

- the foreign and security policy arena;
- the individual citizen's feelings of meaningfulness of, and commitment to, defence-related issues; and
- external factors.[36]

The top axis of Figure 10.1 shows the security policy arena in which the SAF acts, ranging from a national to an international focus. The bottom axis presents the individual citizen's feelings of meaningfulness of, and commitment to, the SAF, ranging from higher experience of proximity to higher experience of distance. External factors are suggested to be central in determining how the public interprets the importance of the military organization. These external factors are continuously subject to change and consequently affect both the SAF's emphasis and individuals' feelings of meaningfulness of, and commitment to, the military organization. External factors might comprise peace, crisis, war, whether there is a threat panorama or not, and clarity of the threat. Other external factors that might affect the perception of the SAF are history as well as socio-economic conditions. For example: during a financial crisis, individuals tend to be more occupied with matters other than defence-related issues.

Jonsson et al., also identify favourable and unfavourable conditions for public support (see Figure 10.2). Typically, a national emphasis is related to the individual experiencing higher proximity to defence-related issues while an international focus relates to individuals' experiencing higher distance. However, this need not be the case, as a person might work within the SAF and thus have personal relations to the organization whereupon he/she might experience proximity to the military organization in spite of an international emphasis.[37]

		Defence and Security Policy Arena (SAF)	
		National Emphasis	International Emphasis
Feelings of Meaningfulness	Higher Experience of Proximity	+/+ (1)	+/- (2)
	Higher Experience of Distance	-/+ (3)	-/- (4)

Figure 10.2: Favourable (+) and unfavourable (-) conditions for public opinion of the armed forces.[38]

In terms of Swedish conditions, as based on Figure 10.2, public opinion of the SAF has been reasonably favourable due to the notion that the Swedish welfare state and the conscript system gave most citizens a direct or indirect relation to the military organization during the postwar period until the late 1990s. The military has been present and active in society while, up to 1996, a majority of young men were selected for compulsory military service. The SAF did then guarantee a social representation of all (men) in society. Consequently, the SAF is assumed to have enjoyed regional/national support for a considerable amount of time due to the "man in the street" having experienced the mental and physical proximity to and feelings of meaningfulness and commitment with regard to the military organization.

Ever since the transformation of the SAF into a mission-oriented force, the international emphasis of military commitment has increased. Today, the military task comprises operations abroad to a greater extent. There is also research that shows how the Swedish defence and security policy arena demands new solutions to secure what is referred to as "common security," which has increased the importance of the United Nations, European Union and North Atlantic Treaty Organization. In parallel with a greater emphasis on global perspectives, the importance of the nation state as an international actor has diminished. Additionally, and as noted above, the SAF has been considerably downsized, which means that fewer citizens experience a natural relation with the military. This development has reduced the visibility of the SAF in society and resulted in less attention, meaning the SAF is perceived as less important in people's day-to-day lives. Today, Swedish citizens in general, appear to lack an opinion on defence-related issues or no longer consider national security a priority, a trend of growing indifference that is noticeable in most European states. For this reason, former favourable conditions for public support appear to have declined.

In keeping with Figure 10.2, it appears that conditions for public opinion of the SAF during the past decades have moved from box one toward box two. It is too early to determine whether this path might continue toward the most unfavourable conditions for public opinion (box four; conditions characterized by an international emphasis and citizens experiencing higher distance to the military organization).[39]

There are studies that show attitude changes of defence- and security-related issues of the SAF. For example, there was a general decline in the Swedish citizens' confidence in public authorities in the beginning of the 21st century,[40] and of these, the military organization is among those that suffered

SWEDEN

the greatest decline in public support.[41] However, one is cautioned not to interpret the drop in confidence as an increase in distrust. Citizens are most likely not distrustful, rather, they are not concerned by authorities such as the military organization.[42]

The above-presented trend of declining public support of the SAF is supported by public opinion surveys which demonstrate that there are just as many Swedish citizens that lack interest in defence-related issues as those that are interested; many state that they have "a very little interest" in defence-related questions. In general, national defence is perceived as being much less important than, for example, education, health or nursing. One explanation might be that defence-related issues no longer concern the man in the street. Such trends are supported by the fact that close to a third (29 percent) of the Swedish population lacks an opinion of the national defence policy, approximately a fifth (22 percent) lack an opinion of whether it is right or wrong to send forces to international operations, and almost half (47 percent) lack an opinion of the scope of international commitment. It is debatable whether such an absence of opinion is based on a lack of interest, ignorance, or both. In any case, it appears that there is a wide body of opinion that believes that national security is no longer an issue of great importance.[43]

Confidence and Credibility

It was noted above that professionalism comprises "a monopoly of credibility with the public."[44] Jonsson, Nilsson and Larsson[45] examined the Swedish public's confidence in the SAF, the SAF's credibility in society, the public's willingness to show commitment for security and defence-related issues, and the public's view of the SAF as a relevant societal function.[46] The results of this empirical interview study showed that public support for military organizations is on the decline. For example, having knowledge of the SAF is central to an understanding of the military organization which, in turn, is necessary as an informative basis for having or not having confidence in the military. However, the picture of Swedish citizens' knowledge of, and confidence in, the SAF stands out as somewhat complex. When specifically asked, the respondents considered themselves to have a thorough and satisfying knowledge of, and thus sufficient insight into, the SAF. However, follow-up questions showed that such knowledge and understanding tended to be rather limited, traditional, and stereotyped whereas younger respondents seemed to lack, to a greater extent, an understanding of the SAF. In keeping with the Swedish National Audit Office's report,[47] Swedish society appears to perceive the relevance of the SAF as relatively unclear.

In a similarly ambiguous manner, many respondents stated that they have confidence in the way the SAF manages its tasks and for those working within the military organization. Nevertheless, many perceived a discrepancy between what the SAF in fact does and what they expect the SAF to do. Hence, they lack confidence in the SAF task, which points to a credibility gap. Among those that question the SAFs task, the majority wish to see a greater national emphasis.

An additional problem that is closely related to the credibility of the SAF refers to the *raison d'être* of the Swedish military system. There were many respondents who discuss difficulties in justifying the existence of the military organization as there are no perceived immediate threats. The inability to see a clear purpose for the national defence once more raises the question of what the military does, relative to what they ought to be doing in the eyes of the public. Today, the perception is that the SAF concerns only a few citizens (mostly military personnel themselves) and therefore, society lacks commitment to its services. The respondents indicated that they are content with their relation to the military organization even though there is hardly any relation at all. Hence the state of the profession's relation to the Swedish society seems, similarly to the attitude trends presented above, characterized by indifference, potentially moving toward distrust and an increasingly challenged officers' corps as the public questions the very *raison d'être* of the SAF.[48]

Long-Term Value Shifts

There are many studies that illustrate a trend of growing societal indifference toward defence-related issues. In a similar manner, research has shown that in spite of having confidence in the SAF, respondents question the SAF of today in terms of the utility of the military organization, in general, and the military task, in particular.[49] Changes in people's attitudes toward various public phenomena, so-called long-term value shifts, happen slowly and over time. Thus, for a deeper understanding of long-term value shifts in defence-related issues, one needs to examine several periods in history.

In Sweden, older generations grew up during relatively unstable conditions when compared to today. Subsequently, defence-related issues were then a more natural part of everyone's day-to-day lives. The two World Wars were succeeded by the Cold War, a period characterized by power balance and a relatively stable geopolitical context. The Cold War came to an end, whereupon the world picture was altered. These changes gradually reduced the threat to the Swedish nation state and the need for a national defence was no longer as prominent. Obviously, these external conditions challenged the SAF and the transformation of the military organization began in order to meet the challenges of the new world order.

As noted above, research has demonstrated that respondents perceive that the main military task has moved away from the Swedish arena to conflict areas abroad.[50] Additionally, military work is increasingly carried out within military alliances such as the EU, the UN and the NATO, making the SAF no longer an explicitly national phenomenon. This development seems to have created a distance between the SAF and Swedish society. Even so, many respondents are positive toward an international emphasis of the military organization as long as this does not occur at the expense of national military presence and security. The Swedish public needs confirmation that the SAF is of use to Swedish society as it is financed by government revenue. Also, democratic grants set aside for the SAF have been, and are still being reduced, illustrating political prioritizations that, in turn, are thought to indirectly signal the importance and relevance of defence-related activity to the Swedish society. Furthermore, the respondents perceive that the local and regional anchoring of the SAF has diminished due to budgetary constraints since the SAF is no longer as visible in society.

Several respondents indicated that the aforementioned development has gradually led to defence-related issues receiving less attention in political debates while the public opinion has become more or less non-existent. Often, the generally negative media picture of the SAF appears to be the main way the public gets information on the SAF. Additionally, some respondents reported that the new personnel staffing system has reduced the SAF from being a publicly important question to one of concerning only its own personnel. The importance of people's individual experience and relation to the SAF in shaping their attitudes of the military organization has been demonstrated.[51] The relation is no longer being perceived as self-evident, which becomes problematic when it comes to long-term value changes in terms of public support of the SAF.

It appears as if insufficient public control, knowledge and understanding of the SAF have made individuals recognize the military organization as being "confidential and strange." Research has provided , in accordance with the trends presented above, evidence of a growing indifference in society regarding defence-related issues in parallel with a lack of interest and subsequent unwillingness to commit to the military organization.[52]

There appears to have been long-term changes in values from a more materialistic to a more post-materialistic society. Since the 1970s, political scientist

Ronald Inglehart has studied whether generations that have grown up during the postwar period (post-materialists) differ in how they prioritize values as compared to older generations (materialists).[53] Sweden appears to be ahead of other countries regarding this development.[54] A great number of young people (the post-materialist generation) have grown up in a safe and well-off society. To take one's own survival for granted has, in general, shown to affect all aspects of one's own view of life, as compared to those growing up during more insecure and unstable conditions. Inglehart has studied two hypotheses. The first, the scarcity hypothesis, concerns the fact that individual prioritization is influenced by the socioeconomic environment as the individual is prone to ascribe the highest value to things that are perceived as being out of reach. The other, the socialization hypothesis, states that the relation between the socioeconomic environment and prioritization of values is not constant: it evolves over time, with some delay.[55]

The two hypotheses generate a number of predictions when it comes to long-term value shifts. First, changes in values are supposed to take place when older generations in society are replaced by younger generations. Inglehart's studies have shown that value changes are related to generations as one discerns a greater difference between generations than within the lifespan of a person. Individuals tend to stick to their values throughout their life. Inglehart asserts that when generations grow up in the absence of war or direct outer threats to national security, security is more or less taken for granted. This tends to result in the man on the street paying little attention to questions of defence and security.[56] The above cited research on public opinion of the SAF supports Inglehart's hypotheses, as respondents state that they do not to think about questions concerning the SAF (i.e., why they exist, what they do, who works within the military organization, one's own relation to the SAF, etc.,).[57]

There are many that question the younger generations' knowledge of the SAF and whether or not they have an understanding of the value of democracy.[58] The results on Swedish conditions can be explained by a study that shows how questions that concern national security are valued as less important by younger citizens and that there are great differences between the perceptions of younger and older generations.[59] Identified deficiencies regarding knowledge of the SAF among young people might result in an even greater distance between the military organization and society in the future. The older generation differs in that it clings to a more "out of date" picture of the military. These results support the presumptions made in Jonsson et al.'s 2010 study.[60] Both approaches are problematic when it comes to public support of the SAF

SWEDEN

in a long-term perspective and, as a result, for the maintenance and the promotion of military professionalism.

COMPETENCE AND EXPERTISE

Recruitment

Harries-Jenkins states that the professional characteristics of the officer corps do "change over time and are variable in that they encompass norms and skills."[61] Obviously, the transformation of the SAF to an AVF has brought demands for changes in selection procedures to the SAF, as well as changes in the education and training system. As it was assumed that the second key set of indicators of professionalism comprise the notion of a "monopoly of competence legitimized by officially sanctioned 'expertise',"[62] a decline in the monopoly of military competence and expertise of the SAF might, apart from a decline in public support, come to threaten military professionalism.

As mentioned above, Inglehart states that generations that lack firsthand experience of war-like conditions tend to take security for granted.[63] Today, this might be problematic as it has been shown that individuals with an interest in joining the SAF armed forces are not focused on defending security, rather they are increasingly motivated by self-interest. For example, a questionnaire study conducted on units that had served in Afghanistan showed that the main reason for participating in international service was the possibility for personal development.[64] Likewise, an interview study with soldiers and officers that had also served in Afghanistan revealed that there was an obvious lack of altruistic motives.[65] Other studies illustrate that interest in the SAF often is derived from relatives and friends with experience from the armed forces.[66]

In the current volunteer system, the main reason for joining the SAF is stated to be challenges, a prior interest in compulsory military service, and comradeship.[67] This might have implications for military professionalism. During the previous conscript system, officers had eleven months during which they tried to convince competent conscripts to continue within the armed forces after release. In the current system, the basic military training is minimized to three months before individuals are offered employment or officer education training. Military officers state that three months is not enough to get to know their recruits in order to recommend which continued military education and organizational position would be most suited to the recruits.[68] Studies show that one important reason for conscripts continuing within the SAF was, in fact, related to being personally encouraged by an officer.[69] If officers lack personal knowledge of their recruits, this might negatively affect the recruits' motivation to continue within the Armed Forces.

To look at more positive and favourable aspects of the new system, officers state that the new recruits are more motivated as compared to conscripts. They are often carrying out their education at the unit where they will be employed, which facilitates a sense of loyalty and solidarity.[70] Even so, individuals motivated by self-interest might negatively affect the competence of the military profession in the future. Even though the SAF aims at shorter lengths of service (compared to today where there is a surplus of officers in certain categories, like for example, lieutenant-colonels), the turnover might occur too rapidly to guarantee a solid transfer of this foundation of competence. A third of those selected for basic military training expressed an interest in continuing in the armed forces for only three to five years.[71] This in turn can be assumed to affect public support. Future recruits appear to primarily seek excitement and development instead of long-time commitment to serve the nation.

Retention

Statistics from the first year of the volunteer system show that the number of drop-outs from the basic military training varies between ten and 25 percent[72] with an average of 14 percent.[73] Accordingly, it has been fairly easy to recruit new military personnel.[74] However, taking into consideration that individuals often are interested in what is new (read: the AVF), such positive experiences might not continue for future recruitment. It might instead, lead to difficulties in meeting the requirements of recruiting individuals in terms of motives and qualifications.

Concerning physical and psychological qualifications, the majority of drop-outs cited physical problems or injuries as reasons for leaving. Even though recruits met the criteria in selection procedures, many military officers, who are involved in basic military training, are of the opinion that the qualifications are set too low as recruits are often injured. One should bear in mind, however, that the tempo is higher today as compared to when the conscript system was operating. This could mean that recruits might lack the necessary time required to build strength and muscle. However, officers and recruits also noted that it might be easier to blame injuries as a cause of dropping out, rather than admitting motivational issues.[75]

To Serve in International Operations

Today, the international focus of the SAF obliges employees to serve in international operations, or in other words, it presumes individuals are willing to serve abroad. Consequently, individuals seeking excitement and personal development might strive for frequent operations and come to constitute a

SWEDEN

dominant category of those applying to the military in the future. Research has shown that the personal trait of sensation-seeking might affect the degree to which individuals expose themselves to stress,[76] which in turn might result in them exposing themselves, their comrades or perhaps the whole group to dangerous situations and unnecessary risks.[77] Those seeking excitement might also come to be a problem since individual units do not serve abroad annually or even biannually[78] and there is a clear risk of these individuals losing motivation in periods between operations. Officers in the SAF are concerned that this might cause a competitive situation where units with an operation in the near future will recruit employees from other units, leaving the latter with vacancies. Another concern expressed by officers involved in educating the new volunteer soldiers is that soldiers will lose their motivation and quit/leave the armed forces once their operations are accomplished.[79] This might in turn lead to a scarcity of individuals with the necessary experience in international operations.

Between international engagements, the units are in need of joint training. Although permanently employed soldiers should see increased opportunities for joint training, officers in the SAF expressed a concern about defective in-service training when units are decreased, making large-scale training impossible. With the previous conscript system, large batches of conscripts facilitated large-scale training, not only for conscripts, but also for officers at different hierarchical levels.[80]

MILITARY PROFESSIONALISM IN DANGER?

Profession-State Relationships and Public Support

It was assumed that professionalism requires "a monopoly of credibility with the public." On the basis of such theoretical starting points, a decline in public support was suggested to be a threat to military professionalism. Thus it is somewhat ambiguous to find that the societal/social, technological, economic and geopolitical changes that are claimed to have spurred the transformation of the SAF into an AVF and promoted military professionalism appear to be the same factors that challenge military professionalism by eroding prerequisites for public support. So, how is it that recent changes are said to give rise to, as well as have shown to undermine, military professionalism are in parallel? One explanation might be given by the specific course of professionalization and professional activity that it was suggested to have occurred in most European countries.

In keeping with the "specific way of professionalism" in most European countries, politicians have the overall responsibility for the SAF. Principally, politicians manage the SAF by distributing government revenue. As noted above, research has demonstrated that many respondents see a problem in budgetary constraints and financial cutbacks as well as a decrease in personnel numbers, as these hint at the prioritization of the military organization, evincing its societal value from a political perspective.[81] Many respondents accuse politicians of not understanding or taking enough responsibility for the SAF. Additionally, it is felt that defence-related issues are not prioritized and for this reason, they are made invisible in political election campaigns and debates whereupon the military organization receives a continuously smaller amount of the budget. One former Swedish Minister for Defence chose to leave his position as a consequence.[82] Many respondents think that it is socially tolerable to cut-back on defence-related expenses as such reductions in public expenditures do not affect people's private economy. Nonetheless, many feel that politicians lack information on, and insight into, how budgetary constraints and financial cut-backs affect military capability. Respondents show concern for the lack of genuine political support of the SAF, because stability is perceived as vital for a favourable strategic development of military engagement, both nationally and internationally. There is simply no long-term strategy behind decisions and investments when it comes to meeting the needs of the SAF today.

The transformation of the SAF is essentially a result of political decisions (e.g., responses to changes in external factors) that, according to Evetts is constructed and imposed "from above" by politicians and military advisers. Armed forces personnel are thought to grasp the discourse of professionalism since it is perceived to be a way of improving the military occupations' prestige, status and rewards individually and collectively.[83] There are, however, studies that contradict such comprehensions as military personnel are no longer in agreement on what constitutes the main military task and not everybody supports recent organizational changes.[84] Hence, occupational changes appear to have created an identity crisis within the military organization that is expressed as forms of discontent perceived particularly by the older and more experienced groups of workers.[85] In turn, a lack of internal legitimacy has proven to impede the quest for external legitimacy.[86]

In keeping with the aforementioned discussion, it appears that the state has brought constraints onto the military organization by eroding prerequisites for military professionalism instead of facilitating recent changes with regard to the same. This line of reasoning implies that the discourse of professionalism itself is not only an attempt to rationalize organizational change, but that things have even reached such a state that it threatens military professionalism from both within and without the military organization. Subsequently, it appears that politicians have succeeded in motivating neither the international emphasis of military commitment nor the transformation of a conscript-based system to an AVF.[87] Evetts notes that "the reconstitution of employees as professionals involves more than just a process of re-labeling."[88]

Both Evetts and Harries-Jenkins suggested a slightly different approach to military professionalism as they perceive the ideal-type model of professionalism to be inadequate for assessing military professionalism. Harries-Jenkins notes that "a critical evaluation of the postulated characteristics of military professionalism against the ideal-type model leads to the conclusion that armed forces are currently undergoing a measure of de-professionalization."[89] Such assumptions make the author "doubt upon the validity of previously formulated theoretical constructs."[90] However, if military professionalism is approached as a "total fusion of profession and organization," this acknowledges the specific state-profession relationship; it appears that potential threats to military professionalism persist. The state has been shown to use the instruments of legitimization and financial and institutional support to address recent external changes and to promote the transformation of the SAF. Such changes seem essential and justified from both a profession and organization perspective. However, it appears similarly problematic from both perspectives that the state refrains from employing the same instrument to adhere to the potential threats toward military professionalism that have shown to arise during the course of the recent transformation.

In spite of potential threat to military professionalism, research has demonstrated that the majority of respondents are concerned with prevailing budgetary constraints and financial cut-backs, since the military organization is perceived to be the ultimate guarantor of Swedish democracy.[91] Accordingly, respondents appear somewhat undetermined with regard to their attitudes towards the SAF. Thus, creating and maintaining military professionalism appears to be a matter of politicians considering the public's standpoints and needs by framing and communicating the *raison d'être* for the SAF in the context of today while, at the same time, providing supportive measures in the process of organizational change to meet external demands, among themselves, the public, and those working within the military organization.

Monopoly of Military Competence and Expertise

An additional key element of professionalism was ascribed to ensuring that training and education in the armed forces meet the need for having properly qualified and experienced personnel capable of carrying out defence policy requirements.[92] In keeping with this, it was assumed that a decline in the monopoly of competences and expertise might come to threaten military professionalism.

Experiences from the SAF's first year as an AVF show positive results, even though there might be problems with regard to both previous experience (individuals with no prior experience of international operations or national military service) and the quality of future military personnel. Considering that the management of violence is a core element in military professionalism, by extension this might, if we bring matters to a head, result in the abuse of this management due to inexperienced and untrained individuals.[93] Exploiting knowledge and expertise for "evil purposes" would most certainly come to threaten society's confidence in the military professional workers which, in turn would erode military professionalism further.

Throughout this chapter, technological incentives have been brought forward as factors that have spurred the transformation of the SAF into an AVF. As there is an increasing need for technological expert competence within the SAF, some scholars[94] note that "the armed forces are experiencing a long-term transformation toward convergence with civilian structures and norms [...] military skills have become more socially represented."[95] Seen strictly from a military professionalism perspective, it appears that one, on the basis of such comprehensions, is no longer in a state to talk about a monopoly of competence legitimized by officially sanctioned expertise which theoretically was defined as a requirement for military professionalism. However, in parallel, there appears to be a reverse process taking place in the core area dealing with combat tasks. For example, military sociologists Haltiner and Klein noted that:

> The actual military combat capability is concentrated in a downsized organizational nucleus. This creates the paradox that with the increasing civilianization and economization of the military, a reverse process is taking place in the core area dealing with combat tasks. The combat core of the military is undergoing a remilitarization and the combat soldier's role-definition is newly discussed and promoted. Military professionalism is becoming the measure of all thinking and acting, the importance of military functional imperatives, as opposed to socio-economic ones, is again stressed, and allegedly perceptual military virtues are revitalized.[96]

It is too early, however, to say whether the above-mentioned development is "simply a tolerable compensatory strategy of traditionally combat-oriented military domains" or whether we are dealing with a "politically not altogether harmless – counter-cultural isolationistic tendency."[97] In any case, convergence with civilian structures and norms might erode the monopoly of military competence and expertise, thus threatening military professionalism. Combined with the general trend of a weakening of the classical professions, it could be predicted that the future status of the officer profession will be reduced.[98]

CONCLUDING REMARKS

This chapter has drawn upon recent societal/social, technological, economic and geopolitical changes by emphasizing the transformation of the SAF from a conscript-based force to an AVF and its subsequent consequences from a military professionalism perspective. The particular emphasis has been to develop a deeper understanding of potential threats to the military professionalism of the SAF. It was hypothesized that a decline of public support and a weakened monopoly of military competence and expertise would threaten military professionalism. In the case of the SAF, public support for the SAF has shown to be in decline while problems related to the introduction of an AVF and its effects on military competence and expertise, as encountered by other European armed forces, are still difficult to foresee. However, it appears that there is a need to address and assess future military professionalism with regard to the SAF as the military organization constitutes the utmost guarantor of Swedish democracy. The state-profession relationships would gain by political action that promotes not only the transformation, but also the adaptation, of the SAF to external factors on the basis of military professionalism.

ENDNOTES

1. Karl Haltiner and Paul Klein, "The European Post-Cold War Military Reforms and their Impact on Civil-Military Relations", in Frans Kernic, Paul Klein and Karl Haltiner, eds., *The European Armed Forces in Transition: A Comparative Analysis* (Frankfurt am Main: Peter Lang, 2005), 9-30.; Tibor Szvircsev Tresch, *Europas Streitkräfte im Wandel: Von der Wehrpflichtarmee zur Freiwilligenstreitkraft – Eine empirische Untersuchung europäischer Streitkräfte 1975 bis 2003* [The European Armed Forces in Change: From Conscript Based Armies to All-Volunteer Forces – One Empirical Study of the European Armed Forces 1975 to 2003] (Zürich: Faculty of Arts, University of Zürich, 2005).

2. Michael Moore, *Nu har vi ett unikt tillfälle att ställa om det svenska försvaret* [Now We Have a Unique Opportunity to Transform the Swedish Defence], FOA-tidningen, No. 6 (1999). Note: Today, Michael Moore is a Major-General in the Swedish Armed Forces, holding a leader position at the Unit for Military Capabilities and Operations at the Ministry of Defence since September 1st, 2010.

3. Karl Haltiner and Paul Klein, 2005.

4. Michael Moore, *Försvar i Förändring* [Defence in Change] (Stockholm: The Ministry of Defence, 2003).

CHAPTER 10

5. Swedish Ministry of Defence, *Ett användbart Försvar* [A Usable Defence], Prop 08/09:140 (Stockholm: The Ministry of Defence, 2009).

6. Keith Stewart, Hannah Clarke, Peter Goillau, Neil Verrall and Marc Widdowson, *Non-technical Interoperability in Multinational Force*, paper submitted to the 9th International Command and Control Research and Technology Symposium: The Power of Information Age Technologies (Hampshire: Defence Scientific and Technical Laboratory (dstl) and QinetiQ plc, 2004).

7. Tibor Szvircsev Tresch and Karl Haltiner, "New Trends in Civil-Military Relations: The Decline of Conscription in Europe", in Alice Weibull and Bengt Abrahamsson, eds., *The Heritage and the Present – From Invasion Defence to Mission Oriented Organization* (Karlstad: The Swedish National Defence College, Department of leadership and management, 2008), 169-188.

8. Karl Haltiner and Paul Klein, 2005.

9. Tibor Szvircsev Tresch and Karl Haltiner, 2008.

10. Rafael Ajangiz, "The European Farewell to Conscription?", in Lars Mjoset and Sephen Van Holde, eds., *The Comparative Study of Conscription in the Armed Forces* (Oxford: Elsevier Science, 2002), 330-333.; Karl W. Haltiner, "The Definite End of the Mass Army in Western Europe?", *Armed Forces and Society*, Vol. 16 (1998), 329-350.; Jaques van Doorn, "The Decline of the Mass Army in the West – General Reflections", *Armed Forces and Society*, Vol. 1 (1975), 147-157.

11. See for example, Julia Evetts, "Explaining the Construction of Professionalism in the Military: History, Concepts and Theories", *Revue Française de Sociologie*, Vol. 4 (2003/4), 759-776.

12. See for example, Regina L. Hindelang, Michael J. Schwerin and William L. Farmer, "Quality of Life (QOL) in the U.S. Marine Corps: The Validation of a QOL Model for Predicting Reenlistment Intentions", *Military Psychology*, Vol. 16, No. 1 (2004), 115-134.; Eva Johansson, *The Unknown Soldier: A Portrait of the Swedish Peacekeeper at the Threshold of the 21st Century* (Karlstad: Karlstad University Press, 2001).; James A. Knowles, Greg H. Parlier, Gregory C. Hoscheit, Rick Ayer, Kevin Lyman and Robert Fancher, "Reinventing Army Recruiting", *Interfaces*, Vol. 32, No. 1 (2002), 78-92.; René Moelker, "Restructuring and Resilience: Cadet's Opinions on their Future Profession in a Perpetually Changing Organization: The Dutch organization", in Frans Kernic, Paul Klein and Karl Haltiner, eds., *The European Armed Forces in Transition* (Frankfurt am Main: Peter Lang, 2005), 45-64.; Rudy Richardson, Desiree Verweij and Donna Winslow, "Moral Fitness for Peace Operations", *Journal of Political and Military Sociology*, Vol. 32, No.1 (2004), 99-113.; Johan Österberg and Emma Jonsson, "Recruitment to International Military Service: The Officers' View", in Gerhard Kümmel and Joseph Soeters, eds., *New Wars, New Militaries, New Soldiers? Conflicts, the Armed Forces and the Soldierly Subject* (Bingley, UK: Emerald, in press).

13. Swedish Ministry of Defence, *Det nya försvaret* [The New Defence], Prop. 1999/2000:30 (1999).

14. Swedish Ministry of Defence, 2009.

15. Swedish Ministry of Defence, *Totalförsvar i förnyelse - etapp 2* [Total Defence in Renewal – Stage 2], Prop. 96/97:4 (1996).

16. Emma Jonsson, *Erfarenheter avseende personalförsörjning från länder som övergått från pliktbaserat till frivilligbaserat försvar* [Experiences Relating to Recruitment of Personnel From Countries that have made the Transition From a Force Based on Conscription to an All-Volunteer Force] (Karlstad: Swedish National Defence College, Department of Leadership and Management, 2009).

17. Ibid.; See for example, Miepke Bos-Bakx and Joseph Soeters, "The professionalization of the Netherlands' Armed Forces", in Marjan Malešič, ed., *Conscription vs All-Volunteer Forces in Europe* (Baden-Baden: Nomos Verlagsgesellschaft, 2003), 83-99.; Regina L. Hindelang, Michael J. Schwerin and William L. Farmer, 2004.; James A. Knowles, Greg H. Parlier, Gregory C. Hoscheit, Rick Ayer, Kevin Lyman and Robert Fancher, 2002.; René Moelker, 2005.; Rudy Richardson, DesireeVerweij and Donna Winslow, 2004.; Johan Österberg and Emma Jonsson (in press).

18. See for example, Miepke Bos-Bakx and Joseph Soeters, 2003.; John Eighmey, "Why do Youth Enlist? Identification of Underlying Themes", *Armed Forces & Society,* Vol. 32, No. 2 (2006), 307-328.; Regina L. Hindelang, Michael J. Schwerin and William L. Farmer, 2004.; Henrik Jedig Jørgensen and Henrik Ø Breitenbauch, *What If We Gave Up Conscription?* (Copenhagen: Dansk Institut for Militær Studier. Danish Institute for Military Studies, 2009).; Emma Jonsson, 2009.; Philippe Manigart, "Risks and Recruitment in Postmodern Armed Forces: The Case of Belgium", *Armed Forces & Society,* Vol. 31, No. 4 (2005), 559-582.; Tibor Szvircsev Tresch, "Challenges in the Recruitment of Professional Soldiers in Europe", *Strategic Impact,* Vol. 3 (2008), 78-86.; Tibor Szvircsev Tresch, "Recruitment of Military Professionals by European All-Volunteer Forces as Exemplified by Belgium, the Netherlands, and Slovenia", in Tibor Szvircsev Tresch and Christian Leuprecht, eds., *Europe Without Soldiers? Recruitment and Retention Across the Armed Forces of Europe* (Montreal and Kingston: Queen's Policy Studies Series, McGill-Queen's University Press, 2010), 145-164.; Johan Österberg and Emma Jonsson, (in press).

19. See for example, Philippe Manigart, 2005.; Emma Jonsson, 2009.; Tibor Szvircsev Tresch, 2010.

20. Emma Jonsson, Berit Carlstedt and Eva Johansson, "Outcomes of Soldier Recruitment to the Swedish Armed Forces After the End of Conscription", in Philippe Manigart, Chair, *The Impact of Demographic Change on the Recruitment and Retention of Personnel in European Armed Forces* (Session conducted at the Inter-University Seminar on Armed Forces and Society, Chicago, October, 2011).

21. See for example, Julia Evetts, 2003/4.

22. The Swedish Armed Forces, *Försvarsmaktens uppdrag* [The assignment of the Armed Forces] (2012), retrieved on 7 February 2012 from <http://www.forsvarsmakten.se/sv/Om-Forsvarsmakten/uppdrag/>.

23. Julia Evetts, 2003/4.

24. Eliot Freidson, "Occupational Autonomy and Labor Market Shelters", in Phyllis L. Stewart and Muriel G. Cantor, eds., *Varieties in Work* (Beverly Hills, CA: Sage, 1982), 39-54. The excerpt was retrieved from: Julia Evetts, 2003/4, 771.

25. Magali Sarfatti Larson, *The Rise of Professionalism* (California: University of California Press, 1977), 38.

26. Julia Evetts, "A New Professionalism? Challenges and Opportunities", *Current Sociology,* Vol. 59, No. 4 (2011), 406-422.; Daniel Muzio and Ian Kirkpatrick, "Introduction:

Professions and Organizations – A Conceptual Framework", *Current Sociology*, Vol. 59, No. 4 (2011), 389-405.

27. See for example, Anna Bolin, *The Military Profession in Change: The Case of Sweden*, Political studies No. 151 (Lund: Political studies, 2008).

28. Julia Evetts, 2003/4, 771.

29. Gwyn Harries-Jenkins, "The Concept of Military Professionalism", *Defense Analysis*, Vol. 6, No. 2 (1990), 117-130.

30. Ibid.

31. Julia Evetts, 2003/4, 761.

32. Nora K. Stewart, *South Atlantic Conflict of 1982: A Case Study in Military Cohesion - Research report 1949* (Washington, DC: US Army Research Institute for the Behaviour and Social Sciences, 1988).

33. Magali Sarfatti Larson, 1977.

34. Gwyn Harries-Jenkins, 1990.

35. Emma Jonsson, Sofia Nilsson and Gerry Larsson, *Försvarsmaktens folk-och samhällsförankring: Trender, drivkrafter och bakgrundsförhållanden som **kan** påverka det svenska försvarets folk- och samhällsförankring i ett långsiktigt strategiskt perspektiv,* Serie I:61 [The Public Opinion of the Swedish Armed Forces – Trends, Driving Forces, and Basic Conditions That **Can** Influence the Public Support of the Swedish Armed Forces From a Long-Term Strategic Perspective] (Karlstad: Swedish National Defence College, Department of Leadership and Management, 2010).

36. Ibid.

37. Ibid.

38. Ibid.

39. Ibid.

40. Sören Holmberg and Lennart Weibull, "Samlande institutionsförtroende" [Gathering Institutional Trust], in Sören Holmberg and Lennart Weibull", eds., *Ju mer vi är tillsammans* [The More We Are Together], SOM-rapport No. 34 (Gothenburg: SOM-institutet, 2004), 51-74.

41. Sören Holmberg and Lennart Weibull, "Svenskt institutionsförtroende på väg upp igen?" [Swedish Institutional Trust on the Rise Again?], in Sören Holmberg and Lennart Weibull, eds., *Skilda världar* [Separated worlds], SOM-rapport No. 44 (Gothenburg: SOM Institute, 2008), 39-57.

42. Sören Holmberg and Lennart Weibull, 2004, 51-74.

43. The Swedish Civil Contingencies Agency (MSB), *Opinioner 2009. Om allmänhetens syn på samhällsskydd, beredskap, säkerhetspolitik och försvar* [Opinion 2009. About the Public's View on Social Security, Preparedness, Security Policy and Defence], in Sören Holmberg and Lennart Weibull, eds., *Svensk höst. Trettiofyra kapitel om politik, medier och samhälle* [Swedish Autumn. Thirty Four Chapters About Politics, Media and Society], SOM-rapport No. 46 (Gothenburg: SOM Institute, 2009).

44. Julia Evetts, 2003/4.

45. Emma Jonsson, Sofia Nilsson and Gerry Larsson, *Samhället och Försvarsmakten: Försvarsmaktens samhällsförankring i ett långsiktigt strategiskt perspektiv* [The Society and the Armed Forces: The Armed Forces' Achoring in Society from a Long-Term Strategic Perspective], Series I: 71 (Karlstad: Swedish National Defence College, The Department of Leadership and Management, 2011).

46. It should be noted that the Swedish public refers to politicians, representatives for institutions and enterprises at the national and local level.

47. Swedish National Audit Office, *Försvarsmaktens stöd till samhället vid krise* [Defence Force Support for Society During Crises], RiR 2011/15 (Stockholm: Riksdagstryckeriet, 2001).

48. Emma Jonsson, Sofia Nilsson and Gerry Larsson, 2011.

49. Ibid.

50. Ibid.

51. Ibid.

52. Ibid.

53. Ronald Inglehart, "Globlization and Postmodern Values", *The Washington Quarterly*, Vol. 23, No. 1 (1999), 215-228.

54. Ibid.; and Ronald Inglehart, *Modernization and Postmodernization: Cultural, Economic, and Political Change in 43 Societies* (Princeton, NJ: Princeton, U.P, 1991).

55. Ronald Inglehart, *The Silent Revolution: Changing Values and Political Styles Among Western Publics* (Princeton, NJ: Princenton, U.P, 1977).

56. Ronald Inglehart, 1999.

57. Emma Jonsson, Sofia Nilsson and Gerry Larsson, 2011.

58. Ibid.

59. Henrik Oscarsson, "Långsiktiga värdetrender" [Long-Term Value Trends], in Sören Holmberg and Lennart Weibull, eds., *Lyckan kommer, lyckan går* [Happiness Comes, Happiness Goes], SOM-undersökningen No. 36 (Gothenburg: SOM-institutet, 2005), 39-52.

60. Emma Jonsson, Sofia Nilsson and Gerry Larsson, 2010.

61. Gwyn Harries-Jenkins, 1990.

62. Magali Sarfatti Larson, 1977.

63. Ronald Inglehart, 1999.

64. Maria Fors and Gerry Larsson, *Svenska förband i Afghanistan – ledarskap, tillit och motivation* [Swedish Units in Afghanistan – Leadership, Trust and Motivation], PM ILM-K 10-2009 (Karlstad: Swedish National Defence College, Department of Leadership and Management, 2009).

65. Maria Fors and Gerry Larsson, *Den osynliga fienden – IED-attentats påverkan på ledarskap, tillit och motivation* [The Invisible Enemy – IED-Attacks Influence on Leadership, Trust and Motivation], ILM Series I:57 (Karlstad: Swedish National Defence College, Department of Leadership and Management, 2010).

66. Johan Österberg, Emma Jonsson and Peder Hyllengren, *Förhållanden som bidrar till att värnpliktiga jägarsoldater söker internationell tjänst* [Contributing Factors to the Willingness to Apply for International Military Service Among Conscript Army Rangers], ILM Series I:49 (Karlstad: Swedish National Defence College, Department of Leadership and Management, 2008).

67. Claes Wallenius, Aida Alvinius, Maria Fors, Peder Hyllengren, Emma Jonsson, Johan Österberg and Gerry Larsson, *Upplevelser av Grundläggande Militär Utbildning (GMU): Intervjustudie med utbildningsbefäl och rekryter* [Experiences of Basic Military Training (GMU): An Interview Study With Educational Officers and Recruits], Series I:73 (Karlstad: Swedish National Defence College, Department of Leadership and Management, 2011).

68. Ibid.

69. Johan Österberg and Emma Jonsson and Peder Hyllengren, 2008.

70. Ibid.

71. Emma Jonsson, Rose-Marie Lindgren and Gerry Larsson, *Rekryteringsunderlaget 2011: Det första året med ett frivilligbaserat försvar* [Outcomes of Soldier Recruitment to the Swedish Armed Forces 2011: The First Year With an All-Volunteer Force], ILM Series I:70 (Karlstad: Swedish National Defence College, Department of Leadership and Management, 2011).

72. Mikael Holmström, "Var fjärde hoppade av" [One In Four Dropped Out], *Svenska Dagbladet*, (28th January, 2012), retrieved on 7 February 2012 from <http://www.svd.se>.

73. Swedish Armed Forces, *Avgångssamtal rekryter, genomförda under 2011* [Exit Interviews With Recruits, Carried Out During 2011], unpublished paper (2012).

74. Emma Jonsson, Berit Carlstedt and Eva Johansson, 2011.

75. Claes Wallenius, Aida Alvinius, Maria Fors, Peder Hyllengren, Emma Jonsson, Johan Österberg and Gerry Larsson.

76. Yuval Neria, Zahava Solomon, Karni Ginzburg and Rachel Dekel, "Sensation Seeking, Wartime Performance, and Long Term Adjustment Among Israeli War Veterans", *Personality and Individual Differences*, Vol. 29 (2000), 921-932.

77. Claes Wallenius, Curt R. Johansson and Gerry Larsson, "Reactions and Performance of Swedish Peacekeeping Soldiers in Life-Threatening Situations", *International Peacekeeping*, Vol. 9 (2002), 133-152.

78. Note that maximum Operation Tempo is 1:4 for permanent units and 1:7 for contracted units, see for example, Swedish Armed Forces, "Försvarsmaktens inriktning för internationell tjänstgöring avseende personal" [Defence Force Approach to International Service Regarding Personnel], *Försvarsmaktens direktiv 02072010*, HKV beteckning:16 100:60762.

79. Claes Wallenius, Aida Alvinius, Maria Fors, Peder Hyllengren, Emma Jonsson, Johan Österberg and Gerry Larsson, 2011.

80. Ibid.

81. Emma Jonsson, Sofia Nilsson and Gerry Larsson, 2011.

SWEDEN

82. The Minister for Defence Mikael Odenberg (right-wing politician) chose to leave his position the 5th September in 2007.

83. Julia Evetts, 2003/4.

84. Emma Jonsson, Sofia Nilsson and Gerry Larsson, 2011.

85. Julia Evetts, 2003/4.

86. Magnus Peterson, "Defence Transformation and Legitimacy in Scandinavia After the Cold War: Theoretical and Practical Implications", *Armed Forces and Society*, Vol. 37, No. 4 (2011), 701-724.

87. Emma Jonsson, Sofia Nilsson and Gerry Larsson, 2011.

88. Julia Evetts, 2003/4.

89. Gwyn Harries-Jenkins, 1990.

90. Ibid.

91. Emma Jonsson, Sofia Nilsson and Gerry Larsson, 2011.

92. Randall Collins, *The Credential Society* (Orlando, FL: Academic Press, 1979).; Randall Collins, "Crises and Declines in Credential Systems", in Randall Collins, *Sociology Since Midcentury: Essays in Theory Cumulation* (New York, NY: Academic Press, 1979), 191- 215.

93. Claes Wallenius, Aida Alvinius, Maria Fors, Peder Hyllengren, Emma Jonsson, Johan Österberg and Gerry Larsson, 2011.

94. See for example, Gwyn Harries-Jenkins, 1990.; Morris Janowitz, *The Professional Soldier* (New York, NY: Free Press, 1960); Charles C. Moskos, "The Military", *Annual Review of Sociology*, Vol. 2 (1976), 55-77.

95. Gwyn Harries-Jenkins, 1990, 121.

96. Karl Haltiner and Paul Klein, 2005, 24.

97. Ibid.

98. Julia Evetts, 2011.; Daniel Muzio and Ian Kirkpatrick, 2011.

CHAPTER 11

The Dynamic Five-Factor Model as a Compass for Military Professionalism: a Comparison Between Switzerland and the Netherlands

Andres Pfister, PhD
Miriam C. de Graaff, MSc
Marc J. van Gils, MSc*

INTRODUCTION

In this chapter, the current state of affairs regarding the perceived threats to military professionalism in Switzerland and the Netherlands are discussed. It shall offer insights on possible differences and similarities in the perceived threats to military professionalism in two countries that share a comparable culture,[1] are similar in size and economic development, but differ in their military missions as well as the degree of professionalization within their armed forces. Switzerland, for example, still has a conscript army, whereas the Dutch forces transformed into a professional army in 1996.

First, we describe the historical background of both armed forces focusing on two major global changes affecting European armies over the last 30 years (i.e., the end of the Cold War as signified by the fall of the Berlin Wall and the 9/11 attacks on the United States. Second, the concept of military professionalism and what it encompasses will be examined using the approach established by Don Snider and Gayle Watkins and another by Thomas-Durell Young.[2] Third, to have the appropriate framework to understand the possible threats described by Snider and Watkins, we categorized it using the five factors of the Dynamic Five-Factor Model of Leadership developed by Psychologists Stefan Seiler and Andres Pfister.[3] We do not attempt to analyze all possible threats to military professionalism but instead, focus on threats already described in the literature and on threats confronted by both countries. While describing and categorizing the threats, data from two small surveys conducted in both armed forces is presented. Finally, conclusions

---

* The views expressed in this chapter represent those of the authors and do not necessarily reflect those of the Swiss or the Royal Netherlands Armed Forces.

SWITZERLAND & NETHERLANDS

are drawn from these interpretations and the commonalities and differences are discussed between the Dutch (professional) armed forces who deploy to combat zones, and the Swiss (conscript) armed forces, which deploys only to post-conflict areas in peace support operations.

HISTORICAL BACKGROUND OF TWO EUROPEAN MILITARY ORGANIZATIONS

Events taking place in the world have a major influence on defence organizations. After all, these organizations serve society and operate globally. Two events that had a major impact on defence organizations around the world were the fall of the Berlin Wall (1989), which led to the end of the Cold War, and the 9/11 attacks in the United States. These events led to a shift in the focus of military operations in terms of prioritizing terrorist activities. Events like these have changed the habitus of "The Enemy". Conflicts appear to have changed from symmetric to asymmetric, meaning belligerents differ significantly in relative military power, strategy or tactics and exploit each other's weaknesses in order to complete their mission. This is expressed in terrorist attacks and guerilla tactics.

At the end of the Cold War, the Swiss Army Forces had to deal with political and social movements that wanted to abolish the army as a whole. The perceived utility of the armed forces was publicly questioned. The Group for a Switzerland without an Army (GSoA) launched an initiative during the Cold War that was brought to a vote in November 1989. Of the voting population, 35.6 percent wanted a Switzerland without an army. This marked a major turning point for the Swiss Armed Forces, as its goals, size, budget, etc., were widely questioned for the first time. Since then, several political initiatives and referenda which explicitly focused on the armed forces, were cast to a vote.

As a consequence, the Swiss Armed Forces was subjected to two major re-organizations and a massive reduction in size. In the 1980s, there were over 800,000 militia and in 2010 approximately 190,000 remained. Further reductions to around 100,000 are planned in the next few years. Contrary to the reduction of the militia forces, the number of professional officers has doubled in the first years after the millennium. Currently, about 3,750 professional officers form the core of the armed forces. The annual military budget has remained below 10 billion since the end of the Cold War, however, military spending represented 35 percent of the over all federal budget in 1960. Today, it is around 7 percent.[4]

While reducing its size and financial resources, other than its traditional defence of the country position, two further objectives became increasingly important for the Swiss Armed Forces. These included the fostering of peace around the world through international cooperation and assisting Switzerland during disasters (subsidiary missions). After the 9/11 attacks, an additional discussion ensued that focused on the question, is conventional warfare was still applicable to the new terrorist threat? To date, it is not clear for which kind of operations Swiss soldiers should be trained. The discussion as to whether the armed forces have to prepare their personnel for the most probable scenario (i.e., disaster relief, peace support, support of the security organizations within Switzerland), or for the most extreme operations (i.e., country defence in case of a full scale foreign attack), still continues.

During the same period, the Netherlands Armed Forces had also changed. Policy within the Dutch forces was based on the Atlantic framework since the Netherlands has been a part of NATO since 1949. Due to the fall of the Berlin Wall, the "enemy-perception" changed and structural modifications were made. Since 1997, the Royal Netherlands Armed Forces was no longer a conscript Army. In addition, the organization was reorganized dramatically several times. It was divided into four separate "force" departments: Army (land force); Navy (including Marine Corps and the Naval Fleet); Air Force; and the Marechaussee (including Military Police tasks). In addition to these force departments, several civil institutions were established that increased the number of departments within the defence organization to seven. The size of the armed forces was also reduced considerably. From a force of 130,715 in the 1980s (1985: 250,000 when including the reserve component), it was reduced to 109,000 in 1993. Since then, the Dutch defence organization has further down-sized to 75,964 in 1997 (at the beginning of the "professional" non-conscript Army). In 2010, the entire defence organization was approximately 50,000 employees (both military as well as civil support). It is still reducing its numbers.

In the Netherlands, the goals of the defence organization have changed since the end of the Cold War. The organization is now focused on three main goals: 1) protecting the integrity of its own and allied territory; 2) improving international legal order and stability; and 3) supporting civil authorities in law enforcement, disaster relief, and humanitarian aid both in the national as well as the international context. Dutch military performance, since the beginning of the 21st century, is characterized by four features: worldwide, expeditionary, joint, and multinational. This means that military personnel are deployed worldwide, in both humanitarian and combat operations and in international teams in which all the different departments of the defence organization participate.

Like Switzerland, the Royal Netherlands Armed Forces left the traditional notion of being a warfighting or combat force to that of being peace operations and national homeland security. The difference between the Dutch and Swiss forces, however, is that Dutch troops are sent to conflict areas in order to establish or keep peace, whereas the Swiss are only deployed in post-conflict areas where they participate in peacekeeping missions. For this reason, the Dutch Armed Forces are deployed to countries such as Afghanistan, where they run the risk of getting killed or wounded. For example, military operations between 2006 and 2010 in Uruzgan (one of Afghanistan's provinces) and service in the ISAF's Regional Command South, has resulted in twenty-two Dutch fatalities. The developments described above, as well as several others, have changed the view of military professionalism.

WHAT IS MILITARY PROFESSIONALISM?

A profession is not the same as an occupation. Snider and Watkins suggest that the traditional definition of professionalism has two main characteristics that separate professions from occupations,[5] the application of *abstract knowledge* to *specific situations*.[6] Another characteristic of the military profession is the structured way of organizing the occupation, extensive education of its members, the goal of service to society as a whole, and a set of values and shared ethics among the members of the profession.[7]

Snider and Watkins are not alone in studying military professionalism. Others that study this concept have approached it from several perspectives. For example, a historical one, that involves traditional military virtues such as honour and loyalty,[8] or a philosophical one.[9] The concept of normative professionalism,[10] which refers to the competency of individuals to think critically about issues regarding their job assignments; meaning they are able to distinguish moral dilemmas within their professional environment.[11] Others used, like Snider and Watkins, an organizational perspective. For example, Young argues that military professionalism has four components: 1) expertise; 2) responsibility; 3) corporateness; and 4) essential duties.[12] We used these categories to partially describe how the threats mentioned in the following paragraphs could influence military professionalism. To categorize the different threats that are described in the literature or were additionally identified, we build on Snider and Watkins' multi-level approach[13] as well as the dynamic five-factor model proposed by Seiler and Pfister.[14]

DIFFERENT FORMS OF THREATS

Snider and Watkins build on a multi-level conception[15] to categorize threats to professionalism. Essential in this conception, is the use of three perspectives when addressing military professionalism. These include: 1) *the client* (society); 2) *the professional institution* (Armed Forces); and 3) *the professional member* (officer, non-commissioned officer, soldier, army civilian). In addition, Snider and Watkins defined two horizontal boundaries (*civil-military relations* and a*rmed forces-soldier relations*) that divide the three perspectives.[16] Finally, they see a vertical division between these components, defining three main issues that are relevant in each component. These issues are *military-technical* (doctrinal), *moral-ethical* (a matter of institutional values), and *political-social* (a matter of adapting to unhelpful political guidance).

However, the multi-level framework of Snider and Watkins has the shortcoming in that not all threats can be deducted using this approach (e.g., what remains under-represented are the quality of people that are hired, their military education and training, and specific organizational cultures that threaten the individual perception of military professionalism).[17] In order to broaden the scope of threats we combined this categorization with the Seiler and Pfister Dynamic Five-Factor Model of Leadership.[18] This model defines five broad categories that influence leadership behaviour or behaviour in general. Within the Dynamic-Five Factor Model of Leadership, Seiler and Pfister state that 1) the individual's competence, 2) the group/team, 3) the organization, 4) the general context, and 5) the immediate situation will influence leadership behaviour. The three levels described by Snider and Watkins above correspond to the factors of context, organization, and individual competence, but lack the factors group and the immediate situation. As such, it was decided to use these five factors to categorize the possible threats to military professionalism.

SURVEY DATA

In addition to describing the different possible threats, data from a Swiss and Dutch survey completed by military professionals is presented. In this survey, the participants had to rate the perceived impact of the threats that were described. In Switzerland, 14 military professionals having the rank of lieutenant-colonel from different elements of the Swiss Armed Forces completed the survey. In the Dutch Armed Forces, six professionals filled out the questionnaire and another four participated in interview-sessions in which the survey items were transformed into interview questions. The Dutch respondents varied in rank from master sergeant to lieutenant-colonel and two civil servants participated. A five-point scale ranging from 1 (not at all important) to 5 (very important) was used. For each level, the most important threats perceived by the Swiss and Dutch participants are summarized. The survey participants do not represent in size or in rank for the Swiss nor the Dutch Armed Forces. Nevertheless, both samples do provide valuable initial insight into how professionals from both forces perceive different threats to their professionalism. Hence, they provide an overview and a first attempt for evaluating the importance of the different threats presented in this chapter.

INDIVIDUAL LEVEL THREATS

As previously mentioned, military professionalism consists of four key features (i.e., expertise, responsibility, corporateness, and essential duties).[19] Each of these key features face several different threats on the level on the individual military professional.

Expertise

Expertise, for example, is comprised of several different sub-categories such as technical, social, tactical, and training expertise. Deficiencies in any one of these important sub-categories poses a severe threat to the professionalism of the individual. Technical expertise on military weaponry is important[20] as it is the main expertise that differentiates the military profession from other professions. However, technical weapon expertise is not sufficient to ensure military expertise.[21] A military professional also has to know what dangers are faced when using specific military material and know enough about the assets that are under his/her control to be able to effectively put those assets into action.

Social expertise is also important, as military professionals are often in leadership positions in which they are required to act in culturally critical situations (e.g., with the local population in a mission area). Hence, effective command, control, communication and leadership skills are necessary to professionally execute military missions.[22] Besides having the relevant knowledge and skills to work with and motivate subordinates, leaders have to organize the placement of their subordinates in such a way that the right person in the right place at the right time. This requires a considerable amount of planning skills. Military professionals, therefore, need to have sufficient expertise in tactics, operations planning and execution. In its fullest extent, they need the necessary skills to plan and execute military operations in the field while under pressure. Hence, they need experience with the efficient command and control of complex military organizational units. Sufficient tactical and operational proficiency and skills in the formation and management of large military organizational parts,[23] provides the basis for being able to plan large scale operations. Planning and execution, however, has always been accompanied by bureaucracy. According to Young, mastering bureaucracy is a necessary competence as military personnel are part of and are constantly confronted with an enormous amount of bureaucracy.[24] In addition to all these different competencies, which are mission critical, military professionals must have sufficient expertise to train others. Professionals also require sufficient experiences at various organizational levels.[25] This also requires the competency and skill to plan, execute, survey, and ameliorate training for the troops under their command.

Swiss participants saw the lack of individual knowledge and leadership experience at the individual level as a severe threat to military professionalism. According to the Dutch respondents, the lack of training in general poses a severe threat to their professionalism. Consequently, participants from both armies fear that they are not well enough trained in their military skills and drills. Bureaucracy is generally not seen as a large threat by either the Swiss or Dutch force participants.

Responsibility

A military professional is trained in the disciplined application of legal (lethal) force.[26] Therefore, they need to show discipline in order to responsibly operate and manage lethal weapons and equipment. At the same time, operating weapons themselves and leading people who operate such weapons and equipment also requires self-responsibility. Irresponsible behaviour, especially with potentially lethal equipment, was identified as a main threat to professionalism. Besides discipline and self-responsibility, taking social responsibility is just as important.[27] Military professionals, as part of their duty, have to respect the connection between the armed forces and the civil society and fully understand their final objective is to serve the society as a whole. While being a professional, they are at the service of society and therefore have a responsibility to that society. Once assigned to a leadership role, they have to take responsibility for their followers, showing respect, being a good role model and, if needed, intervene if their followers do not act responsibly. They must work and lead professionally, take responsibility, and foster a feeling of corporateness.

The Swiss participants rated lack of responsibility as being important, but it was not seen as a main threat to military professionalism. For the Dutch, they rated responsibility as being high as they believe responsibility for their own troops, as well as for society and the local population in the mission area, is a crucial characteristic for all service members, not only military leaders. The Dutch, like the Swiss, do not consider responsibility as being a major threat to military professionalism.

SWITZERLAND & NETHERLANDS

Corporateness

Corporateness is closely tied to the personal motivation of the individual to serve in the military profession. In fact, corporateness is a positive motivator, apart from gaining new experience, for young recruits.[28] Therefore, motivation to serve and an alignment of the individual with the professional identity of the organization are factors which foster corporateness or an *esprit de corps*. Corporateness often shows itself in camaraderie. If camaraderie is missing or the personal motivation is diminished, corporateness is at risk. Besides camaraderie, trust in the organization and in superiors also fosters corporateness.[29] Hence, threats to this trust such as the unethical behaviour of superiors or the organization itself, or general distrust among the members can create major problems to maintaining military professionalism. Tied to trust and motivation is loyalty toward the organization, comrades and superiors. If this loyalty is threatened, for example from ethical principles that are not shared among the individual professional and the organization, leader, or comrades, then corporateness is at stake.

Swiss and Dutch participants rated a lack of trust in superiors as an important factor that might threaten military professionalism. However, both the Dutch and Swiss did not consider a lack of trust in the subordinates as being a considerable threat. The same goes for a lack of trust in the organization and the trust in society. Within the Dutch forces, trust is a major issue. The Dutch respondents consider camaraderie as one of the major characteristics of the forces and one of the major reasons they joined the armed forces. With respect to threats to military professionalism, the Dutch service members consider motivation as being very important although, for leaders, it is hard to keep their followers motivated due to cut-backs that result in less training and exercises, fewer missions and less challenge. This might explain why the respondents scored high on these scales.

Essential Duties

As already stated, the core essential duty of the military professional is to serve and protect society. A further essential duty is to master communication ranging from the individual face to face interactions to the use of highly complex technical communication systems.[30] Young states that the military professional has to keep pace with the newest technological advances to be able to successfully fulfill their duties. A further duty lies in the generation of training to establish tasks, conditions and standards. Planning field operations is another essential duty. This encompasses the effective use of intelligence, interpreting doctrine, the developing operations or mobilization plans, planning logistics, and managing complex organizational relationships. Young sees a final duty of being a good role model and being able to intervene if their comrades or followers do not act responsibly.

Swiss participants see considerable threats to professionalism resulting from the lack of experience with large-scale operations as well as the lack of communication skills. As already stated, a lack of individual leadership skills is seen as the main threat for military professionalism. Swiss and Dutch participants do not perceive a lack in general management skills, military planning skills as well as technological knowledge as a threat to professionalism. The Dutch respondents did not share the issue of lacking operational experience in large-scale military operations as a threat. They note that during deployments, however, that as leaders they had to monitor moral disengagement. According to them, this is quite difficult since the leaders' own moral compass is gradually and unwittingly deteriorating as well.

GROUP LEVEL THREATS

Threats to professionalism explored at the level were also addressed at the group level (i.e., expertise, responsibility, corporateness, and essential duties), especially when one is obliged to work with others. Hence, team members, subordinates or superiors who a lack in expertise can pose a severe threat to ones own professionalism, as the team tasks cannot be fulfilled in a professional way. When rating the possible threats at the group level and therefore the threats originating from other military professionals, Swiss participants rated the lack of job motivation, the lack of a positive view of the army, and the lack of experience with large scale operations as considerable threats. Similar to the individual level threats, a lack of trust in the superior, organization, subordinates, and the lack of trust in society by other military members were also seen as considerable threats to professionalism at the group level. Finally, the lack of responsibility, lack of conflict resolution competence, and a lack of leadership skills were reported as considerable threats. Although similar threats were perceived at the group level, none were seen as severe as the lack of leadership competence at the individual level. In addition to these, however, other threats exist at the group level such as changes in group dynamics and the multiculturality of group composition.

Changes in Group Dynamics

Conformity pressure has always existed, especially among young people. This pressure has risen over the last 20 years. In Switzerland, for example, this peer pressure results in either an increase or decrease in the number of recruits from different parts of the nation.[31] Young adults from the city are much less willing to serve in the army than are young adults from the more rural regions. This greatly influences the composition of the force. The same is true regarding the level of education. People with higher education levels tend to withdraw from armed service, for many reasons, while people with lower education levels tend to fulfill their compulsory service. Swiss participants do not see changes in group dynamics as one of the main threats to professionalism.

Since the Dutch military is a professional organization without "compulsory military service," these problems and threats are not recognized in the organization. However, within the Dutch Armed Forces, servicemen consider the hardening of society as a threat toward military professionalism. The Dutch believe that traditional (military) values such as respect are diminishing, which might eventually lead to morally irresponsible behaviours. The Dutch respondents believed that the young lack respect for and knowledge of possibilities that exist within the forces. On the other hand, new military personnel come from a more harsh world that makes leaders fear morally irresponsible behaviour might occur during missions and in the barracks. According to the Dutch, respect is a key value that is necessary in these contexts. Within the Royal Netherlands Armed Forces, respect is addressed in two different ways. First, Dutch military personnel believe respect is a value of significant importance to the military. They consider respect amongst each other as being very important. The second way that respect is addressed entails the perceived respect the military gets from Dutch society. They remark that society is losing its respect for authorities and as a consequence, the Dutch Forces. The respondents do not consider this to be a major influence on military professionalism, however, they fear that when this continues to affect the organizational image, the organization will no longer attract the right professionals.

Multiculturalism

The cultural background of the men and women serving in the army has drastically changed over the last few decades within the Swiss as well as the Dutch Armed Forces. While 30 to 40 years ago most of the armed forces were composed of citizens whose families originated from the country they served, globalization, migration, and naturalization have changed the cultural background of societies and, of course, this has led to a more multicultural face of the armed forces. As the young recruits, now raised in a variety of culturally different manners, serve in the armed forces, professional officers have to take multiculturalism into account. Having Muslims, Christians, Buddhists, Atheists and other (religious) practices present within one armed force, requires the organization to adapt to this new troop composition. Hence, the armed forces can no longer be led or organized as they were

30 years ago when the composition of the troops was predominantly from one single cultural background, namely the national culture. The pressure to adapt to this multiculturalism may pose a threat to the traditional view of military professionalism.

Swiss participants did not at all see multiculturalism as a threat to military professionalism. This was an expected result since Switzerland has been a multicultural country with four language regions for many centuries. Within the Dutch Forces, about 10 percent of the servicemen have a culturally diverse background and about 14 percent are women. The Dutch participants in this study did not consider multiculturality as a threat to military professionalism as they state they would rather work in a multicultural vice a homogenous team. This can probably be explained by the fact that the Dutch troops operate in multinational teams during deployments (e.g., patrol missions with German forces in Kunduz, Afghanistan). This finding may also be in part due to the fact that the Dutch society has for centuries been a melting pot of different cultures.

ORGANIZATIONAL LEVEL THREATS

Apart from individual and group level threats, major threats to professionalism originate from organizational changes in the armed forces which directly influence the individual's expertise, responsibility, corporateness, and essential duties. These threats can generally be separated into threats based on processes, culture, knowledge generation and transfer, strategy, mission and goals, and resources.

Processes

Within the last few decades, armed forces have embraced a wide range of business methods to increase efficiency and cost control.[32] Total quality management, HR processes for achievement appraisal, personnel selection and promotion, total cost analysis, and many more have shown their potential in both the private and public sectors. At the basis of these organizational changes lies a change in the view of the military professional. Snider and Watkins suggest that military professionals are no longer seen as professionals, but instead, as employees.[33] The shift from the traditional perspective on military tasks toward a more managerial perspective has resulted in a shift of focus away from effectiveness in executing military power toward efficiency. In many departments, however, this shift also resulted in increased bureaucracy. Bureaucracy of course, is in itself useful and needed;[34] too much bureaucracy, however, often denies the elements of professionalism.

SWITZERLAND & NETHERLANDS

Swiss participants rated a lack in adequate managerial administration as a considerable threat. The Dutch considered the managerial perspective to be a threat toward military professionalism since it may lead to an inaccurate perceptions of the military job itself (i.e., thinking it is a "normal" managerial job). Moreover, it may lead to thinking in costs and efficiencies which is not always appropriate since military personnel have to concern themselves with their personal and collective safety and security; lives are at stake and they are not dealing with "real products."

Culture

The success of the armed forces is strongly dependent on the positive image the military generates in society, especially when they need to attract high quality people to military service. This positive image has diminished in Europe since the end of Second World War.[35] The existing military values need to be lived and communicated within the organization as well as externally in order to generate an appropriate image of the military culture. As an example, military leadership focuses on instruction and command relationships. However, a gap exists between military leadership values and the participative leadership style fostered in current management and leadership theory, which is commonly experienced in society. New members entering the military organization are more accustomed to a participative leadership style and they do not know the culture and organizational values that are expected. Confronted with a more direct leadership style, new members are often irritated. Subsequently, the armed forces are then viewed as old-fashioned and a constant pressure exists for the armed forces to adapt its leadership behaviour according to the current view of society. Not being able, as an organization, to actively communicate their culture, goals, and values, both internally and externally, can lead to a false image of the organization.

It has also been argued that the military professional culture has to incorporate faithfulness, unlimited liability, and a strong respect for the connection between the armed forces and the society it serves.[36] Further, the organization has to take responsibility for its employees. Even if such values exist, not being able as an organization to communicate these internally and externally as well as not being able to foster the desired culture can threaten military professionalism.

Swiss participants see the lack of a positive image within and outside of the organization, as well as a lack of organizational values, as considerable threats. The same is true for the lack of adequate communication with the Swiss society. The Dutch forces, in contrast, see the lack of a positive image

CHAPTER 11

within and outside of the organization as severe threats to military professionalism. In both armies, the lack of responsibility the organization takes for its employees is seen as a problem. Within the Netherlands defence organization, the employees often complain about the organization being too bureaucratic and that it is losing the "human-component"; the Dutch participants consider this to be a major threat to professionalism.

Knowledge Generation and Transfer

The shift in culture and the organizational approach has also led to changes in knowledge generation and management. Today, the emphasis is less on developing knowledge, which is the core of becoming an expert to that of a more pure knowledge application within the armed forces.[37] This decreases the expertise of the individual and reduces the capability of the organization to learn as a whole. One main objective of the armed forces, according to Young, is it to systematically create a class of people for whom war is a profession.[38] Essential here is knowledge on the art and the science of conflict. There needs to be training to establish tasks, conditions and standards so that the individual, the group, as well as the organization as a whole are able to resolve conflict professionally. Hence, a lack of training or sufficient education for individuals, groups, and the organization itself, can pose a major threat to military professionalism. An interesting aspect of this that influences training and knowledge generation results from a more organizational view that develops. For example, the Swiss Armed Forces often have to think about which military leadership education and training will provide the practical management experience that can then be applied to the civil realm.[39] The reason lies in the lack of prestige of the armed services and the lack of support of the economy, which directly influences the quality, and indirectly the quantity, of personnel within the Swiss Armed Forces.

The lack of adequate education and training are seen as considerable threats by the Swiss and the Dutch participants. Even though they consider these elements crucial for their profession, they believe the current educational system is sufficient. They also, however, consider the continued cut-backs and, as a consequence, less training opportunities as a threat to their professionalism.

Strategy, Mission, and Organizational Goals

Further threats to professionalism stem from changes in strategies, missions, and organizational goals. For example, many armed forces have shifted away from the goal of mission accomplishment to that of force protection (e.g., zero casualties).[40] This leads to a shift in the view of what responsibility the individual, the group and the organization have to take. More importantly, the main responsibility of the armed forces, namely protecting society, may be at risk due to this shift in goals. Armed forces are nowadays confronted with a multitude of missions within and outside of their own country. The increased use of the armed forces for non-combat, internal security missions could diminish the military warfighting expertise.[41] The individual professionals, having to focus on national missions see a decline in or do not acquire the necessary competences for a possible future war. One major problem is that the tasks, expertise, roles and missions of the armed forces start to blur due to subsidiary missions and it becomes more and more unclear what the army has to do and what not to do.[42] The essential duties of the individual professional as well as the organization, therefore, are harder to define and to communicate internally and externally.

The lack of organizational goals in "true" military operations was seen as a considerable threat to the Swiss participants. For the Dutch, this threat is not as apparent. Since the Royal Netherlands Armed Forces are participating in UN and peace-missions abroad, they are still confronted with an unstable conflict environment, even though warfighting missions no longer represent a large part of their tasks. Within the Dutch society and within the military, a discussion is ongoing as to what the main tasks of the defence organization should be. One can distinguish a shift toward more national activities of late, however, an official decision on this matter has not yet been made. The Dutch respondents consider clearly defined goals as an important element in military professionalism.

Resources

Perhaps one of the most severe threats to professionalism is the lack of resources due to budget cuts, reorganizations, and the downsizing of the armed forces. Lack of funding makes it impossible to execute multiple missions in a professional manner as the organization has to focus its resources.[43] Lack of funding also results in a loss of technological competence leading again to a decrease in professionalism. This greatly affects the responsibility as well as the expertise factors that define military professionalism. Downsizing can lead to a major loss in expertise in the development and maintenance of the competence and the capability to maneuver large formations.[44] It also greatly influences the professional interplay of all the elements of an armed force. This is a key expertise which is quickly lost but very hard to regain. The difficulty in regaining these competences lies in the loss of knowledge and experience when the forces are down-sized and large scale manoeuvres are no longer trained. It is critical to understand all the small caveats and problems that arise when commanding large-scale manoeuvres.

In addition, the development of problem-solving skills for these leadership situations is of high importance. The interplay between the different people within the command chains also has to be exercised and the different leaders have to learn how to efficiently work together. Building up experience, getting to know each other, training the leadership processes, and improving the problem-solving skills requires time and considerable dedicated effort. Both the Swiss and Dutch participants reported the lack of resources as a severe threat to their military professionalism.

CONTEXT LEVEL THREATS

Many of the developments and threats described so far originate from various changes in the general context in which the military organization is embedded. These can be separated into global developments, social developments and support, political support and economic support.

Global Developments

One of the major developments in the last century, for many armed forces, was the loss of the great enemy. This greatly impacted the corporateness of the armed forces. Snider and Watkins claim that with the dissolution of the great enemy and the according societal developments, the need for a military function has drastically diminished.[45] Without a single large enemy, many armed forces were forced to start to justify their existence as well as their budgets. At the beginning of the new millennium, terrorist attacks, although always present, reached a new level. In addition to the loss of the great enemy and the evolution of a new blurry enemy, international operations experienced today have many more constraints as compared to earlier missions.[46] Like the need for zero casualties and increased processes leading to more bureaucracy, more constraints within missions has resulted in situations where responsibility has shifted away from mission accomplishment. Swiss and Dutch participants did not consider these points as posing an immediate threat to military professionalism.

Social Developments and Support

Many citizens don't want to be part of the armed forces. Hence, armed forces have to fight in the "war" for talent, where other economic-oriented organizations often have far better resources and competence. Social commitment plays a major role for recruiting good soldiers and cadre.[47] The reduction of the size of the armed forces reduces visibility that can result in less desire to serve their country. As a result, shorter military service reduces public visibility and could lead to the gradual exclusion of the army from society. If most young people complete military service, pressure to do so will remain high. Today, young people know fewer people who have completed service than they did during the time of conscript armies. After the fall of the Soviet Union, societal values began to change.[48] Obedience and discipline are today seen as less important than autonomy, self-determination and self-development. These values, however, can only be adhered to or combined with military professionalism to a certain degree. As a result of these factors, active sympathy for and the prestige of the military from a societal perspective becomes challenged. This was extremely visible after the Vietnam War, in which US operations gradually received less and less support. This loss in visibility, prestige, and support for the military can of course, have a negative influence on the expertise of the individual soldier, on their overarching responsibility and on their feeling of corporateness. Swiss and Dutch participants, however, did not view these social developments as great threats to their professionalism.

Political and Economic Support

As politicians are directly responsible for setting the strategic goals of military organizations, deciding on defence budgets, and the definition of the specific missions that have to be accomplished.[49] Due to budget cuts and the economic crisis, defence budgets have been among the first to be reduced. At the same time, national needs have surged, the result of an increase in natural disasters. Therefore, agreement has to be reached between political parties on the different goals, missions, and budget for the military. If this political agreement is not reached, the organization will continue to be confronted with conflicting goals. This can lead to great insecurity within the organization. A further development is that conscription has lost its significance within Europe.[50] Many countries have already abolished conscription, which directly influences the quantity and potential quality of personnel available for its armed forces. As already mentioned, this reduces the visibility of the armed forces in society since fewer people are actively pursuing a military career and are less likely to be seen in uniform in the streets.

For the Dutch military, the problems described above are not apparent since it no longer is a conscript army. Of course, the organization still has to deal with the "Battle for Talent" and the political influences on decision-making and missions. Swiss participants mainly see the lack of agreement within the political parties regarding the armed forces and their missions and goals as well as the political influence in military decisions as considerable threats. Additionally, financial reductions in the military budget and the resulting lack of adequate reorganizations are also seen as considerable threats by the

Swiss and Dutch participants. A last threat identified on the context level by both groups of participants was the vanishing visibility of the armed forces within the public.

SITUATION LEVEL THREATS

Finally, several threats to military professionalism exist when it comes to the situations encountered in missions or military life. The encountered situations have become more complex, less known and more and more reflect non-military situations.

Complexity

Today, more actors are involved in military situations than 40 years ago. Missions are generally multinational, led by NATO, EU, UN, or others, in very different parts of the world. Many Non-Government Organizations (NGO) are also present. At the same time, as already stated, enemies are often not recognizable. No longer do they wear clearly identifiably uniforms. An insurgent may look like a farmer when one passes by in a convoy. Also, confrontation is less open. Mines, bombs, IEDs, and ambushes are the preferred tactic of war. In all these situations, civilians, NGOs, Government Organizations (GO) and other troops are involved. Complexity can make it difficult to behave responsibly and professionally.[51] Also in the non-combat zone, the professional situation encountered has become more complex.

Unknown Situations

It has been argued that current military situations encountered are less clear than they were a few decades ago – when people expected a full-sized tank attack from the east.[52] Today, the enemy is not as clearly defined as during the Cold War. Similar problems are encountered when defining the threats to the country and society. Currently, Switzerland has no serious foreign aggressor. Compared to the Cold War, where the enemy came from the east, the movements of a possible modern enemy are not predictable. As these military situations are less clear, training for this complexity is not easy and traditional education and training sessions are no longer sufficient.

Non-Military Situations

Most situations encountered by the army are not military in nature. Current training and instruction does not necessarily reflect war-time situations. Militaries focus increasingly on training for possible situations encountered during subsidiary missions (i.e., situations the Swiss Armed Forces are mostly confronted with). The threat then lies with the potential lack of experience

SWITZERLAND & NETHERLANDS

should a traditional combat mission be encountered. None of these situational level threats were seen as being of considerable or even of high importance by the Swiss participants. The Dutch consider the complexity of the mission area and the unclear insurgency, as an indicator that their personnel should be prepared to be adaptable.

DISCUSSION

Although the samples in both countries were small, the two surveys represent the first attempt to gather data on the perceived threats to professionalism. Some trends for the two nations, similar and dissimilar, were found. Many threats are seen as equally important or unimportant in both countries. For example, the lack of resources for the armed forces is seen as a main threat for military professionalism in the Netherlands as well as Switzerland. Similarly, the lack of a positive image of the armed forces poses a threat both to the Dutch and Swiss armed forces. The threat is more severe for the Dutch forces since the abolition of conscription as they have to compete to recruit their personnel from the regular job market. A poor image increases the difficulty to recruit adequate staff. Interestingly, however, the Dutch troops (referred to as *"onze jongens"* meaning, our sons) are quite popular, whereas, the political decisions and the military missions are not. Both groups of participants also see the lack of organizational responsibility toward the employees as a threat. Not feeling responsible for your organizational members may lead to decreasing motivation, dissatisfaction, focus more on the individual rather than on organizational goals, and a decrease in corporateness. These factors will result in a decrease in professionalism. Both the Swiss and the Dutch participants see the lack of training and expertise as threats. Swiss participants regard insufficient leadership expertise as well as the planning and command of large scale operations as problems. Dutch participants reported that reduced training opportunities were the direct result of budget cuts. Only the Swiss participants perceived the absence of organizational goals stemming from political disagreement and the influence of politics in the military decision-making process as being threats to professionalism. This threat stems from the transformation phase that the Swiss Armed Forces has been engaged in since the end of the Cold War. Contrary to the Dutch forces, the Swiss forces are not participating in any full-risk missions and do not have a clear enemy. Additionally, the Swiss Armed Forces are confronted with three main missions (national defence, subsidiary missions, and fostering peace) and neither the public nor the politicians have decided which has the highest priority. As a consequence, the armed forces are unable to determine operating costs and parliament is unable to agree on the military budget.

Interestingly, and contrary to the views of Snider and Watkins, bureaucracy is not seen as a threat to professionalism by either the Dutch or Swiss participants. Multiculturalism at the group or situational level is also not seen as a threat to both groups of participants. Generally though, in both countries, the financial and budgetary constraints are seen as the fundamental problems that could lead to several threats within the armed forces (i.e., a lack in training and a lack of knowledge on large scale operations). Hence, although not explicitly stated, we conclude that the lack of funding for the armed forces may pose the most severe and acute threat to both the Swiss and the Dutch armed forces. The lack of funding, however, stems from different origins. For Switzerland, it stems from the lack of agreement on the goals and missions for the forces and for the Netherlands, it stems from the larger financial problems of the state itself which has resulted in sweeping cut-backs in all ministries.

CONCLUSION

Both the Swiss and the Dutch Armed Forces report similar threats to their military professionalism; the lack of funding being the most significant concern. The lack of funding, though having different origins in both the countries, leads to similar problems and threats. It is not an increase in salary or insufficient pay that is the basis for the perceived threat, but rather, the fear that military personnel will not be sufficiently trained and equipped to face the most severe danger, namely a large scale foreign attack or anti-guerilla/ terrorist operation on their home soil. Therefore, although the two Armed Forces differ in size, history, experience, professionalization, and combat experience, they share common problems and similar threats to the development and sustainment of their professionalism.

ENDNOTES

1. Robert J. House, Paul J. Hanges, Mansour Javidan, Peter W. Dorfman and Vipin Gupta, *Culture, Leadership and Organizations: The GLOBE Study of 62 Societies* (Thousand Oaks, CA: Sage, 2004).

2. Don M. Snider and Gayle L. Watkins, "The Future of Army Professionalism: A Need For Renewal and Redefinition", *Parameters,* Vol. 3, (2000), 5-20.; and, Thomas-Durell Young, "Military Professionalism in a Democracy", in Thomas C. Bruneau and Scott D. Tollefson, eds., *Who Guards the Guardians and How?* (Austin, TX: University Press, 2006), 17-33.

3. Stefan Seiler and Andres Pfister, "Why Did I Do This? Understanding Leadership Behavior Based on the Dynamic Five-Factor Model of Leadership", *Journal of Leadership Studies*, Vol. 3, (2009), 41-52.

4. Tibor Szvirscsev-Tresch, "The Transformation of Switzerland's Militia Armed Forces and the Role of the Citizen in Uniform", *Armed Forces & Society,* Vol X, (2010), 1-22.

5. Snider and Watkins, 2000.

6. Alexander M. Carr-Saunders and Paul A. Wilson, *The Professions* (Oxford: Oxford University Press, 1933).

7. Geoffrey Millerson, *The Qualifying Associations* (London: Routledge, 1964).

8. David. J. B. Trim, "Introduction", in David J. B. Trim, ed., *The Chivalric Ethos and the Development of Military Professionalism* (Leiden: Koninklijke Brill, 2003), 1-40.

9. Harry Kunneman, "Normatieve Professionaliteit: Een Appel", *Sociale Interventie, Vol. 5, No. 3,* (1996), 107-112.

10. Ibid.

11. Jos M.H. Groen and Desiree E.M. Verweij, "De Onlosmakelijke Band Tussen Professionaliteit en Ethiek", *Militaire Spectator,* Vol. 177, No. 6, (2008), 349-360.

12. Young, 2006.

13. Snider and Watkins, 2000.

14. Seiler and Pfister, 2009.

15. Samuel C. Sarkesian, *The System of Profession: An Essay on the Division of Expert Labour* (Chicago: Pergamon Press, 1981).

16. Snider and Watkins, 2000.

17. Ibid.

18. Seiler and Pfister, 2009.

19. Young, 2006.

20. Lawrence Freedman, *The Revolution in Strategic Affairs, Adelphi Paper 318* (London: International Institute for Strategic Studies and Oxford University Press, 1998).

21. Richard Swain, *The Obligations of Military Professionalism: Service Unsullied by Partisanship* (Washington, DC: National Defence University, 2010).

22. Young, 2006.

23. Snider and Watkins, 2000; and Young, 2006.

24. Young, 2006.

25. Ibid.

26. Swain, 2010.

27. Snider and Watkins, 2000.

28. Szvirscsev-Tresch, 2010.

29. Swain, 2010.

30. Young, 2006.

31. Szvirscsev-Tresch, 2010.

32. Snider and Watkins, 2000.

33. Ibid.

34. Young, 2006.

35. Young, 2006.

36. Swain, 2010.

37. Snider and Watkins, 2000.

38. Young, 2006.

39. Szvirscsev-Tresch, 2010.

40. Snider and Watkins, 2000.

41. Young, 2006.

42. Snider and Watkins, 2000.

43. Ibid.

44. Young, 2006.

45. Snider and Watkins, 2000.

46. Szvirscsev-Tresch, 2010.

47. Ibid.

48. Ibid.

49. Snider and Watkins, 2000.

50. Szvirscsev-Tresch, 2010.

51. Snider and Watkins, 2000.

52. Szvirscsev-Tresch, 2010.

CHAPTER 12

Complacency: A Threat to (Canadian) Military Professionalism

*Craig Leslie Mantle**

In a short article that appeared in the early 1960s, *The New York Times Magazine* offered a collection of quotations from Eugene O'Neill, the 1936 Nobel Laureate in Literature. The various nuggets of wisdom, which were gleaned from letters written and interviews given between 1920 and 1946, were essentially the "views of America's most famous playwright on the Broadway of his time." The authors *cum* editors, a husband and wife team that shortly thereafter published what is still considered to be the definitive biography of O'Neill, selected comments that spoke to the "Stuff of Plays," the "Writing of Plays," "Critics," the "Theatre as Business" and the "Theatre's Future." One of the quotations included within this brief anthology of musings was particularly prescient, speaking as it does across the years:

> A man's work is in danger of deteriorating when he thinks he has found the one best formula for doing it. If he thinks that, he is likely to feel that all he needs is merely to go on repeating himself. ... And so long as a person is searching for better ways of doing his work he is fairly safe.[1]

In effect, O'Neill had identified what he considered to be a significant challenge to success as a writer, being stuck in one's ways and refusing to search for different, perhaps even better, approaches to one's craft. Removed from their literary context, his words apply with equal relevance to other fields of human endeavour where the need for innovation and improvement are constants. Although he was speaking of literature, not the military, his comments are nevertheless germane to both. As it does for the creative process in the liberal arts, complacency, what different dictionaries define as either "extreme self-satisfaction"[2] or being "overcontented,"[3] also represents a real and significant threat to military professionalism in the early 21st century. In an institution like the military where the need for professionalism is paramount – recall that its *raison d'être* is the lawful, ordered application of force

---

* The views expressed in this chapter are those of the author and do not necessarily reflect those of either the Canadian Forces or the Department of National Defence.

CANADA

on behalf of a national government in pursuit of its legitimate objectives – a *laissez faire* approach to the development, maintenance and improvement of core standards in the face of changing circumstances does not bode well for the future. As will be seen, the changes that might possibly occur in the immediate future within the Canadian Forces and the Department of National Defence appear to be evidence of the initial stages of regression. In the years ahead in Canada, military professionalism may be accorded much less attention than what it once received.

Before proceeding further, a few definitions are required for it is impossible to discuss threats to professionalism without first understanding the meaning of professionalism itself. As perceived by the Canadian military, a profession is:

> … an exclusive group of people who possess and apply a systematically acquired body of knowledge derived from extensive research, education, training and experience. Members of a profession have a special responsibility to fulfill their function competently and objectively for the benefit of society. Professionals are governed by a code of ethics that establishes standards of conduct while defining and regulating their work. This code of ethics is enforced by the members themselves and contains values that are widely accepted as legitimate by society at large.[4]

Stemming from this, the profession of arms in Canada is:

> … composed of military members dedicated to the defence of Canada and its interests, as directed by the Government of Canada. The profession of arms is distinguished by the concept of service before self, the lawful, ordered application of military force, and the acceptance of the concept of unlimited liability. Its members possess a systematic and specialized body of military knowledge and skills acquired through education, training and experience, and they apply this expertise competently and objectively in the accomplishment of their missions. Members of the Canadian profession of arms share a set of core values and beliefs found in the military ethos that guides them in the performance of their duty and allows a special relationship of trust to be maintained with Canadian society.[5]

What both definitions reveal, when considered together, is that *all* men and women of both the Regular Force and Primary Reserve, regardless of individual rank or specific occupation, are professionals in the profession of arms, each possessing specific responsibilities and obligations to themselves, the military and Canada. Subordinate to civilian authority and the rule of law, members of Canada's military must master the specific knowledge and skills, both intellectual and technical, which will allow them to perform their duty competently and with honour. Set apart from the remainder of Canadian society through their contract of "unlimited liability,"[6] sailors, soldiers and air personnel must also embody the four key military values (duty, loyalty, integrity and courage) and be actuated at all times by the military ethos. The conduct of military members must be irreproachable, being informed as it is by the values that the larger society itself cherishes. Much is expected from every individual who wears the uniform.

For the Canadian military, as for all militaries, the list of threats to professionalism is long indeed, with complacency being only one of many. Several of the challenges that have the potential to impair the ability of the CF to function successfully in complex operating environments, in both domestic and international settings, are "external" in the sense that they are imposed on the institution from the outside. As an organization, the CF is, to a very significant degree, at the mercy of forces beyond its control. Stated differently, assaults upon professionalism can come from a variety of directions. Being unable to either prevent or stop their onset, the military can only hope to adapt to such menaces and limit their insidious effects. Canadian military professionalism has been, and in some respects continues to be, assailed on a number of diverse fronts, some of which include:

- Declining federal budgets that ultimately threaten to erase financial support for vitally important professional development and educational programs;[7]

- Reduced opportunities for military personnel to participate in higher level education and training, to deploy at home or abroad, and to participate in military and civilian exchanges (in other words, to gradually gather and refine through multiple avenues the expertise required to competently fulfill their special and complex responsibilities); and,

- An evolving geo-strategic environment for which the military is largely unprepared.[8]

Yet not every challenge has a similar origin. To be sure, many threats emanate from within the military itself and are nothing less than "internal" and self-inflicted. Self-imposed threats to military professionalism include, but are certainly not limited to:

CANADA

- A prevailing culture that fails to value professional development and education, foster an ethical climate or treat military service as a noble profession rather than a mere occupation;[9]

- An attitude of elitism, wherein members believe themselves to be "above the law" and thus able to operate with impunity, regardless of the norms by which they are governed and the ultimate consequences of their actions;[10] and,

- Scandals or high-profile incidents that throw the veracity of the profession of arms into question, erode public support and reduce morale within the military itself.[11]

That professionalism can at times thrive in such a hostile environment is nothing short of remarkable.

Perhaps the greatest internal threat of all, as has been suggested, is self-congratulatory smugness, or in other words, complacency. A sense that a crisis has passed, that all deficiencies have been duly rectified and that nothing therefore remains to be done is just as much of a threat to military professionalism as any other. Like its allies and partners throughout the world, Canada's military must be continually introspective and not shy away from self-criticism, reform, change and progress. As is certain, a lack of vigilance, wherein threats to professionalism are allowed to emerge unchallenged or to persist unchecked, must be guarded against. The process of review and renewal must therefore be ongoing, not employed merely in response to emergencies and then promptly abandoned once calm returns. Exercising initiative and being proactive rather than reactive are fundamental prerequisites in the process of protecting military professionalism.[12] Without doubt, such is an extremely tall order since large organizations, by their very nature, tend to be slow-moving, inclined to tradition and resistant to fundamental change. That the task at hand is difficult in no way absolves the military, or the government, from seeing to its completion.

Within society at large, a vast array of disturbing trends is, and has been for some time, threatening the foundations of the professional ethic. In some quarters, the very definition of what it means to be professional is being questioned. Principals within the fields of medicine, law and public administration, including the military, have come to understand that the idea of professionalism can not simply be taken for granted. The present International Military Leadership Association volume is evidence enough of that. The many specialized journals that serve these diverse disciplines often include hot debates over the erosion of professionalism in contemporary society – its genesis, its manifestations, its remedies and its preventatives.[13] Charged with the defence of the nation and its interests, perhaps nowhere are the threats to professionalism more serious than in the military.

That complacency is indeed a significant threat to military professionalism can be illustrated and understood through a very brief examination of recent Canadian military history. Over the past two decades, the CF has transformed itself considerably, becoming much more professional than what it once was.[14] The military of 2012 is barely recognizable from the military of 1992. Despite such significant gains, however, the *potential* for "backsliding" and regression remains a hazard. In the absence of constant attention and renewal, the high standard of professionalism that the CF has recently attained might, piece by piece, begin to slowly erode.

Without question, the CF reached its absolute nadir in the 1990s. The torture-murder of a young Somali national, Shidane Arone, in March 1993 not only shocked the Canadian population, but also, and perhaps more important, revealed fundamental cracks in the Canadian military edifice. Other troubling incidents, both overseas and in Canada, further eroded the CF's reputation. Over the winter of 1993-1994 in Bosnia-Herzegovina, some Canadian soldiers who were responsible for protecting two hospitals at Bakovici and Drin allegedly participated in the black market, abused patients, drank heavily, had frequent sex with nurses and interpreters, fired their weapons indiscriminately, held wild parties and altered operational logs to hide their illegal and less-than soldierly activities. At home in Canada, certain senior officers engaged in practices that were anything but ethical.[15] Other unsavoury episodes likely occurred that did not see the light of day, failing to be uncovered by the nation's media outlets or the military's investigative services. Collectively, such shortcomings indicated that the problems facing the CF were systemic rather than isolated.[16] In a few short years, owing to a mix of both high-profile and less noticeable episodes, the Canadian military lost much of the sheen and polish that it had gained over the past century owing to its important and costly contributions to the First and Second World Wars (1914-1918; 1939-1945), the Korean War (1950-1953) and numerous United Nations peacekeeping operations throughout the world starting with the United Nations Emergency Force that deployed to the Sinai in 1956.[17] Although not everyone could be tarred with the same brush – there were many competent, dedicated and professional individuals within its ranks still who were unfortunately overshadowed by events – the military, for all intents and purposes, was teetering on the verge of becoming a national embarrassment. Some might argue that it already was.

CANADA

The causes of the so-called "Decade of Darkness" were numerous indeed. Many of the challenges of the 1990s stemmed from a culture in which careerism, anti-intellectualism and a "ticket-punching" mentality prevailed. Rather than focusing on the acquisition, development and refinement of professional skills, some, but certainly not all, of the military's leadership was more concerned about how best, and how quickly, their next promotion or "plum" posting might be achieved. For them, the military was a means to an end, not an end in itself. A general lack of informed and healthy debate on matters of professional importance, coupled with an absence of higher-level encouragement of the same, only reinforced feelings of general apathy. The condoning of unethical behaviour had a similar effect. Experience was preferred over education; to many, a campaign medal was much more important than an academic degree. Declining budgets, pay freezes, aging equipment and a brutally high operational tempo (owing principally to the Canadian commitment in the Balkans to the United Nations Protection Force, and later the Implementation Force and Stabilization Force) put considerable stress on the military and its members to do more and more with less and less. Soldiers worked multiple jobs just to "make ends meet." Military families were all but ignored. By the last decade of the 20th century, it is fair to say, the military had lost sight of traditional martial values, the soldierly ethos and its purpose. Such an environment was ripe for abuses to occur.[18]

In the time since, however, considerable human and financial resources have been devoted to improving professionalism within the CF. The regenerative initiatives that were undertaken in the wake of the numerous scandals aimed to correct the obvious failings within the military and, in the process, attempted to ensure that the conditions that ultimately contributed to the debacle of the 1990s never again became manifest. Beginning in 1997, a number of important documents appeared in quick succession that offered a suite of recommendations aimed at improving the military in most relevant respects – from quality-of-life, to leadership, to training, to accountability, to ethics, to military justice.[19] At no other time in its history had the Canadian military undergone such a searching and comprehensive examination. Nor, for that matter, had the proposed changes been so sweeping. The sheer number of recommendations – 160 from the Somalia Commission alone – revealed just how profoundly "broken" the military institution in Canada truly was.

Following closely upon the release of the many reports, the *Minister's Monitoring Committee on Change in the Department of National Defence and the Canadian Forces* (the MMC, which counted among its members such prominent Canadians as The Honourable John A. Fraser, Dr. David J. Bercuson,

Peter Archambault, Daniel "Bev" Dewar and Sheila-Marie Cook) was established to follow the implementation of the recommended reforms, in effect to ensure that implementation happened and happened correctly.[20] From 1997 to 2000, the MMC watched intensely as the CF began the painful process of rebuilding not only itself, but also trust with Canadian society. Between 2000 and its termination in 2003 however, the purpose and focus of the MMC shifted somewhat; it moved away from monitoring the implementation of institution-wide reforms and toward assisting with the restructuring of Canada's army reserves and focusing on issues related to leadership and education.[21] Working in a five or so year period that straddled the turn of the millennium, the MMC oversaw many important changes to Canada's military that affected its organization, its infrastructure, and most significant of all, its culture.

The implemented reforms were broad and sweeping in both scope and content. In 2002, the Canadian Defence Academy (CDA), the educational "hub" of the CF that delivers and oversees a host of training and educational programs, became a reality; soon thereafter, the Canadian Forces Leadership Institute, a directorate of CDA, penned the profession of arms manual and a suite of documents on leadership;[22] with its Terms of Reference dated to late 1997, the Defence Ethics Programme encouraged the creation of an ethical climate within DND and the CF;[23] making its debut in early 2000, the *Canadian Military Journal* provided a transparent forum for debate and discussion, to "stimulate the intellectual growth and development of our profession," that had hitherto been missing;[24] and the list goes on.

Lest the wrong impression be left, it must also be acknowledged that a small cadre of reform-minded senior officers, such as Lieutenant-General Roméo Dallaire and Vice-Admiral Gary Garnett, pushed for change from inside the military; the MMC, in other words, was not alone in its quest to see the CF emerge from the "Decade of Darkness" a better, stronger and more professional institution overall. Regardless of how change was ultimately achieved, whether monitored from the outside or encouraged from within, the CF had by 2005 come a considerable distance from where it found itself only ten to fifteen years earlier. Collectively, such structural and cultural changes over the past decade and a half have brought the CF to a high standard of professionalism, a standard that Canada's most important allies freely acknowledge, as do many of its citizens. The CF is still a less-than perfect organization, yet it is considerably more perfect than what it once was.[25]

And now to the crux of the matter … to ensure that Canadian military professionalism remains high, both the CF and DND must not allow these and

CANADA

other important changes to go by the wayside. For its part, the military can not allow regression to occur. It must be ever vigilant. Individual initiatives may change and evolve (they probably should to better reflect the current environment), but a general spirit of constant monitoring, continual reform and overall improvement must remain. Vital programs and personnel that aid in the professional development of military members must not be eliminated. If the will to improve is allowed to fade and wither, worrying trends, like those witnessed around the time of Somalia and Bosnia, might potentially re-emerge with disastrous consequences. Stated differently, the military must not let itself become a victim of its own success, being content with victories, no matter how small, and simply leave the matter at that. The spirit and knowledge that facilitated the achievement of particular goals must not be lost in the warm glow of accomplishment. A self-congratulatory attitude may indeed jeopardize future success. Resting on hard-won laurels is just as much of a threat to professionalism as any other.

Myopic and complacent attitudes are certainly not without precedent within the Canadian military. To take perhaps the best known and frequently cited example, Canada's army in the immediate aftermath of the First World War failed to systematically record the many lessons that it had learned over the past four years for the edification of the next generation of soldiers. The Western Front, replete with its own unique challenges, was quite unlike anything that had been seen in the past. By the time of the Armistice in November 1918, the Canadian Corps had achieved considerable competence in conducting operations in both static and manoeuvre-type warfare.[26] Despite the high cost of attaining this expertise, the spirit of innovation and the resolve to continually improve was, for whatever reason, allowed to dissipate. The corps commander, in addition to his subordinate officers at all levels, including the staff, failed to systematically record what had and had not worked in the field. Nor, for that matter, was there any higher direction from government that mandated the same. Of that time, one of Canada's foremost historians has written:

> By the end of the war the Canadian Corps had taught itself, or adopted, advanced techniques of assault and defence that rivalled those of any other army on the western front. When the war ended, neither Canadians nor their government had showed any inclination to maintain the magnificent instrument they had created.[27]

Canada (and its allies) had unlocked the secrets to success in battle, yet few thought it important to keep the key safe.[28] Commenting on the *interbellum*, another Canadian historian has similarly remarked that "Keeping alive the art of warfighting, especially against a first-rate enemy, was not accorded a high priority."[29] Such collective negligence ultimately had many negative consequences. Come the Second World War, Canada's army was forced to re-learn much of what it had once known and since forgotten, wasting valuable time, resources, and no doubt lives, in the process. Indeed, "Canada had to rediscover the hard way just what armies and military professionalism were all about."[30] Canada had done exceedingly well in the first major conflict of the 20th century but failed to ensure that it retained the knowledge that would allow it to begin the second great struggle from where it had left off some twenty years earlier (or, optimistically, from an even better position!).[31]

This discussion, about complacency as a threat to military professionalism, is by no means speculative or purely hypothetical. From first impressions, the potential for a significant amount of "backsliding" to occur in the immediate future seems to exist, the result of the 2012 federal budget that announced the need to husband financial resources and adjust fiscal priorities.[32] Reducing government expenditure will, so it is understood, be partly accomplished through substantial reductions in the total number of public servants in DND and the gradual expiry, without renewal, of the contracts of many CF reservists on full-time service. A number of important organizations, programs and services related to education and professionalism have apparently been earmarked for dissolution in anticipation of fewer employees, whether military or civilian, being on the government's payroll. A few examples will suffice. What must be remembered, however, is that it is entirely too early to state with any authority that the changes detailed below will actually come to pass and in the exact form described; all that can be offered now is a few informed comments based on the latest information at hand as of the time of writing (the middle of 2012). With that being said, however, some worrying changes seem to be in the offing that might negatively affect the professionalism of Canada's military should they occur. Some of the more significant include:

- A considerable number of positions at CDA Headquarters and elsewhere within DND, many of which are occupied by civilians holding master's or doctoral degrees, have apparently been slated for elimination as part of overall cost-reduction strategies;

- Funding for the Security and Defence Forum, which is "mandated to develop a domestic competence and national interest in defence issues of current and future relevance to Canadian security"[33] may all but disappear to the ultimate detriment of the military;

- At the Royal Military College of Canada, where a sizeable portion of the CF's newest officers are trained and prepared for military service, it is expected that a significant number of professors, including a handful of deans, will be identified as "surplus;" and,

- The Officer Professional Military Education Programme[34] that "inculcates many of the core values held by the CF as essential to responsible leadership, quality of service, and quality of life"[35] is to be phased-out over the next three years to be replaced with another initiative.

Such reductions are only the tip of the proverbial iceberg. On the whole, education and professional development within the military might not fare well at all in the aftermath of the recent budget. Only with the passage of time and the settling of dust will the budget's true implications be known with any certainty. If these and other changes occur, the Canadian military and the Canadian government may be taking the first steps down a very precarious path in which professionalism might ultimately again suffer, if not immediately, then in the long-term. *One cannot expect the military to be a highly professional organization when some of the more important mechanisms by which professionalism is developed and sustained are accorded low priority or eliminated altogether.* Some of the reductions in programs and personnel, as outlined above, certainly have the potential to jeopardize future success by weakening the military's professional foundations.

The need to combat complacency seems more than evident; what has been gained thus far must not be allowed to disappear through inattention or laxity. In order to ensure that the CF is capable of achieving the missions assigned by government in an honourable and praiseworthy manner, that is, competently and professionally, individual leaders, *at all rank levels*, must cultivate and attend to the many values that collectively contribute to effectiveness.[36] For the CF to achieve mission success, so it is understood, leaders must to a greater or lesser degree: 1) respond to change and actively engage their operating environments; 2) demonstrate concern for their people and the quality of their conditions of service; 3) coordinate unit or system functioning so as to reduce chaos to predictability; and 4) ensure that all conduct is governed by, and conforms with, the military ethos. When attention and effort are actively devoted to all four value dimensions by all leaders throughout the entire organization, mission success, the primary and often overriding objective, is more likely to be realized. Complacency in any area, however, threatens success by weakening the foundations upon which that success is ultimately predicated. When through negligence leaders work in physical or psychological isolation from the world around them, when they fail to limit or redress their personnel's dissatisfaction with military service, when the unit or system within which they work is dysfunctional, and when the military ethos stands as more of a "catch phrase" rather than a guiding concept, success is truly jeopardized. Ensuring that complacency does not exert a caustic influence is both an organizational *and* an individual responsibility. Although leaders will naturally pursue different activities at the highest, middle and lowest levels of the military institution depending on their rank, the ultimate purpose of their collective activities, of ensuring that the CF is well-positioned for success, is truly identical. Four strong pillars can easily support a roof, but when one or more columns are weakened, the chances of collapse are indeed that much greater.

The Canadian Forces has changed profoundly over the past 20 years; such is an indisputable truth. At no other time, except perhaps during war, has the military witnessed such fundamental shifts in terms of its overarching culture and professionalism. So profound have the changes been that the military, which failed to command the admiration of many Canadians during the 1990s, is now an institution that warrants national respect.[37] The recent performance of the Canadian Army, the Royal Canadian Air Force and the Royal Canadian Navy in the world's troubled regions, most notably in Afghanistan, but also in Libya, Haiti, the Gulf of Aden and elsewhere, has helped garner this support. Would these and other successes have been possible without the earlier reforms? Probably not. Now, however, the challenge for leaders, both military and civilian alike, is to not let the many gains slip away through self-congratulation and complacent attitudes. The CF has not won the race, but rather only begun it. It will certainly be interesting to see what the CF looks like in 2032, some 20 years hence. If the military is constrained in some respects by forces beyond its immediate control, it is also, at the same time, master of its own destiny and quite capable of deciding, for itself and on its own, how it will proceed into the murky and unknowable future. Allowing old habits and cultural artefacts to re-emerge simply through a lack of vigilance is as much a threat to Canadian military professionalism as any other.

ENDNOTES

I should like to thank Dr. Bill Bentley, Lieutenant-Colonel Jeffrey Stouffer, Dr. David J. Bercuson and Dr. Jim Wood for their assistance; all errors and omissions, however, remain mine and mine alone.

1. Arthur and Barbara Gelb, "As O'Neill Saw the Theatre", *The New York Times Magazine* (Section 6), 12 November 1961, 32, 34, 37 and 39; Arthur and Barbara Gelb, *O'Neill* (New York, New York: Harper & Brothers, 1962).

2. *Collins English Dictionary*, 6th ed. (2003), 346.

3. *Webster's II – New Riverside University Dictionary* (1988), 290.

CANADA

4. Canada, *Duty with Honour: The Profession of Arms in Canada*, 2nd ed. (Kingston, Ontario: Canadian Forces Leadership Institute, 2009), 6.

5. Ibid., 10.

6. Unlimited Liability means that all military members "accept and understand that they are subject to being lawfully ordered into harm's way under conditions that could lead to the loss of their lives." See Ibid., 27.

7. That an insufficient budget for DND represents a threat to military professionalism is beyond doubt. In 1922, the Liberals returned to Ottawa where they would remain firmly ensconced as the national government for approximately the next 30 out of 35 years. In accordance with good liberal practices and owing to the fact that the nation had just emerged from four years of total war, the new Prime Minister, William Lyon Mackenzie King, sought to economize by significantly reducing the federal budget. The newly-christened DND, which had recently evolved from the Department of Militia and Defence, was an obvious, plump and easy choice. So deep and drastic were the ensuing cuts that, in the 1920s and 1930s, the Royal Canadian Navy and Royal Canadian Air Force, both of which were in their infancy, were forced to abandon much of their *raison d'etre*. The former lost its sea-going capability, becoming in the process little more than a land-locked training establishment. The latter fared little better, with flying operations being severely curtailed by a lack of personnel and inadequate equipment. Rather than focus their energies on the defence of Canada and its interests, both services, thusly distracted, struggled for mere survival in the fiscally-restrained postwar world. See James George Eayrs, *In Defence of Canada: From the Great War to the Great Depression*, Vol. 1 (Toronto, Ontario: University of Toronto Press, 1964).

8. The end of Cold War in the late 1980s and early 1990s witnessed a profound transition in the nature of warfare, from "war between the people" to "war amongst the people." See General Sir Rupert Smith, *The Utility of Force: The Art of War in the Modern World* (New York, New York: Knopf, 2007). In Canada, owing to the lack of a highly educated officer corps that was capable of grappling with and adjusting to the new environment, the military struggled as it attempted to impose an older paradigm (preparing to fight set-piece battles against Warsaw Pact countries, inter-state conflict) on a new and vastly different environment (operating in theatres marked by ethnic and religious conflict, intra-state conflict). So-called "whole of government" operations in the new security environment, where the lines of demarcation between purely military and civilian spheres of activity are blurred, also pose a significant challenge to the CF and other government departments given their relatively novel nature. The main Canadian actors – the military, trade, finance, international development, foreign affairs and so on – are now attempting to identify best practices in order to increase efficiency and effectiveness, or in other words, to meet the challenges of such operations in a professional manner.

9. William L. Hauser, "Careerism vs. Professionalism in the Military", *Armed Forces & Society*, Vol. 10, No. 3 (1984), 449-463. The 1990s, as will be discussed, is a prime example drawn from the Canadian experience.

10. Colonel Bernd Horn, "A Law Unto Themselves? – Elitism as a Catalyst for Disobedience", in Craig Leslie Mantle, ed. *The Unwilling and The Reluctant: Theoretical Perspectives on Disobedience in the Military*, (Kingston, Ontario: CDA Press, 2006), 127-143.; and Colonel Bernd Horn, "The Dark Side to Elites: Elitism as a Catalyst for Disobedience", *Canadian Army Journal*, Vol. 8.4 (2005), 65-79. The Canadian Airborne Regiment, both in Somalia and immediately afterwards, stands as the most obvious Canadian example.

11. In October 2010, now ex-Colonel Russell Williams was convicted on multiple charges of first-degree murder, sexual assault, forcible confinement and burglary. The graphic and shocking nature of his crimes, not surprisingly, cast a temporary pale over the CF.

12. What this paragraph suggests, indeed what this entire chapter suggests, is that the military must become a true learning organization, one that rejects the maxim, "if it isn't broke, don't fix it." For a discussion of learning organizations, see Peter M. Senge, *The Fifth Discipline: The Art and Practice of the Learning Organization*, revised and updated (New York, New York: Doubleday/Currency, 2006).

13. William Sullivan and Patricia Benner, "Challenges to Professionalism: Work Integrity and the Call to Renew and Strengthen the Social Contract of the Professions," *American Journal of Critical Care*, Vol. 14, No. 1 (2005), 78-84.; Jay M. Shafritz, "The Cancer Eroding Public Personnel Professionalism," *Public Personnel Management*, Vol. 3, No. 6 (1974), 486-492.; Ronald D. Rotunda, "Lawyers and Professionalism: A Commentary on the Report of the American Bar Association Commission on Professionalism," *Loyola University of Chicago Law Journal*, Vol. 18, No. 4 (1987), 1149-1180.; Wayne Kondro, "Threats to medical professionalism tackled in Canada," *The Lancet*, Vol. 360, No. 9329 (27 July 2002), 316.; Richard L. Abel, "The Decline of Professionalism," *The Modern Law Review*, Vol. 49, No. 1 (1986), 1-41.; Warren E. Burger, "The Decline of Professionalism," *Fordham Law Review*, Vol. 63, No. 4 (1995), 949-958.; Frank P. Sherwood, "Responding to the Decline in Public Service Professionalism," *Public Administration Review*, Vol. 57, No. 3 (1997), 211-217.; Deborah L. Rhode, "The Professionalism Problem," *William and Mary Law Review*, Vol. 39, No. 2 (1998), 283-326.; Philip C. Kissam, "The Decline of Law School Professionalism," *University of Pennsylvania Law Review*, Vol. 134, No. 2 (1986), 251-324.; John G. Hervey, "The Decline of Professionalism in the Law: An Exploration into Some Causes," *New York Law Forum*, Vol. 3, No. 4 (1957), 349-371.; Steven H. Miles, "On a New Charter to Defend Medical Professionalism: Whose Profession Is It Anyway," *The Hastings Center Report*, Vol. 32, No. 3 (2002), 46-48.; Colonel Robert N. Ginsburgh, "The Challenge to Military Professionalism," *Foreign Affairs*, Vol. 42, No. 2 (1964), 255-268; Thomas D. Morgan, "Real World Pressures on Professionalism," *University of Arkansas at Little Rock Law Review*, Vol. 23, No. 2 (2001), 409-421.; Alden N. Haffner, "Professionalism endures though dentistry is changing. Societal pressures affect traditional concepts of professionalism," *The Journal of the American College of Dentists*, Vol. 48, No. 3 (1981), 151-155.; and, Edwin A. Deagle, "Contemporary Professionalism and Future Military Leadership," *The Annals of the American Academy of Political and Social Science*, Vol. 406, No. 1 (1973), 162-170.

14. Measuring and quantifying the level of professionalism now extant in the CF is admittedly difficult. The activities undertaken by elements of the Canadian population in support of the military (as outlined in endnote 37), the success of recent Canadian operations throughout the world (as briefly listed in the concluding paragraph) and high levels of public opinion (as judged by a completely non-scientific assessment of Canadian media outlets) all seem to suggest that the CF is doing "something" right.

15. Lieutenant-General Armand Roy, the Deputy Chief of the Defence Staff, was dismissed from the military for making fraudulent claims totaling some $86,000. See *Esprit de Corps*, "Segregation not always a bad thing," retrieved on 4 June 2012 from <http://www.espritdecorps.ca/index.php?option=com_content&view=article&id=332:segregation-not-always-a-bad-thing&catid=39:personnel&Itemid=96>.

16. For details surrounding the climate in the CF in the 1990s, and the underlying causes of what would come to be derogatorily known as the "Decade of Darkness," see, as a very preliminary start: David J. Bercuson, *Significant Incident: Canada's Army, the Airborne, and the Murder in Somalia* (Toronto, Ontario: McClelland and Stewart, 1996).; Barry Came with Luke Fisher and Mark Cardwell, "Shamed in Bosnia," *Maclean's*, Vol. 109, No. 31 (29 July 1996), 10-12.; Donna Winslow, "Misplaced Loyalties: The Role of Military Culture in the Breakdown of Discipline in Peace Operations," *The Canadian Review of Sociology and Anthropology*, Vol. 35, No. 3 (1998), 345-367.; Canada, *Dishonoured Legacy: The Lessons of the Somalia Affair:*

CANADA

Report of the Commission of Inquiry into the Deployment of Canadian Forces to Somalia (Ottawa, Ontario: Public Works and Government Services Canada, 1997).; and, Major-General Lewis Mackenzie, *Peacekeeper – The Road to Sarajevo* (Vancouver, British Columbia: Douglas and McIntyre, 1993).

17. Michael K. Carroll, *Pearson's Peacekeepers – Canada and the United Nations Emergency Force, 1956-67* (Vancouver, British Columbia: University of British Columbia Press, 2009). Brief synopses of the missions in which Canadian peacekeepers have been involved, up to the early 1990s, can be found in Colonel John Gardam, *The Canadian Peacekeeper* (Burnstown: General Store Publishing House, 1992).

18. See endnote 16.

19. Foremost amongst them, the 1997 *Dishonoured Legacy*; the 1997 *Report to the Prime Minister on the Leadership and Management of the Canadian Forces* (the Young Report, after Minister of National Defence Douglas Young); and the 1997 *Report of the Special Advisory Group on Military Justice and Military Police Investigation Services* (the Dickson Report, after former Chief Justice the Right Honourable Brian Dickson).

20. See the October 1997 *A Commitment to Change: Report on the Recommendations of the Somalia Commission of Inquiry* where then-Minister of National Defence Arthur C. Eggleton revealed initial details about the MMC. Significant collections of archival material pertaining to the MMC and its various activities can be found at the *Library and Archives Canada* (Ottawa, Ontario), Minister's Monitoring Committee on Change, R112-891-8-E, and, *The Military Museums* (Calgary, Alberta), David J. Bercuson papers and John A. Fraser papers.

21. For a larger discussion of reserve restructuring, in which the MMC is mentioned briefly, see Jack L. Granatstein and Lieutenant-General (Ret'd) Charles Belzile, *The Special Commission on the Restructuring of the Reserves, 1995: Ten Years Later* (Calgary, Alberta: Canadian Defence and Foreign Affairs Institute and Centre for Military and Strategic Studies, University of Calgary, September 2005).

22. Canada, *Duty with Honour* (2003 and 2009). See also, Canada, *Leadership in the Canadian Forces: Doctrine* (2005); Canada, *Leadership in the Canadian Forces: Conceptual Foundations* (2005); Canada, *Leadership in the Canadian Forces: Leading the Institution* (2007); and Canada, *Leadership in the Canadian Forces: Leading People* (2007).

23. See especially, Canada, Defence Ethics Programme, *Statement of Defence Ethics*, which encourages everyone to respect the dignity of all persons, serve Canada before self, and obey and support lawful authority. See also, Terms of Reference for Defence Ethics Program, dated 21 December 1997 and signed by General Maurice Baril (Chief of the Defence Staff) and Louise Fréchette (Deputy Minister of National Defence), and, Defence Administrative Order and Directive 7023-1, Defence Ethics Program.

24. The Honourable Art Eggleton, "Message from the Minister of National Defence", *Canadian Military Journal*, Vol. 1, No. 1 (Spring 2000), 3.; General J.M.G. (Maurice) Baril, "Message from the Chief of the Defence Staff", *Canadian Military Journal*, Vol. 1, No. 1 (Spring 2000), 4.

25. David J. Bercuson, "Up from the Ashes: The Re-Professionalization of the Canadian Forces after the Somalia Affair", *Canadian Military Journal*, Vol. 9, No. 3 (2009), 31-39.

26. Ian M. Brown, "Not Glamorous, But Effective: The Canadian Corps and the Set-Piece Attack, 1917-1918", *Journal of Military History*, Vol. 58, No. 3 (1994), 421-444.; Shane B. Schreiber, *Shock Army of the British Empire: The Canadian Corps in the Last 100 Days of the Great War* (Westport: Praeger, 1997).

27. David J. Bercuson, *Maple Leaf Against the Axis. Canada's Second World War* (Toronto, Ontario: Stoddart, 1998), 6.

28. It would appear that Canada failed to systematically record the lessons of the Great War owing to: 1) war-weariness (the nation had just emerged from four years of total war, the mood of the nation being generally anti-militaristic during the early years of peace and for some time thereafter); 2) economics (the military's budget was drastically reduced, thus preventing what would have undoubtedly been an expensive exercise); and 3) few senior soldiers remained in the military (the Corps Commander, Sir Arthur Currie, became the Inspector-General of the Canadian Army, but left military service in 1920 to become Principal and Vice Chancellor of McGill University in Montreal, Quebec), with even fewer still writing any type of publishable memoir. Whatever the reasons, Canada missed a prime opportunity to institutionalize knowledge; by default, a large number of aging and dwindling veterans became its sole repository, a wholly inadequate means of retaining and transmitting professional knowledge.

29. John A. English, *Canadian Institute of International Affairs* 3, *Lament for an Army: The Decline of Canadian Military Professionalism* (Toronto, Ontario: Irwin, 1998), 22.

30. Ibid., 25.

31. A quick examination of the most important military journal extant in Canada during the *interbellum*, the *Canadian Defence Quarterly*, published between 1923 and 1939, reveals only one substantive debate of any importance. Argued between Lieutenant-Colonel E.L.M. Burns and Captain Guy G. Simonds, both future corps commanders during the Second World War, their exchange centred on the use of armour in the defence and in the attack. As one historian has commented, the debate, which ran over four issues, was the "the absolute high point of interwar military thinking in Canada." See Jack L. Granatstein, *The Generals: The Canadian Army's Senior Commanders in the Second World War* (Toronto, Ontario: Stoddart, 1993), 125. Such a statement may be a slight over-generalization, as information received by the present author suggests that there were many more "thinking officers" besides Simonds and Burns alone in the years between the wars (phone conversation between Dr. David J. Bercuson and Craig Leslie Mantle, 18 May 2012). Nevertheless, from first impressions, it does not appear that professional concepts like "the way of war" received much attention in the years prior to the Second World War. For the articles themselves, see Lieutenant-Colonel E.L.M. "Tommy" Burns, "A Division That Can Attack", *CDQ* (April 1938); Simonds, "An Army That Can Attack – A Division That Can Defend", *CDQ* (July 1938).; Lieutenant-Colonel E.L.M. "Tommy" Burns, "Where Do The Tanks Belong?", *CDQ* (October 1938).; and, Guy Simonds, "What Price Assault Without Support?", *CDQ* (January 1939).

32. Budget 2012, "Jobs, Growth and Long-Term Prosperity", retrieved 10 on May 2012 from <http://www.budget.gc.ca/2012/home-accueil-eng.html>.

33. Security and Defence Forum, retrieved on 5 June 2012 from <http://www.forces.gc.ca/admpol/SDF-eng.html>.

34. The Officer Professional Military Education Programme is offered through the Division of Continuing Studies at the Royal Military College of Canada. Open to all ranks, although geared toward junior officers, its purpose is to provide students with a common body of knowledge, generally at the university level, that is specific to the military profession. Six courses are offered: 1) defence management; 2) military law; 3) military history; 4) civics, politics and international relations; 5) technology, society and warfare; and 6) leadership and ethics. So flexible is the Programme that students can take courses online from anywhere in world, for instance during a posting to the Canadian Embassy in Cairo or on a deployment to Afghanistan or in a classroom at Canadian Forces Base Petawawa.

35. Officer Professional Military Education Programme, retrieved on 9 May 2012 from <http://www.opme.forces.gc.ca/au-ns/index-eng.asp>.

CANADA

36. The CF Effectiveness Framework is discussed at length in Canada, *Conceptual Foundations*, 18-23. In this model, for mission success to be achieved, the values of internal integration, member well-being and commitment, external adaptability and military ethos must be positively actuated.

37. As evidence, the military is now a more visible element of Canadian society. "Red Fridays" (the wearing of red t-shirts to show support), CF appreciation days (usually held at professional sporting events), the "Highway of Heroes" (a renamed stretch of Highway 401 between Trenton and Toronto), vehicle magnets and bumper stickers that implore the viewer to "Support Our Troops," military discounts on various goods and services at local establishments, increasing attendance at Remembrance Day ceremonies (although there may be other factors at play here), amongst a handful of others, all stand as evidence of the high regard in which the military is now held. Such marks of respect would likely have been all but impossible fifteen to twenty years ago.

CONTRIBUTORS

Dr. Mie Augier an associate professor at the Naval Postgraduate School (NPS). She works on research on economics and security, strategy, and net assessment. She also is a founding director of the centre for new security economics and net assessment. Before joining NPS, she was a research associate & post doctorate at Stanford, and a senior research fellow and director of strategy research at the Advanced Research and Assessment Group in the UK defence Academy and has consulted for government institutions, businesses and business schools in the US and abroad on issues relating to strategy, organizational structure and leadership. She has published more than fifty articles in journals and books, and co-edited several special issues of journals and books. Her current research interests include: the links between economics and security; the development of an interdisciplinary framework for strategic thinking & New Security Economics; Organizational Theory and behaviour.

Dr. Bill Bentley is a retired Lieutenant-Colonel who served over 30 years in the Canadian infantry. During his career Dr. Bentley had extensive experience with both the United Nations and NATO. He served as a Professor of Military Science at the US Army Command and Staff College and a three-year secondment with the Department of Foreign Affairs. Dr. Bentley has been with the CF Leadership Institute since its creation in 2001. He received the Deputy Minister/Chief of the Defence Staff Innovation Award for writing *Duty With Honour: The Profession of Arms in Canada* and the Meritorious Service Medal for his contribution to the reform of the CF Professional Development System.

Piet Bester is a registered Industrial Psychologist and the Officer Commanding of the South African National Defence Force's Military Psychological Institute. He holds a D Phil degree from the University of Johannesburg and is also a part-time lecturer at the University of Pretoria.

Maria Fors Brandebo (MA, Karlstad University, Sweden) is a research assistant at the Department of security, strategy and leadership at the Swedish National Defence College, and is a doctoral student in psychology at Karlstad University, Sweden. She has published journal articles, book chapters and research reports within the field of psychology and leadership, motivation, trust and organisation.

Major James Do, United States Air Force, is an Assistant Professor for the Department of Behavioral Sciences and Leadership at the United States Air

CONTRIBUTORS

Force Academy. He is a USAF behavioral scientist and psychological operations officer, who has deployed to the Central Command area of responsibility to conduct military information support operations. Major Do also worked as a human factors analyst in operational testing and was the program manager of the USAF pilot selection program. He received his Master's degree in sociology from the University of Colorado in Colorado Springs and will begin his doctorate at the University of Colorado in Boulder in the fall of 2012. His research interests include gender bias in the military, the impact of e-resources on student learning, and cynicism within military organizations. A 2000 Air Force Academy graduate and former editor of the cadet humour magazine, *The Dodo*, Major Do uses his experiences to address cynicism and attack the root causes in order to improve organizational military culture and pride in the profession of arms.

Abel Esterhuyse is an associate professor of strategy in the Faculty of Military Science of Stellenbosch University at the South African Military Academy. He holds a PhD from Stellenbosch University and regularly publishes on contemporary (South African) military issues.

Dr. Craig Foster is a Professor in the Department of Behavioral Sciences and Leadership at the United States Air Force Academy. He is a graduate of Washington University in St. Louis, where he completed an undergraduate major in Psychology and a minor in German. He then completed his Master's Degree and PhD in Social Psychology at the University of North Carolina in Chapel Hill. His Master's thesis focused on the role that perceived injustice plays in motivating individuals to seek power. His doctoral dissertation examined how individuals perceive others who seek power. Dr. Foster taught several undergraduate courses while pursuing his graduate degrees, including Introduction to Psychology, Research Methods in Psychology, and Social Psychology. He also won a university-wide award for excellence in undergraduate teaching. After completing his doctoral degree, Dr. Foster joined the Department of Behavioral Sciences and Leadership at the United States Air Force Academy. He has taught several courses at USAFA including Introduction to Behavioral Sciences, Statistical Principles in Behavioral Science, Social Psychology, Personality, Psychology in Film, Psychological Operations, Foundations of Leadership Development, and Advanced Leadership. He has served in a variety of Departmental roles, typically in the areas of assessment and leadership. Dr. Foster continues to conduct research in the areas of relationships, power, and leader development. He has also won a Department teaching award and twice been a finalist for a USAFA-wide teaching award.

CONTRIBUTORS

Marc van Gils (MSc) received his academic degree in Human Resource Management (HRM) in 2002. Since then, he has worked in the field of HRM policy, leadership development and research, mainly within the Dutch government. His main interests are out-of-the box thinking, originality and vision development. He is also highly interested in the question of "what makes humans do what they do and think what they think?", especially when it seems ineffective or even hinders them in reaching their goals. Currently, he works as a project manager and personal coach within the Dutch Armed Forces. In his private life he loves the outdoors, climbing, mountaineering in all its facets and exploring his own thinking and motives.

Miriam de Graaff (MSc) received her academic degree in both Psychology and Communication Studies (*Cum Laude*) in 2008 from the University of Twente, The Netherlands. Since then, she works in the field of leadership development and research within the Netherlands Ministry of Defense. Currently, she is employed at the Royal Netherlands Army Centre of Excellence for Leadership and Ethics as a project manager and researcher. Miriam is also affiliated as a PhD student to the University of Twente. Her doctoral dissertation combines moral psychology with ethical philosophy and focuses upon issues related to moral judgement such as identity and emotions. She has published several articles, reports and book chapters dealing with leadership and ethics in the Dutch forces.

Jerry Guo is a Research Associate in the Center for New Security Economics and Net Assessment at the Naval Postgraduate School. His research interests include the influence of culture on individual and organizational decision-making. He holds an MA in Security Studies (Defense Decision-Making and Planning) from the Naval Postgraduate school and a BA in Economics from Dartmouth College. He is proficient in Chinese speech.

Lieutenant-Colonel Doctor Eri Radityawara Hidayat is currently heading the Psychological Development Institute, the Psychological Service of the Indonesian Army. He has a Bachelor of Science from the University of Wisconsin Madison, an MBA from the University of Pittsburgh, a Master's of Human Resource Management and Coaching from the University of Sydney, Australia, and a Ph.D. in Psychology from the University of Indonesia. The title of his dissertation was "Choice of decision mode and cognitive cross-cultural competency in international peacekeeping operations: Comparative study of Indonesian and French peacekeepers," and he was awarded a Fulbright Doctoral Dissertation Research Scholarship at Columbia University, New York. A graduate of the Indonesian Defence Forces Officer's School in 1990, Colonel Hidayat attended the Indonesian Army Command and Staff School in 2006.

CONTRIBUTORS

Colonel Bernd Horn, OMM, MSM, CD, PhD, is an experienced infantry officer who has commanded at the unit and sub-unit level. He has filled key command appointments such as the Deputy Commander Canadian Special Operations Forces Command, Commanding Officer of the 1st Battalion, The Royal Canadian Regiment and Officer Commanding 3 Commando, the Canadian Airborne Regiment. Dr. Horn has a PhD from the Royal Military College of Canada where he is also an Adjunct Professor of History. He has authored, co-authored, edited and co-edited in 32 books and over 100 chapters and articles on military history and military affairs.

Dr. R. Jeffrey Jackson is a Professor for the Department of Behavioral Sciences and Leadership at the United States Air Force Academy. He is a 20-year veteran of the United States Air Force serving as chief of psychological services, director of counseling and leadership development, deputy department head, and department head. He now supports a Master's degree curriculum for preparing Academy commanders. He received his doctorate from Loyola University Chicago and maintains a license as a clinical psychologist. His research activities have generally followed two tracks. His clinical focus has addressed topics such as airsickness, anxiety sensitivity, and post-traumatic stress with publications in the *Journal of Abnormal Psychology, Military Medicine,* and the *Journal of Personality.* His leadership emphases have been on coaching, leader development, and early leader experience with publications in the *Journal of Management Development, Industrial and Organizational Psychology,* and the *Journal of Leadership Education.* He serves as a co-editor for the *Journal of Character and Leader Integration* and *Military Behavioral Health: An International Journal of Research and Community Study.*

Emma Jonsson works as a research assistant at the Department of security, strategy and leadership at the Swedish National Defence College. She graduated from Uppsala University, Sweden with an MA in social science. She conducts research primarily on recruitment and selection with an emphasis on the personnel supply to the Swedish Armed Forces as well as the public opinion of the Swedish Armed Forces and its anchoring in society.

Gerry Larsson, PhD is a licensed psychologist and professor of leadership at the Swedish National Defence College. During the period 2004 - 2009 he also served as Vice President of the college. He has published over 100 journal articles, 75 books or chapters in books, and more than 500 research reports. His main research and teaching areas include leadership, stress, personality, organization, and health.

CONTRIBUTORS

Lieutenant-Colonel Psalm Lew is currently Head of the School Leadership Development with the responsibility to review and develop the Leadership Curriculum in all SAF schools. An Infantry Officer by vocation, he is concurrently the Commanding Officer of a National Service Infantry Battalion in the SAF Armed Forces. His past appointments include being the Chief Researcher of the Army Museum of Singapore, a Principal Staff Officer in the 3rd Singapore Division and Training Development Officer of the Officer Cadet School. Lieutenant-Colonel Lew holds a Bachelor of Science (1st Class Honors) in Psychology from the University of Birmingham, U.K. and a Diploma in Learning Science from the National Institute of Education, Nanyang Technological University.

Lieutenant-Colonel Douglas Lindsay, PhD, US Air Force, is the Deputy Department Head and an Associate Professor for the Department of Behavioral Sciences and Leadership at the United States Air Force Academy. He is a career Behavioral Scientist and has had held positions as a test psychologist, research psychologist, occupational analyst, military assistant, inspector general, deputy squadron commander, professor, and executive officer. He recently returned from a deployment to Afghanistan where he was the Deputy Communications Director in support of Operation Enduring Freedom. He received his doctorate degree in Industrial/Organizational Psychology from The Pennsylvania State University and his research interests are in the areas of leadership, leadership development, leader-follower dynamics, and followership. He has over 50 publications and presentations on these topics and has been published in journals such as *Military Psychology, Journal of Leadership Education, International Journal of Training and Development, Human Resource Development International*, and has presented at such venues as the American Psychological Association, American Psychological Society, Society for Industrial & Organizational Psychology, International Military Testing Association, and International Leadership Association. In addition, he is the co-founder and co-editor of the *Journal of Character and Leader Integration*.

Craig Leslie Mantle graduated from Queen's University (Ontario, Canada) with his MA in Canadian History in 2002 and has been employed by the Canadian Forces Leadership Institute as a research officer ever since. He is also a PhD candidate under the supervision of Dr. David Bercuson at the University of Calgary (Alberta, Canada) where he is currently studying leader-follower relations in the Canadian Expeditionary Force during the First World War. He has authored, edited or co-edited a number of publications that deal with a variety of military topics, ranging from the historical to the contemporary.

CONTRIBUTORS

Robert M. McNab, Associate Professor, received his Bachelor of Arts from California State University, Stanislaus in 1991 and his PhD in Economics in 2001 from Georgia State University in Atlanta, Georgia. He has served as a consultant on tax policy, tax administration, and revenue estimation and forecasting issues for the United States Agency for International Development and the World Bank. He has published articles in the *Applied Economics, Defense and Security Analysis, National Tax Journal, Journal of International Trade and Economic Development, Public Budgeting and Finance, Small Wars and Insurgencies,* and *World Development,* among others. He has served as a referee for *Defense and Peace Economics, Journal of Policy Analysis and Management, Journal of Public Economics, Public Finance and Management, Public Finance Review, Public Finance and Budgeting, Review of Financial Economics, World Development* and other journals. His research interests include the outcomes of fiscal decentralization, the reform of budgeting and tax administration systems in developing and transitional countries, and the economics of insurgent movements. Professor McNab joined the faculty of the Defense Resources Management Institute and the Naval Postgraduate School in August 2000 and was promoted to Associated Professor in 2006. He currently holds a joint appointment with the Global Public Policy Academic Group.

Sofia Nilsson is currently working as a research assistant at the Department of Security, Strategy and Leadership at the Swedish National Defence. She studied at Växjö University and Karlstad University in Sweden and at the University of Westminster in London and graduated with a PhD in Education in working life and an MA in political science. Her primary research focuses on leadership during trying situations in general and moral stress in particular. She has published journal articles, chapters in books and several research reports at the Swedish National Defence College dealing with management, leadership, organization, and stress.

Andres Pfister currently holds the Chair for "Leadership and Communication Studies" at the Swiss Military Academy (MILAK). He teaches courses for future professional military officers of the Swiss Armed Forces as well as for interested students at the ETH in Zurich. Andres began his academic career at the University of Basel where he studied Psychology and Business Economics and received his Master's Degree in Social and Business Psychology in 2004 and his PhD in Psychology from the University of Zurich in 2011. In his thesis he researched and tested a new model of leadership and studied how individual personality and national culture affect leadership behaviour. Before starting his PhD at the MILAK in 2006, he was a recruitment professional in an executive search company. Apart from his duties at the Military Academy he further acts as a consultant on leadership and communication topics for mid-sized and global companies, NGOs, Swiss police forces, and for several departments within the Swiss Armed Forces. As a special officer and team leader in the Pedagogic Psychological Service of the Swiss Armed Forces, Andres also works to prevent stress and drug use in the recruitment schools around Zürich.

Lieutenant-Colonel Rich Ramsey is an Army officer serving as an Instructor in the Air Force Academy's Department of Behavioral Sciences and Leadership where he teaches the Academy's core leader development course. He was commissioned as an Armor Officer in 1994 through the Reserve Officer Training Corp Program. He previously served as a Tank Platoon and Scout Platoon Leader, Tank Company and Headquarters Troop Commander, Tactical Officer at the United States Military Academy at West Point, Air Officer Commanding at the United States Air Force Academy, Operations Officer in a Cavalry Squadron, and on multiple occasions as an Advisor to the Iraqi Army and Police Forces. He has deployed to Iraq three times, twice as an Advisor and once as a Cavalry Squadron Operations Officer. In addition to teaching leadership, he also serves as the Director of Air Officer Commanding Master's Degree Program and advises the Cadet Commander's Leader Enrichment Seminar, a Leader Development Program for emerging leaders. He earned his BA in Political Science from The University of Michigan and his Master of Science degree in Counseling and Leader Development from Long Island University.

Dr. Hugh Smith is a graduate of the London School of Economics and the Australian National University. He joined the University of New South Wales in 1971, lecturing first at the Royal Military College and from 1986 at the Australian Defence Force Academy until his retirement as Associate Professor in 2004. His publications include *On Clausewitz: A Study of Military and Political Ideas* (Palgrave Macmillan, 2005) and numerous articles on topics relating to ethics and war, the military profession, armed forces and society, strategy, intelligence, and peacekeeping. He is a Visiting Fellow at the University of New South Wales and the Centre for Defence Leadership and Ethics.

Lieutenant-Colonel Brett Waring, United States Air Force, is the Deputy Chief, Weapons and Tactics Branch, Headquarters United States Air Forces in Europe. He is an A-10 Weapons and Tactics officer who has deployed to the Central Command area of responsibility to conduct combat and combat support operations on six deployments since 2001. He is a graduate of the USAF Weapons Instructor Course at Nellis AFB, NV, where he also served as an

CONTRIBUTORS

instructor. He received his Master's degree in military arts and science from the Air Command and Staff College at Maxwell Air Force Base, Alabama, and a second degree in Humanities from California State University, Dominguez Hills. His research interests include war literature, military leadership, and cynicism within military organizations. A 1996 Air Force Academy graduate and former editor of the cadet humor magazine, *The Dodo*, he uses his experiences to address cynicism across various training venues in order to better understand leadership opportunities and the inherent pride in the profession of arms.

Lieutenant-Colonel Daniel J. Watola, PhD, US Air Force, is an Assistant Professor and Director of Leadership Curriculum and Programs in the Department of Behavioral Sciences and Leadership, United States Air Force Academy, Colorado Springs, Colorado. He is responsible for the core leadership development course for 4,400 undergraduate cadets as well as leadership concentration course sequence within the Behavioral Sciences major. He is also the Program Manager for the Air Officers Commanding Master's Program, a $570K joint Air Force Intermediate Development Education Program and Air Force Institute of Technology graduate degree program that prepares high potential Air Force Majors to command cadet squadrons at the United States Air Force Academy. He oversees the Cadet Commanders' Leadership Enrichment Seminar, a leadership development workshop for 160 cadet commanders and intercollegiate team captains per year. He graduated from the United States Air Force Academy in 1993 with a Bachelor of Science Degree in Human Factors Engineering. He has served in several science and engineering positions throughout the Air Force, including flight test engineer for the Northrup-Grumman B-2A Spirit, Occupational Analyst, and Research Laboratory Division Chief. He has also served as a Staff Officer and Executive Officer in Air Education and Training Command's Directorate of Operations, and obtained Master of Arts and Doctorate of Philosophy degrees in Industrial and Organizational Psychology. Prior to his current assignment, he was the Deputy Commander of Detachment 5, Air Force Research Laboratory at Brooks City-Base, Texas.

GLOSSARY

ADF	Australian Defence Force
AFSC	Air Force Specialty Code
AFRICOM	African Command Centre
ANC	African National Congress
AOCs	Air Officers Commanding
APLA	Azanian People's Liberation Army
AVF	All-Volunteer Force
BCT	Basic Cadet Training
CBHRM	Competency-Based Human Resource Management System
CDA	Canadian Defence Academy
CDS	Chief of Defence Staff
CEO	Chief Executive officer
CF	Canadian Forces
CFC	Canadian Forces College
CFLI	Canadian Forces Leadership Institute
COCOM	Coordinating Committee
COIN	Counter-Insurgency
COSATU	Congress of South African Trade Unions
DISBINTALAD	*Dinas Pembinaan Mental Angkatan Darat* (Mental Guidance Service of the Army)
DISPSIAD	*Dinas Psikologi Angkatan Darat* (Psychological Service of the Army)
DM	Deputy Minister
DMD	Department of Militia and Defence
DND	Department of National Defence
EFP	Explosively Formed Projectiles
EU	European Union
FOB	Forward Operating Base
GDP	Gross Domestic Product
GO	Government Organization
GO/FO	General Officers/Flag Officers
GSoA	Group for a Switzerland Without an Army
HRM	Human Resource Management

GLOSSARY

ICBM	Intercontinental Ballistic Missile
ICT	In-Camp Training
IED	Improvised Explosive Device
IFOR	Implementation Force
IMF	International Monetary Fund
IMLA	International Military Leadership Association
IMTA	International Military Testing Association
ISAF	International Security Assistance Force
KNIL	*Koninklijk Netherlands-Indische Leger* (Dutch Colonial Army)
KZPF	KwaZulu-Natal Self protection Force
MEF	Minimum Essential Force
MK	*Umkhonto we Sizwe*
MMC	Minister's Monitoring Committee
MND	Minister of National Defence
NATO	North Atlantic Treaty Organization
NCO	Non-Commissioned Officer
NGO	Non-Government Organization
NPS	Naval Postgraduate School
NS	National Service
NSmen	National Servicemen
OPEC	Organization for the Petroleum Export Countries
PCAP	Position Competencies Assessment Programs
PE	Physical Education
PPKJ	Program *Penilaian Kompetensi Jabatan*
PUSDIKIF	*Pusat Pendidikan Infantri* (Infantry Training Centre)
PUSDIKTER	*Pusat Pendidikan Teritorial* (Territorial Training Centre)
REEs	Rare Earth Elements
REOs	Rare Earth Oxides
RIP-TOA	Relief in Place – Transfer of Authority
ROEs	Rules of Engagement
RSA	Republic of South Africa
SADF	South African Defence Force
SAF	Singapore Armed Forces or Swedish Armed Forces
SANDF	South African National Defence Force

GLOSSARY

SESKOAD	*Sekolah Staf dan Komando Angkatan Darat* (Army's Staff and Command School)
SFOR	Stabilization Force
SNDC	Swedish National Defence College
SOEs	State-Owned Enterprises
STOMP	Straights Times Online Mobile Print
TBVC	Transkei, Bophuthatswana, Venda and Ciskei
TNI	*Tentara Nasional Indonesia* (Indonesian National Defence Force)
TNI AD	*Tentara Nasional Indonesia Angkatan Darat* (Indonesian National Army)
UDF	Union Defence Force
UK	United Kingdom
UN	United Nations
UNISA	University of South Africa
UNPROFOR	United Nations Protection Force
UP	University of Pretoria
US	United States
USA	United States of America
USAF	United States Air Force
USAFA	United States Air Force Academy
WTO	World Trade Organization

INDEX

INDEX

Cognitive Boundry 52

Cold War 6, 64, **143** *notes*, 171, 179, **188** *notes*, **194** *notes*, 195-197, 211, 212, **228** *notes*

Combat Stress 36, 40

Competency Framework 75-78, **82** *notes*, **84** *notes*

Competency-Based Human Resource Management System 72

Competent, see also Competency, Complacency 27, 44, 52, 71, 74, **83** *notes*, 102, 182, 221

Comprehensive Soldier Fitness 31, **46** *notes*

Conscript Army **193** *notes*, 195, 197, 210

Conscript Military 11

Conscription 5, 8, 87, 169, **189** *notes*, **190** *notes*, 210, 212

Core Values 58, 72, 79, 90-92, **96** *notes*, **98** *notes*, 124, 218, 226

Corporate Army 2, 3

Corporateness 198

Corruption 4, 42, 43

Counter-Insurgency 6, 7, 36-38, 40, 44, **47** *notes*

Counter-Insurgency Warfare 36

Counterfeiting 125, 134, 141

Courage 57, 61, 219

Credibility 14, 43, 89, 141, 156, 159-161, 173, 178, 179, 184

Cultural Awareness 27, 30, 40, 41, 43, 44

Cultural Intelligence 44

Currency Manipulation 125, 133, 136, 137, 140

Cynicism 119, 147-159, 161, 162, 164, 165-166,

166 *notes*-**168** *notes*, 234, 240,

Decolonization 5, 18

Defining Issues Test 40, **48** *notes*

Dehumanization 39, **47** *notes*

Delapan Wajib TNI, see also Eight Military Pledges 77, 80

De-professionalization 186

Differentiation 170

Dinas Pembinaan Mental Angkatan Darat, DISBINTALAD, see also Mental Guidance 78
    Service of the Army 78

Dinas Psikologi Angkatan Darat, DISPSIAD, see also Psychological Service of the Indonesian Army 77-79

Direct Fire 27, 29

Displacement of Responsibility 30

Distortion of Consequences 39

Distributed Learning 44

Diversity 10, 17

Downsizing Wave 170

Dumping 134, 137, 141

Duty 33, 37, 38, 40, 44, **82** *notes*, 87, 89, 91, 104, 107, 113-116, 118, **120** *notes*, 147, 153, 201, 202, 218, 219, **228** *notes*, **230** *notes*, 233

Dynamic Five-Factor Model of Leadership 195, 199, **213** *notes*

East Timor 109, **120** *notes*

Economic Togetherness 123, 124, 135, 138, **142** *notes*

Economic Warfare 124-130, 133-138, 141, 142, **142** *notes*, **143** *notes*, **144** *notes*

INDEX

Integrity 9, 61, 62, 64, 114, 118, 119, **120** *notes*, 197, 219, **229** *notes*

"Intelligent Failure" 63

International Security Assistance Force 41, 198

Iran-Contra 115

Iraq 25, 41, 42, 53, **69** *notes*, 130, 239

Jati Diri, see also Core Identity 77, 80

Just War 106, 107, 116

Kandahar 36

Kejuangan, see also Warrior Code 79, **84** *notes*

Kinetic Operations 26, 29, 36

Korean War 38, 128, 221

Law Enforcement 111-113, 197

Law of Armed Conflict 44, 103, 106, 107, 111

Leadership iii, iv, 3, 8, 16, **22** *notes*, 27, 28, 30-36, 43, 44, **45** *notes*, **46** *notes*, 49, 50, 54, **54** *notes*, 60, 61, 64, 67, 68, **69** *notes*, 77, 78, **83** *notes*, 84, 89, 90, 92, **97** *notes*, **98** *notes*, 117-120, **120** *notes*, 137, 139, 149, 154, 156-162, 164, 166, **167** *notes*, **168** *notes*, 169, **189** *notes*-**193** *notes*, 195, 199-201, 203, 206, 207, 209, 212, **213** *notes*, 220, 222, 223, 226, **228** *notes*-**231** *notes*, 233-240, 253

Loyalty 4, 8, 10, 11, 59, 67, 90, 103, 104, 113-118, **120** *notes*, 183, 198, 202, 219

Materialists 181

Medieval Times 57, 110

Mentoring 26, 34, 42, 43, 75

Military Ethics **19** *notes*, **48** *notes*, **68** *notes*, **85** *notes*, 101, 103, 117, **120** *notes*

Military Task-Oriented Model 71

Military Unions 16

Military Weapons Systems 29

Minimum Essential Force, see also MEF 71, 72, **82** *notes*

Mission Command 2, 13, 62, 65, **120** *notes*

Mission-Oriented Defence 171

Modularization 170

Money as a Weapon System 29

Moral Battlefield 44

Moral Behaviour 40, 44, 109

Moral Development 27, 37, 40, **48** *notes*, 60

Moral Dilemmas 198

Moral Disengagement 39, 40, **47** *notes*, 203

Moral Inversion 63

Moral Justification 39

Moral Reasoning 30, 36, 37, 40, 43, 44

Multi-Rater Feedback 35

National Democratic Revolution 9, **21** *notes*

Nazism 107

NCM Corps 2020 50

Normative Professionalism 198

Obedience 30, 37, 38, 40, **47** *notes*, 102, 107, 113, 114, 210

Officership 2020 50

Operation Enduring Freedom 41, 237

Operation Iraqi Freedom 41

Operational Art 49, 51, 52, **55** *notes*

INDEX